LIES THAT GO UNCHALLENGED™
IN POPULAR CULTURE

TYNDALE HOUSE PUBLISHERS, INC., WHEATON, ILLINOIS

LIES THAT GO UNCHALLENGED SERIES . . .

LIES THAT GO UNCHALLENGED™

IN POPULAR CULTURE

CHARLES COLSON

COMPILED BY JAMES STUART BELL

Visit Tyndale's exciting Web site at www.tyndale.com

TYNDALE is a registered trademark of Tyndale House Publishers, Inc.

Tyndale's quill logo is a trademark of Tyndale House Publishers, Inc.

Lies That Go Unchallenged is a trademark of Tyndale House Publishers, Inc.

How Now Shall We Live? is a registered trademark of Tyndale House Publishers, Inc.

Lies That Go Unchallenged in Popular Culture

Designed by Luke Daab

Colson, Charles W.
   Lies that go unchallenged in popular culture / Charles Colson with James Stuart Bell.
      p. cm. — (The how now series)
   ISBN-13: 978-1-4143-0166-2 (sc)
   ISBN-10: 1-4143-0166-9 (sc)
   1. Christianity and culture. 2. Christian ethics. I. Bell, James S. II. Title. III. Series.
   BR115.C8.C556 2005
   261'.0973—dc22   2004030695

Printed in the United States of America

11   10   09   08   07   06   05
 8   7   6   5   4   3   2   1

CONTENTS

Introduction ix

How to Use This Book xi

RIGHTS OF THE INDIVIDUAL

MARRIAGE AND THE FAMILY

SOCIETY AND TOLERATION

THE ARTS

CHRISTIANS IN CULTURE

THE MEDIA

SPIRITUALITY IN CULTURE

INTRODUCTION

When the serpent told Eve that if she ate of the fruit from the tree she would become like God, knowing good and evil, he spoke a half-truth rather than an outright lie. He twisted the truth to make his offer sound attractive and harmless even though it was in direct rebellion against God's laws. Satan does the same thing in our present culture. Casual statements that sound good on the surface often go unchallenged by Christians, not because we're avoiding confrontation, but because the statements appear to make sense and we don't perceive their underlying errors.

"No one has a monopoly on truth, and we'll live in harmony if we tolerate each other."

"Marriage can be between any two people, and it should last only as long as they are happy."

"We have the freedom of choice to become who we want and to do what we want."

There's a partial truth in each of these statements, but each is based on an underlying lie that reflects a cultural worldview strongly opposed to Christian revelation. We must identify and challenge these lies—whether in our personal lives or in the culture at large—because they contribute to the moral disintegration of our society and violate God's good intentions for us.

Contemporary American culture has drifted far from its Judeo-Christian moorings. The church bears some responsibility for this in its failure to be salt and light to the world. Another cause is that the liberal elite want to create a future that bears little resemblance to a Christian model. Over the past generation, the ideas and values of this group have permeated popular culture.

Scientific and technological advances have improved our quality of life in some respects, but our sense of the sanctity of life, the traditional family, and the moral standards of our society have all suffered greatly. As Christians, we have a hard time responding adequately as various laws, events, and people affect popular culture and challenge what we believe and how we live. Thus, we often fail to challenge the implicit lies that drive the changes in our culture.

These lies are found in our churches, families, media, politics, art, and education. They affect us and our families and how we relate to each other at all levels of society. This book identifies seven core lies that shape popular culture. They sound good on the surface, yet they reflect a worldview diametrical to Christianity. Here are some other seemingly harmless and even attractive statements that ultimately divert us from God's purposes for us:

"The arts should break conventional bounds and challenge the status quo."

"Christian beliefs are a private matter and shouldn't be imposed on anyone."

"The media's purpose is to entertain us and gratify our personal desires."

"Spiritual unity is enhanced by realizing that there are many ways to God."

The seven chapters in this book, adapted from a selection of Charles Colson's *BreakPoint* radio commentaries, discuss significant events and changes in our culture over the past decade. These commentaries help us to understand some of the laws, events, and people behind the changes in popular culture and the worldview that informs them. They also help us to examine these cultural currents in the light of God's truth. Supplementary materials in each chapter facilitate the practical application of these concepts, helping Christians to challenge cultural lies and to effectively influence their culture for good.

How do we confront these lies? First, we can be open to the guidance of the Holy Spirit as we seek personal spiritual renewal in these areas. If our own lives are out of line with the truth, we can't witness effectively on behalf of the truth. Second, we need to support one another and work as a Christian community, whether through a small group using this book or through a church that is able and willing to deal internally with these issues. Finally, we need to engage people with other worldviews in dialogue and action. Thus, the application material is in sections titled The Spiritual Dimension, Group Approach, and Influencing Culture.

Charles Colson

HOW TO USE THIS BOOK

All of us are affected by deceptive and antagonistic worldviews. *Lies That Go Unchallenged in Popular Culture* exposes underlying cultural agendas and helps us to interpret what is happening in our society. With these insights, we can interact more effectively with those outside a Christian worldview, expose false and harmful premises, and articulate the merits of our own position. We can also present our faith more knowledgeably when we understand the needs of our contemporary society.

This book can help you to do these things well. The cultural topics addressed in this book àre relevant and interesting, and we need to examine them in the light of God's revealed truth to identify and counteract the lies they promote. The section titled Truths to Consider summarizes some important concepts in a way that makes them easy to understand and recall.

There will be no effective cultural response unless spiritual transformation begins with individuals. The Spiritual Dimension sections consider how fraudulent worldviews challenge the spiritual lives of individuals and groups within the church and helps us to be the salt and light that Jesus asks us to be.

As individuals are spiritually transformed, how can the church provide a vital Christian apologetic? In witnessing to a broken world, how can we counteract Satan's lies and set captives free? The Group Approach sections recognize that group discussion can help us learn to function as a redeemed community in the midst of increasing spiritual darkness. We need to flesh out these principles within the church in order to present a strong and unified witness to our culture.

Finally, we need to offer our contemporaries the living reality of God's Kingdom by boldly confronting and radically serving our enemies and those in need. The Influencing Culture sections suggest persuasive ways to help others see the logic of eventual destruction found in these worldviews as well as alternatives that can liberate their minds and hearts.

I hope that as we are inundated in our society by the effects of negative and destructive worldviews, we won't despair but will see the truth and its life-transforming implications. May God give us the courage to respond in love to the individuals and institutions among whom he has placed us.

RIGHTS OF THE INDIVIDUAL

LIE 1

We have the freedom of choice to be who we want and to do what we want.

Underlying Worldview: Individuals derive their rights from themselves, are responsible to no higher authority, and are free to pursue their own destinies as long as they don't hurt others.

As a culture, we no longer know the Author of life who created us in his image. Instead, we define human beings as the products of a random evolutionary process and we believe that we will survive and grow if we do what is most fulfilling to our selves. This worldview extends to the autonomous shaping of our gendered identities and their outward expression in our sexuality. As an example, you'll see in this section how adolescent girls explore various options of sexual identity, including bisexuality and lesbianism, before settling on a final preference. When they see heterosexual pop icons such as Britney Spears and Madonna kissing intimately, they consider that anything and everything must be acceptable.

When moral guidelines are not based on the holy character of our Creator, we think that we are free to set our own agendas. Apart from our inherent selfishness, this credo gains much of its seductive and deceptive power from the kernel of truth that it distorts. God does want each of us to survive and thrive by doing what is most fulfilling to us. As Jesus put it, "I have come that they may have life, and have it to the full" (John 10:10). The problem lies not with our desire for deeply fulfilled and satisfying lives, but in our failure to understand that God has placed our true desires deep in our hearts. Following the guidelines that our Creator established for us leads to our true fulfillment and happiness, but as philosopher Robert George states the secular belief, "Moral rights cannot come as a divine gift because there is no divine giver."

This section presents the view that no one has the inherent right to tell us not to abort our children, have sex with them, or genetically alter them. According to this view, we come into this world as free persons with no inherent guilt or responsibility, but with a "blank slate" that is filled in by our environment. We find celebrity talk show host Rosie O'Donnell promoting gay adoption by telling us that as a lesbian, she is also a good mother of three adopted children, even though statistics clearly show that children of gay parents suffer from the lack of both gender models in the household.

Since we are our own private universe, as one judge stated, we question whether we can even punish something as barbaric as cannibalism, if both parties consent. In one article in this section, a man who cannibalized another man defended himself because the victim authorized this horrible act. With the complete sovereignty of the individual, we are headed toward the ungovernable chaos of anarchy. In another article, the quadriplegic movie actor Christopher Reeve leads a campaign for cloning and, later, for stem cell research. It seems that if it is for "humanitarian purposes," it is morally acceptable to take the Creator's role into our own hands.

To combat these lies, we need to articulate a Christian worldview that stands squarely against the cult of autonomous individualism. We were created for perfection, intended to be like God and to worship him forever, yet we have disobeyed the just laws of this all-loving Creator and have paid the consequences in our fallen nature. He has redeemed us at the cost of his own life, and when people speak of "rights," we need to recognize that everything we are and have is God's gift to us, intended to be invested in wise stewardship. The more important issue is our obligation to be reconciled to God in order to become all that we were meant to be as individuals.

CHECKING BOXES
Transgender Chic

Members of the next incoming freshman class at Brown University will enjoy a new option when it comes to on-campus housing—what the school calls a "gender-neutral option." Students selecting that option will live in a dorm with "lockable bathrooms for use by one person."

While we all like our privacy, just what kind of student requires these special accommodations? The answer is the newest fashionable minority on college campuses: "transgender students."

Fifty years ago, George Jorgensen stunned the world when he

checked into a Copenhagen hospital and left as Christine Jorgensen after the world's first sex-change surgery. Until recently, claims that someone was "a man trapped in a woman's body," or vice versa, were regarded with skepticism. The reason is clear. Many of the people making these claims suffer from some kind of mental illness, and what they really need is treatment, not radical surgery. Even more important, there was a well-founded reluctance to believe that nature had somehow made a mistake.

Now, as events at Brown demonstrate, we don't hesitate to think that nature might have made a mistake. In fact, we deny that nature has anything to do with a person's sex. That's because of the influence that feminism and "queer theory," as it is called, have on college campuses. For both of these philosophies, the idea that there is such a thing as fixed or biologically determined human nature, especially with regard to sexuality, is the enemy. If we are, as the Scriptures say, created male and female, then this limits our personal autonomy—which is, after all, the *summum bonum* of modern American life. And so postmodern academics replace the word *sex* with *gender*, a word historically associated with classification and description. This enables feminists to claim that the qualities normally associated with the sexes are socially constructed, that is, imposed from without as opposed to being inherent. "Queer theorists" depict human sexuality as a continuum instead of an either-or. So a man, biologically, can choose to be feminine, and vice versa—it's just another life choice.

While these ideas haven't held much sway among ordinary Americans, they've become articles of faith on college campuses and among the elite. They've been added to another staple of postmodern thought—"identity politics"—which views membership in a particular group as the basis for all action. The result is separate dorms for "transgender students"—men who choose to be feminine and women who choose to be masculine.

If this sounds absurd to you, you're not alone. Phillip Johnson tells a story in his great book *The Right Questions*, about a fellow faculty member at Berkeley who taught his students the postmodern line. Then his son began cross-dressing, and Dad, despite his proclamations, was embarrassed to introduce him at a dinner party. All the young man was doing, of course, was following his father's teaching. Even postmodern academics can be awakened when they see where their worldview leads. On some level they still understand that being transgender, as it is called, is a violation not only of the moral order but also of the biological order. It takes a lot more to overcome "male and female he created them" than checking a box on a college housing form.

TRUTHS TO CONSIDER

Exploring various forms of sexuality in order to evolve as a sexual person is destructive of God's intentions. It ends in the brokenness of the inner person and in a compromised capacity for permanent marital relationship.

We were designed in God's image as male and female, and God has always chosen whether we should be men or women. Now many believe that they should decide for themselves which sex they will be.

In today's moral and sexual climate, our young people need encouragement, support, and guidance as they explore and clarify their sexual identities.

GROUP STUDY

The Spiritual Dimension: Have you ever resented or disliked being the sex that you are? Explore the roots of this distress and seek the help of the Holy Spirit in becoming the fulfilled man or woman you were created to be.

Group Approach: Does your church provide venues where sexual issues can be discussed in an informative, prayerful, and supportive setting? How can you be supportive of those who struggle in these areas?

Influencing Culture: The church is the wild card as to which worldview will prevail in light of recent cultural changes. How can the church be salt and light to the secular culture that surrounds it?

FOR WHOSE SAKE?
Rosie and Gay Adoption

In an ABC interview with Diane Sawyer, talk-show host Rosie O'Donnell—who has three adopted children—announced what was already an open secret: that she is a lesbian. Nevertheless, Rosie insisted, "I know I'm a really good mother, and I have every right to parent [these children]." Evidently, anyone who thinks otherwise is wrong.

ABC apparently agreed. On a program that lasted two hours, no one challenged or contradicted Rosie, but the truth—unmentioned on ABC—is that children do not fare as well in homes headed by gays as they do in heterosexual homes, where both genders are present.

According to several independent studies by respected authorities, children raised by homosexuals are more likely to become promiscuous and to engage in substance abuse. They are at higher risk of losing a parent to AIDS and more likely to commit suicide.

By contrast, children raised in homes with married, heterosexual parents enjoy greater health, both physically and emotionally. They do better in school, commit fewer crimes, and are less likely to live in poverty.

As Glenn Stanton writes in *CitizenLink*, children raised in such homes "do far better in every measure than children who grow up in any other family situation. Rarely is the social science literature as conclusive as it is on this point."

Then there's the question of whether kids raised by gays are more likely to become gay themselves. Rosie says no, but the research says otherwise.

One study showed that gay parents "may be four times more likely to produce homosexual children." One teenager who was interviewed said that when she had conflicts with her boyfriend, her lesbian mother "would tell me to try girls." In fact, 64 percent of kids reared by lesbian mothers consider having same-sex relationships, compared with only 17 percent in heterosexual families.

The more we study the topic, the more empirical research supports the wisdom of traditional teaching about married, heterosexual parenting.

Rosie O'Donnell's assertion—"I have every right to parent [these children]"—exposes what this debate is really about. It's not about what's good for kids. It's about the demands of gays for their so-called rights.

O'Donnell is leading an effort to overturn state laws against gay adoption. Before states make any drastic decisions, they need to listen to the real experts: kids raised in gay homes. Jakii Edwards told *CitizenLink* that while the intentions of gays may be good, "it does hurt the children to come up in gay homes. When a child [sees] mom kissing mom and dad kissing daddy, it leaves the child . . . with gender identity issues. We question whether we have to be gay like mommy [or daddy] is gay.

"It causes a lot of turmoil," Jakii says, and she adds that nearly everyone she knows who was raised by a gay parent "has major anger issues."

Jakii reminds us that if we really care about the needs of children, we'll do everything in our power to promote healthy, two-parent, heterosexual families. After all, what made June Cleaver, Donna Reed, and Carol Brady great moms was not the fact that they wore aprons and pearls. It was that they were married to their children's fathers.

TRUTHS TO CONSIDER

Regardless of what Rosie or others say, the evidence demonstrates that children raised in gay and lesbian families have more problems than those raised in heterosexual families.

Children from heterosexual families have fewer problems with AIDS, suicide, anger, poverty, crime, education, and gender identity than children raised by homosexuals. No other factor can override the benefits of parental input from both sexes.

We should boldly put this evidence forward by publishing both the statistics of failure in the context of gay households and the positive qualities our children possess when raised by married, heterosexual, Christian parents.

GROUP STUDY

The Spiritual Dimension: How can you better fulfill the biblical roles of husband or wife and create a clearer gender identity for your children? What will prepare them for a mature love relationship within their future families?

Group Approach: Can you reach out to a gay young person or to a young person raised in a gay family with some of the healthy input they are missing? Does that person know the love and forgiveness of Jesus Christ?

Influencing Culture: Even though gays would like the experience of parenting, be bold when interacting on this issue and point out the true harm caused to children in gay adoptive families.

THE POLITICS OF SUFFERING

Stem Cell Research and Our Moral Ideals

Prior to September 11, the defining moment of the Bush presidency had been the president's decision to limit embryonic stem cell research. And while that issue has been overshadowed by the war in Iraq, it hasn't gone away. In fact, it's back with a vengeance, and that means it is time for Christians to understand the facts and what is at stake in the debate.

On October 4, 2004, Senator John Kerry charged the president with "sacrificing science for ideology and playing politics with people who need cures." He added that treatments for dreaded diseases "could be right at our fingertips" if we lifted "the stem cell ban."

Along the same lines, a writer in the *Baltimore Chronicle* accused "opponents of embryonic stem cell research" of "prolonging the suffering of millions." He labeled the president, and other opponents of embryonic stem cell research, as an "obstacle to hope for a scientific breakthrough, a miracle."

Then came the death of actor Christopher Reeve, who played Superman in the 1978 film. Reeve, who was paralyzed when he was thrown from a horse a decade ago, was a tireless advocate of embryonic stem cell research. He even used his appearance on the latest version of the Superman story, *Smallville*, to promote the reversal of the president's policy.

While my thoughts and prayers are with Reeve's family, it is simply not the case that the president's policy is all that stands between people like Reeve and a miracle.

Someone who knows this is Leon Kass, the chairman of the President's Council on Bioethics. In a *Washington Post* op-ed, Kass wrote that the president's critics are distorting his policy and ignoring the "weighty moral issues involved" in their quest for partisan advantage.

For starters, there is no ban. The president's policy affects only embryonic stem cells. There is nothing in the policy that stops researchers from using stem cells obtained elsewhere, such as adult stem cells.

Second, the policy applies only to projects using federal money for embryonic stem cell research. Private and state money is still available, and Harvard University has just announced that it will clone human embryos.

And the federal policy doesn't prohibit the use of all embryonic stem cells. Federally funded research can be conducted using stem cell lines that were already available in August 2001. As Kass points out, there are enough of these lines "for years of essential basic research."

Worse than the distortion of the president's policy is the false hope its opponents are spreading. Kass calls it "cruel to suggest that stem-cell-based therapies are 'at our fingertips.'" According to "our best scientists," such therapies are "at least several decades" away. But what you will not hear the politicians tell you is that adult stem cells are working now.

While the suffering of our fellow citizens and loved ones is heartbreaking, the answer doesn't lie in "recklessly trampling over [our] most cherished moral ideals," as Kass puts it. Rather, it lies in taking full advantage of the research opportunities we have instead of "playing politics with the sick." As Christians need to make clear, false hopes are often the biggest obstacle to real progress.

TRUTHS TO CONSIDER

When our loved ones are suffering, it is easier to place blame or grasp at straws than to feel our helplessness and pain. God is the only true source of healing and miracles.

It is easy to mislead by subtly distorting or omitting data while purportedly telling the truth. We should not be naive or uninformed in judging the appeals that come our way.

God wants us to understand our world and use our knowledge to help others. However, he will not contradict himself by asking us to pursue or apply knowledge in ways that violate his guidelines for appropriate human conduct.

GROUP STUDY

The Spiritual Dimension: When you are on a campaign for something that you feel you can't live without, do you stop to examine your motives in the light of God's Word with the help of the Holy Spirit? What is the source of this energy?

Group Approach: When we feel that our lives are hopeless or out of control, do we place our trust in God or grasp at stopgap solutions to mask our helplessness? How can we support one another when we are suffering and there seems to be nothing we can do?

Influencing Culture: Are there people in your church who stay abreast of scientific research and medical developments? Do they speak out when research is undertaken in a way that violates the dignity or the rights of other people?

UFOS, LITTLE GREEN MEN, AND CLONED BABIES

It's Time for a Ban

It was no accident that baby girl Eve was born on December 26, missing Christmas by only a day. Eve, whose makers claim she was cloned, is the firstborn in what the Raelians, a UFO cult, believe will be a glorious, brave new world.

The Raelians teach that human beings are clones of extraterrestrials called *Elohim*, a word they say Jews and Christians have wrongly translated as "God." And just as cloning was the beginning of human life, so cloning is the key to human immortality. First, they want to develop cloning to produce children. Second, they hope to speed up the growth process so that an adult can be cloned in a few hours. Third, they will transfer the mind of an aged or infirm person to the new, youthful clone—a process that they can keep repeating forever to give human beings eternal life.

Bizarre, you say? Laughable? The Raelians claim that they have successfully completed step one with baby Eve. They claim that more clones are due in a couple of months, and there's a waiting list of two thousand people waiting to pay $200,000 each for a clone.

The Raelians may not be as far out in the fringe as they seem. Remember that Carl Sagan, Stephen Hawking, and other respected scientists have claimed that human life came from somewhere—perhaps somewhere in outer space—and redemption would come from outer space, as well.

This is an inevitable consequence of suppressing a biblical worldview. Pascal's "God-shaped vacuum" will be filled by something. It's part of our nature, because we're created in the image of God, and thus, we ask ultimate questions. We'll answer those questions one way or another, whether with truth from the Bible or with fanciful nonsense.

The announcement of the cloned baby's birth has thrust cloning onto the front pages of major newspapers. Cloning supporters are scrambling to distinguish so-called therapeutic cloning—in which embryos are created for destruction in medical experiments—from "reproductive" cloning.

I couldn't help noticing that ABC chose Christopher Reeve, who at the time was the country's most visible therapeutic cloning advocate, to release the switch that dropped the ball in Times Square to celebrate New Year's Eve a couple of years ago. In interviews, Reeve talked about his great humanitarian crusade.

But not so fast. The distinction between "therapeutic" cloning and "reproductive" cloning is a smoke screen. All cloning is reproductive. Who is going to enforce whether an embryo goes to a lab for experimentation or is implanted in a womb to be born? The Justice Department has testified that it cannot. In order to ban live-birth cloning, we must ban *all* human cloning. Politically, this is the time to do it because the president has said he wants a cloning ban.

In 2002, the House passed a total ban on human cloning by an overwhelming majority. In the Senate, a similar bill introduced by Senator Bill Brownback of Kansas was blocked by then-majority leader Tom Daschle (D-SD). The new majority leader, Bill Frist (R-TN), is a physician who happens to be on the right side of this issue.

This is the time to call your representative and your two senators and make your opposition to human cloning very clear. Urge them to pass a total ban on all human cloning.

The lid on the Pandora's box of unethical biotechnology has been raised. Now is the time to slam it back down and lock it tight.

TRUTHS TO CONSIDER

When we remove the biblical creator God from the picture, we seek answers to fill the God-shaped vacuum in ourselves and thus can arrive at conclusions originating from outer space.

There is no significant difference between therapeutic and reproductive cloning; the former is just a smoke screen to allow for the latter.

We must do whatever possible to ban all human cloning. We are made in the image of God, who alone has the rights of creation.

GROUP STUDY

The Spiritual Dimension: Perhaps the greatest form of idolatry is to take over the role of the Creator and make ourselves into our own gods. Cloning does this, but in what other ways do you do it by choosing your own will over God's?

Group Approach: The issues related to biotechnology are complex and sometimes confusing, but they have tremendous ramifications for our future. Work with others to identify major issues and stay abreast of trends.

Influencing Culture: There are multiple practical dangers in cloning, such as disease and malfunction. Start with these practical areas to convince others that going against nature is dangerous and could create as many problems as it solves.

DARWIN MADE ME DO IT

An Evolutionist Looks at Rape

The late comedian Flip Wilson used to get laughs when, by way of explaining his misdeeds, he would say, "The devil made me do it!"

Unfortunately, our culture no longer believes in the devil, so it has to look elsewhere to find explanations for the things people do. Increasingly, evolution has emerged as the explanation of choice—but it's an explanation that leaves a lot to be desired.

Psychologists, biologists, and anthropologists have all taken to explaining human behavior in purely Darwinian terms. In the past few years, scientists have argued that behaviors such as jealousy, altruism, and even infanticide have their origins in our ancestors' struggle to survive and pass on their genes.

The newest addition to the list is rape. In their book, *A Natural History of Rape*, Randy Thornhill and Craig T. Palmer argue that rape is "natural." That is, it occurs in nature and can be explained in biological terms.

The authors reject the view, best represented by Susan Brownmiller's 1975 book, *Against Our Will*, that rape is "an act of aggression, designed to intimidate women." Instead, they contend that rape has its origins in what could be called the "Darwinist imperative" to reproduce and pass on one's genes.

According to the authors, rape is "an adaptive reproductive strategy." In other words, males resort to rape when all other efforts to attract a mate fail. The authors cite examples of rape among animals and point to the fact that most rape victims are of childbearing age. They conclude that rape must be motivated, however unconsciously, by the desire to impregnate.

Not surprisingly, feminists are in an uproar. Thornhill has been the object of protests wherever he speaks. And in the latest issue of *Time* magazine, feminist writer Barbara Ehrenreich takes the pair to task.

It's mildly amusing, I must say, to watch the feminists in their uproar. Whether they realize it or not, they're in a logical bind. Most are avowed evolutionists, yet here evolution is being used to justify the exploitation of women. They are impaled on the sword of their own worldview.

The truth is that the whole evolutionist idea that we are manipulated by our genes is nonsense. Evolution can't explain most human behavior, especially those traits that Lincoln called "the better angels of our nature," such as altruism and mercy.

No, if you really want to understand what makes us tick, the only sensible answer resides in a Christian worldview. As I wrote in my recent book *How Now Shall We Live?* this worldview centers on three key ideas: creation, the Fall, and redemption. Since we are made in the image of God, we are capable of kindness and mercy, which reflect the nature of God. Since we are also fallen, we are also capable of great brutality, such as rape.

Books such as *A Natural History of Rape* purport to explain reality without reference to the biblical worldview. They end up demonstrating that only the biblical worldview offers an explanation of reality that makes sense—and that is a message our neighbors need to hear.

In the end, "Evolution made me do it" isn't as funny as Wilson's line. It's also not true.

TRUTHS TO CONSIDER

Blaming evolution or our genes for our misdeeds is as ineffective as any other way of sidestepping responsibility for our actions.

The theory that rape is an "adaptive reproductive strategy" takes no account of the violence done to the women thus assaulted or to the perpetrators, who act against humanity as God created it.

Darwinism is a form of an old Epicurean materialism that says that since everything evolved by chance, there is no good or evil and we can live any way we wish. However, this does not make it morally neutral. It is destructive of individuals and of culture.

GROUP STUDY

The Spiritual Dimension: How often do we play at being pawns of fate and blame our sin on our genetic makeup? Thank God that he has not placed us in an evolutionary mode but has "hardwired" us for him. He wants us to conform us to his image.

Group Approach: Though most Christians don't believe in evolution, feminism and determinism have affected the church. How can we keep up with the latest developments in opposing viewpoints so that we can counteract their negative effects?

Influencing Culture: Evolution is at the heart of diverging worldviews today; it underlies rampant autonomous individualism. It is supposedly a triumph of evolution that we should make our own choices without responsibility to a higher power. How can we model the authentic responsibility for our lives that emerges from accountability to God?

BORN OR MADE?

The Gay Debate

It has become the mantra of the gay lobby—sexual orientation is in our genes, and our biology is our destiny.

According to gay activist Denny Lee, "When people understand that being gay or lesbian is an integral characteristic, they are more open-minded about equality for gay Americans."

The problem is, there's no evidence that homosexuality is an "integral characteristic." It's something to keep in mind on the eve of the latest "gay holiday."

Radical gays are fond of quoting studies that purport to prove that gays are born, not made. For example, ten years ago, Simon LeVay of the Salk Institute announced that he had found a significant difference in the brain structures of homosexual and heterosexual men, but subsequent research by others failed to duplicate LeVay's findings.

The same goes for the research of Dean Hamer, who claims to have found a "gay gene." Hamer—who is gay—was subsequently investigated by the Office of Research Integrity of the U.S. Public Health Service.

Then there's a 1993 study on twins and sexual orientation by Boston University psychiatrist Richard Pillard. Pillard claims to have found evidence that homosexuality is a family trait. But Dr. Paul Ewald, an Amherst College biologist, told the Boston University *Daily Free Press* that Pillard's research made no such genetic connection.

Dr. Ruth Hubbard of the Council for Responsible Genetics says that the gay hype over genetics "is due to the fact that there is money to be made through biotechnology." And she adds that "there's no such thing as a gay gene" and that "it is a waste of time and money" to look for one. So why are researchers spending time on this?

If gays could prove that homosexuality is genetic, there would be, they believe, no excuse for making moral distinctions between homosexual and heterosexual behavior. But suppose there were a genetic connection. Would that justify gay "marriage"? At least one study has established a genetic connection to criminal behavior. Does that excuse crime? Of course not. What about a gene for heterosexual behavior? Does that mean that rape should be condoned? No! Nor does it mean that homosexual behavior is inevitable and acceptable. We are more than the sum of our genes.

Gay groups celebrate the "Day of Silence Project." They are encouraging students around the country to take a nine-hour vow of silence to protest what they consider inappropriate discrimination against homosexuals. We can expect the press to trot out all the same, tired claims about gay genes, which assume that we should just accept this behavior as perfectly normal and give homosexuals full rights to marry and to adopt children.

On that particular day of silence, why don't we do what many other Christians are doing and use the occasion to speak out about couples such as John and Anne Paulk, who both came out of the homosexual lifestyle, married, and raised a Christian family together.

We can also tell people about the phony research on so-called gay genes—and about the truth that God heals homosexuals through groups such as Exodus and Regeneration. True hope for homosexuals does not lie in a gay gene but in the gospel.

TRUTHS TO CONSIDER

There is no scientific evidence of a gay gene that establishes a biological predisposition to homosexual behavior.

Many gays and lesbians have been able to find healing through the power of Jesus Christ; they have left the gay lifestyle, married, and raised children.

Whether gay or not, genetic predispositions don't justify immoral behavior. We are all accountable for the wrong that we do.

GROUP STUDY

The Spiritual Dimension: What excuses of heredity or predisposition to weakness do you employ at times to justify sinful behavior? How can you overcome this with God's power?

Group Approach: Christians should support organizations such as Exodus, Regeneration, and others that help to set believers free from the bondage of addiction to sin. How do these organizations counteract claims that there are no alternatives to homosexual behavior?

Influencing Culture: Be ready to explain that homosexuality has no genetic origin. Communicate that although negative behavior may be related to past circumstances, it can still be overcome by God's grace.

SCIENCE WITHOUT LIMITS
Reinventing Parenthood

Two University of Pennsylvania researchers announced findings that, in the words of the *Washington Post*, "could blur the biological line between fathers and mothers."

Writing in the online journal *Science*, Hans Schoeler and Karin Huebner describe how they turned ordinary mouse embryonic stem cells into eggs capable of being fertilized.

What's more, the stem cells they used were from males. Thus, if the technique used by the two researchers were applicable to humans, it could be possible for a gay couple to have children "with one man contributing sperm and the other fresh eggs bearing his own genes."

That raises a new question. Should the man who contributed the cells for the egg be recognized as the child's "mother"? If not, what is he?

Scientists are abuzz. John Eppig, a mouse geneticist, told the *Washington Post* that "the mind boggles with potential wild applications of this stuff." Lee Silver, molecular biologist and bioethicist at Princeton, told the *Post* that the results "[break] down all the classic barriers in terms of sexual reproduction, with none of the problems of cloning."

But others were less enthusiastic. Douglas Johnson of National Right to Life, for one, called the results a potential big step toward opening "human embryo farms."

Johnson is right. But the even bigger threat comes from the hubris of researchers who feel free to "blur the biological lines between mothers and fathers." Even the risk of fundamentally changing what it means to be human doesn't seem to deter them.

It should, because even dyed-in-the-wool Darwinists would agree that sexual reproduction involving fathers and mothers must serve some important purpose. They would recognize that the only animal species without distinct roles for the sexes in reproduction are lower species such as amoebas and paramecia.

Darwinists such as Stephen Pinker of MIT would affirm that the differences between male and female go beyond their roles in reproduction. They are different in many ways—physically, mentally, and emotionally.

Christians, of course, affirm all of this and more. The respective roles and contributions of both sexes are what Genesis is referring to when it says, "male and female he created them." The history and destiny of life is inextricably tied up in that phrase. It is sheer madness to tamper with the distinction.

Christians shouldn't let anyone say that these concerns make us "Luddites" who fear technology. Bill McKibben, a science writer whom no one would call a Luddite, shares the same concerns. In his book *Enough: Staying Human in an Engineered Age*, he writes that the questions posed by biotechnology threaten to alter what it means to be human and are too important to be left to scientists. He asks, "Must we forever grow in reach and power? . . . Or can we, should we, ever say, 'Enough'?"

Exactly—which is why Christians ought to sound the alarm now, before science without limits blurs lines that were meant to be distinct and achieves what C. S. Lewis called the "abolition of man."

TRUTHS TO CONSIDER

We are at the point of blurring the distinction between fathers and mothers in the reproductive process and the very definition of what it means to be human.

Even Darwinists can see the importance of retaining male and female characteristics for purposes beyond reproduction, recognizing that mainly lower species don't have distinct gender roles.

Science without limits can bring about destruction that we cannot imagine or control. We need to promote genuine respect for the sanctity of life to help provide those limits.

GROUP STUDY

The Spiritual Dimension: If you have been born again, you have been spiritually regenerated by God. Have you tampered with the results by trying to bring about spiritual fruit through your own efforts?

Group Approach: How can we foster within the church a holy fear of tampering with the building blocks of creation? Can we recognize this as human pride and idolatry? Discuss the difficult line between conquering disease and assuming God's place when attempting to achieve that goal.

Influencing Culture: How can we convey that we do not automatically oppose technology but that we must discern which of these processes alter what it means to be human and therefore have negative consequences?

CONSENTING ADULTS
Responding to a Cannibal

In Germany, Armin Meiwes placed a personal ad on the Internet, seeking "a young, well-built man who wants to be eaten."

That's twisted all by itself, but it's not the worst part of the story. The worst part is that someone answered the ad.

Bernd Brandes, a man who is said to have had an obsession with pain, allowed himself to be killed and eaten by Meiwes. As a psychiatrist later determined, Meiwes had severe "emotional problems," and later, he was sentenced to eight-and-a-half years in prison.

But some argue that he didn't commit a crime. In fact, the case raises some very disturbing questions for German and American societies. The idea of an unchangeable moral law given by God has been abandoned. The idea today is that we're autonomous— we're free to do whatever we want, as long as we don't hurt somebody else. That puts us in an awkward position when we try to determine just what Meiwes did wrong. By what standard can a modern secularist argue that Meiwes acted inappropriately?

But didn't Meiwes hurt Brandes? That depends on who you ask. Meiwes's lawyer argued that this was a case of "killing on request." Brandes wished to die, and Meiwes accommodated him. In Holland—and in Oregon, for that matter—it is legal to help fulfill such a wish.

Perhaps the secularist could say that he finds killing and cannibalism repulsive. But that's no argument. Some pro-choice activists, when pressed, will admit that they find partial-birth abortion repulsive. But they'll fight for it because they believe that any restrictions on abortions are a blow to their personal autonomy. So how can they object to the way these two men exercised their personal autonomy, even if it was repulsive?

Columnist and physician Theodore Dalrymple makes exactly this point in *City Journal*. Dalrymple writes, "Meiwes and Brandes were consenting adults: By what right, therefore, has the state interfered in their slightly odd relationship? Of course, one might argue that by eating Brandes, Meiwes was infringing on his meal's rights, and acting against his interests. But Brandes decided that it was in his interests to be eaten, and in general, we believe that the individual, not the state, is the best judge of his own interests."

Once we stop believing in the sanctity of human life or in the dignity of each person created in the image of God or in an absolute moral law, how can we argue with an individual's decision to throw away his own life? How can we ask the state to step in to protect his life, to save him from himself?

I'm reminded of the U.S. Supreme Court decision *Planned Parenthood v. Casey*, in which Justice Kennedy famously wrote, "At the heart of liberty is the right to define one's own concept of existence, of meaning, of the universe, and of the mystery of human life." Armin Meiwes and Bernd Brandes took that morally bankrupt definition of liberty to its logical—if extreme and repulsive—conclusion. And the frightening part is that a world that has largely abandoned the Christian worldview has no meaningful response to give them.

TRUTHS TO CONSIDER

If personal consent and the supreme right of the individual are the criteria in law for what is permissible, then our society will inevitably go beyond pornography or homosexuality to more extreme issues such as euthanasia and even cannibalism.

As a society, we no longer believe in the sanctity of human life but only in our own right to do what we want with it, even if that is vile, inhuman behavior.

Christians believe that their rights emanate from a higher source. The world can find no substitute response that retains civilized behavior. Thus, we don't have the right to do whatever we want just because we want to, even if no one appears to get hurt.

GROUP STUDY

The Spiritual Dimension: How has God enabled you to put a curb on your own fallen tendencies? Are you ever plagued by irrational thoughts that border on perversion or exploitation? Ask for God's healing grace.

Group Approach: How can we explain the fallen tendencies of the autonomous individual to others? Cannibalism is an extreme example, but we need to apply the same logical principles to the small events of our lives.

Influencing Culture: This is a great story to use in dialogue with people of other worldviews, as it illustrates the conclusions of the world's logic. Through disillusionment, a hunger for the Christian alternative may emerge.

BEARING WITNESS
The Martyrs of Uganda

One constant of Christian history is that persecution rarely, if ever, succeeds. While some Christians may succumb to its unimaginable pressures, many others are, as the Bible puts it, faithful unto death. In turn, their witness, which is what the word *martyr* means, draws others to the faith. In the second century, the apologist Tertullian wrote, "Go on, rack, torture, grind us to powder: Our numbers increase in proportion as you mow us down. The blood of Christians is their harvest seed."

A century ago, twenty-six young African Christians proved

Tertullian right. In so doing, they set an example not only for their contemporaries, but also for us. In the late 1800s, Anglican and Catholic missionaries brought Christianity to what is now Uganda. While at first people were free to convert to the new faith, conversion created problems for the converts. Becoming a Christian meant adopting new moral and religious standards and suggested having turned one's back on old allegiances. As a result, Christians were often regarded as rebels.

Mistrust turned to persecution when a new king named Mwanga came to the throne. His court was infamous for homosexual debauchery. Suddenly, Christians were not only undermining the old religious and political order, but they had the temerity to criticize his sexual practices. Events came to a head when the king's pages began to resist his sexual advances. His outrage turned to murderous rage against Christianity when he learned why they had resisted. They had become Christians and were living chastely as their new faith required.

Mwanga gave the new converts a choice: complete obedience to his orders, including his sexual demands, or their new faith and death. They chose martyrdom. On June 3, 1886, twenty-six converts between the ages of thirteen and thirty, Protestants and Catholics, were burnt to death. Their leader, Charles Lwanga, asked to be untied so he could arrange the sticks on his pyre. While few remember the tyrant who martyred these Christians, the Martyrs of Uganda, as they are known, became heroes of the faith. Today, largely because of their witness, Uganda is mostly a Christian nation—one that is offended and scandalized by the easy acceptance of homosexuality that exists in some of our churches.

There's another lesson for us as well. Christians in the West face pressure, albeit nothing like Lwanga and his companions, to play down Christianity's moral demands, especially regarding sexual practices. We're told that things will go better for us if we remain quiet about issues such as abortion, homosexuality, and gay "marriage." Those who do speak out are called bigots, but if Charles Lwanga could tell his executioner that he was glad to die for the faith, being called names, however unfairly, is a small price to pay. Remembering these martyrs, the church in Uganda and other parts of Africa stands firm in resisting same-sex "marriages" and the ordination of homosexuals. It's costing them financial support, and their reputation is being hurt, yet they stand with the martyrs in bearing witness to absolute truth and to God's moral law. As they resist the hostile spirit of the age, they are a model for us all to follow.

TRUTHS TO CONSIDER

Most Western Christians have little concept of being persecuted for their faith. Our brothers and sisters in other parts of the world often inspire and challenge us to remain faithful regardless of the social or political consequences.

Our culture fears death and does everything possible to deny it and distract us from thinking about it. Christ has already conquered death—we do not have to be afraid of it.

In our culture, we are rarely put to death for our beliefs, but we are often asked to compromise our faith in more subtle ways.

GROUP STUDY

The Spiritual Dimension: Our government has departed from laws that take God into account, yet we sometimes forget this. How can we judge the laws we face according to their alignment with God's law and seek what God wishes us to do?

Group Approach: How do we work together to ensure just laws, especially in the interests of those who are powerless to speak for themselves?

Influencing Culture: Do we feature the lives of courageous men and women who have stood up for God's ways to the point of losing their careers, reputations, or lives? Do we promote them as heroes alongside athletic and entertainment stars?

EMOTIONAL RESPONSES
Moral Sentiment Is Not Enough

Are you pro-life? If so, can you explain *why* you're pro-life?

It turns out that most Americans cannot. When sociologist James Davison Hunter interviewed people for his book *Before the Shooting Begins*, he discovered that most Americans base their moral beliefs entirely on private feelings.

Take a young man named Scott, a former Catholic. Scott argues fiercely that the fetus is a human being, yet he insists that abortion should be legal. The fetus is a person to me, Scott said, but it "might not be a person to that mother."

What Scott fails to see is that personhood is an objective fact. The fetus either is or is not a person, regardless of what you and I think.

But Scott is typical of Americans today. They base their moral views on sentiment, not conviction. On the pro-choice side, Hunter asked an architect named Paul why he supports the right to abortion. Paul became agitated. "I don't want to get into philosophical or theological wrangling," he said. "My feelings are based on experiences that are mine alone, and you can't tell me they are wrong."

Notice how Paul begs off from any objective discussion of abortion based on philosophy or theology, even at the most elementary level. Instead, he treats private experience as the final court of appeal.

You know, if Paul ran his architectural firm the way he makes moral decisions—if he based his construction blueprints on sheer feelings—his buildings would collapse. To be a good architect, Paul treats physical facts as qualitatively different from moral values.

But when we separate facts and values, genuine moral debate becomes impossible. If morality is merely a matter of private feelings, then any attempt to reason with people is perceived as a personal attack.

Listen to the words of a young mother named Karen. Karen told Hunter she would never dream of getting an abortion herself. Yet she could not bring herself to say that abortion is morally wrong for everybody. "I don't know how [other people] feel," she said defensively. Apparently Karen's greatest fear is that if she says abortion is wrong, she will hurt someone's feelings.

The majority of Americans, Hunter discovered, are just like Karen—pro-life in their personal lives, yet pro-choice politically. Many are even hostile to the organized pro-life movement because, in their words, pro-life activists "are trying to impose their views on everyone else."

Hunter's book does us a great service by delving into the way most Americans really think about abortion—or I should say, how they feel. Those of us who base our opposition to abortion on conviction instead of sentiment need to know that we are up against the highly articulate pro-choice movement as well as the inarticulate, inchoate opposition of most pro-lifers—those who have lost a sense of objective moral truth.

The battle is no longer just over the status of the unborn; it's over the status of truth itself.

TRUTHS TO CONSIDER

In the prevalent cultural worldview, moral views are based on feelings and experiences instead of on an objective standard. Thus, we feel that we can't tell others that their views are wrong.

Moral judgments are just as true as physical facts if based on absolute truth; they bind us to a higher standard, whether or not it is convenient and whether or not we like it.

Pro-lifers who allow personal preference to replace truth hurt the pro-life movement and compromise any other issue where truth is at stake.

GROUP STUDY

The Spiritual Dimension: Because we feel pressure to be tolerant, we now hesitate to tell others that absolute truth is binding for everyone. How can we follow Paul's admonition to speak the truth in love without compromising any part of the truth?

Group Approach: Let's hold others in the church accountable when they acknowledge the right position based on God's law but are not willing to stand up for it for fear of hurting someone's feelings. Can we discuss the implications of our beliefs with each other without placing blame?

Influencing Culture: An example such as that of Paul and his architectural firm is a great way to make an analogy to facts and feelings. We don't ignore natural laws; we need to show that in the past the Judeo-Christian worldview provided strength and prosperity by observing universal moral laws as well.

WHAT'S REALLY "HARMFUL TO MINORS"

Sex and Worldview

If journalist Judith Levine intended to stir up controversy with her book *Harmful to Minors*, she succeeded in spades. As word about the book spread, it was attacked for presenting pedophilia as an "alternative lifestyle." Levine rejects that characterization, calling it an example of the "hysteria" that prompted her to write the book.

While Levine does not condone pedophilia in its technical sense—that is, sexual relations by adults with prepubescent children—there's little else she rules out of bounds. Levine denies that sex between minors and adults is always wrong. She writes that teens seek out sex with older people for what she considers "understandable reasons."

In an interview with the Newhouse newspapers, Levine demonstrated just how far "understandable" could be stretched. She said, "Yes, absolutely," when asked if a sexual relationship between a priest and a boy could be a positive experience for the boy. She added that some research suggests that such experiences can be positive for even young children.

In Levine's telling, the real danger in sexual relationships between minors and adults comes not from the relationship but from our reaction to the relationship. As the title of one of the book's sections puts it, "The Enemy Is Us."

To fight this "enemy," Levine suggests revising laws governing sexual consent. She holds up Dutch law, which allows kids as young as twelve to consent to sex, as an example for us to follow. This would be just a part of the shift in societal attitudes toward the sexual lives of our kids that she recommends.

In many respects, it doesn't matter if Levine's book does or does not specifically endorse pedophilia, as either way the result is the same. Children will be sexually active and, as a result, exploited and damaged at younger and younger ages.

But is Levine really so radical, or is she just carrying our culture's attitudes about sex to their logical conclusions? She is to sexual liberation, in my opinion, what Peter Singer, the Princeton professor who advocates infanticide, is to the culture of death: She shows us the deadly consequences of this secular worldview.

That worldview denies that sex has anything to do with morality or truth. It considers traditional sexual morality, and most notably biblical morality, as a way of controlling people, especially women.

It views attempts to curb sexual liberties as repressive and, thus, as emotionally harmful.

For Levine and our culture, there are no prohibitions when it comes to sex. What matters is consent and avoiding exploitation or being exploited. Of course, these are thin reeds with which to protect our children—or even ourselves—from harm.

The only way to effectively oppose the pernicious nonsense of Levine's book is to attack the worldview that makes this kind of wrongheadedness possible. Ironically, *Harmful to Minors* may help Christians by giving us an apologetic argument. After all, if we force people like Levine to take their arguments to their logical conclusion, we expose the fallacy of their belief systems. We show that they simply don't work. People must be shown that this book is dangerous and that the presuppositions about life that underlie it are even more dangerous.

TRUTHS TO CONSIDER

We have now moved to the place in our culture where some are proposing that pedophilia is acceptable if there is consent and avoidance of exploitation. However, it is unclear how child sexual abuse can avoid exploitation.

Our negative reaction to pedophilia is not what is damaging; rather, it is the extreme psychological, emotional, and spiritual damage that results from child sexual abuse.

Sex with children is a logical consequence of the culture's view of the unrestricted sexual rights of individuals. This can be used in counter-arguments against sexual permissiveness.

GROUP STUDY

The Spiritual Dimension: As with sex, we often take other good and pleasurable things and pervert or distort them by overindulgence or by using them in the wrong ways, for the wrong reasons. Examine your own life in this regard.

Group Approach: Work with parents you know to help them educate their children and protect them from potential pedophiles.

Influencing Culture: As you interact with others who hold different views on the rights and wrongs of sexual behavior, point to some of the negative consequences of their views, and help them make the logical connection between cause and effect.

APPLES, TEACHERS, AND SERPENTS
Academia's Assault on Our Children

Penn State University made headlines for a sexually explicit event held on its campus. The keynote speaker for Penn State's Conference on Women's Health and Wellness was Patrick Califia-Rice, an outspoken advocate of pedophilia and sadomasochism.

Just how radical is this self-described "transgender bisexual person"? NAMBLA, the North American Man-Boy Love Association, features this quote from Califia-Rice on its Web site: "Boy-lovers and the lesbians who have young lovers . . . are not child molesters. The child abusers are priests, teachers, therapists, cops, and parents who force their stale morality onto the young people in their custody. Instead of condemning pedophiles for their involvement with lesbian and gay youth, we should be supporting them."

Shocking? Indeed. Rare? No. The academic world is becoming increasingly brazen in its attempts to legitimize sex between adults and children.

I have reported on a book called *Harmful to Minors*, published by the University of Minnesota Press. In it, author Judith Levine supports loosening restrictions against sex between adults and minors. While conservatives were rightly outraged, many so-called sexually liberated folks reviewed the book favorably. Levine's book seems to have become a beacon to others who are trying to jump-start public debate about children's sexuality.

One such scholar is Jorja Prover of the University of California at Los Angeles. As she explained to the *Chicago Tribune*, "What we've been talking about in academic circles for a decade has been brought to public attention in a dramatic way."

Levine is not alone in exploring these taboos. Earlier this year, University of Missouri professor Harris Mirkin ignited a firestorm when he published an article in the *Journal of Homosexuality* that dismissed fears surrounding child sexual abuse. He wrote, "Like homosexuality, the concept of child molestation is a culture- and class-specific modern creation." Mirkin also wrote, "Though Americans consider intergenerational sex" [note what they call it] "to be evil, it has been permissible or obligatory in many cultures and periods of history."

As the *Wall Street Journal* responded, human sacrifice was considered normal and obligatory in other cultures and time periods, but that doesn't mean we should embrace it now.

One good thing about Mirkin and Levine is that they are revealing the ugly face of extreme sexual "liberation" that is all too common on college campuses. This worldview claims that the pursuit of sexual gratification need not recognize any social norms, whether laws, age, or species. And unfortunately, what is being whispered among academics today has a way of infecting our culture tomorrow.

To their credit, Missouri lawmakers loudly denounced Mirkin's writings and reappropriated $100,000 from the university's budget to the state's Crime Victim's Compensation Fund. As one legislator put it, "Let Mirkin say what he wants to, but my taxpayer dollars should not go to justify his research." Indeed!

Whether in fashion, court decisions, TV, or academics, when children are being harmed by a dangerous view of sexuality, Christians need to forcefully oppose it. As the wise statesman Edmund Burke once said, "The only thing necessary for the triumph of evil is for good men to do nothing." Let that not be said of us.

TRUTHS TO CONSIDER

The idea that pedophilia or sadomasochism could never be accepted in popular culture is as naive as the earlier thinking that homosexual adoption or marriage could never happen.

Many cultures in the past have accepted pedophilia, but they have also accepted human sacrifice—both of which are abominations to God and destructive of humans.

If no boundaries are to be observed concerning sexual gratification, no one will be considered off-limits, even if they are not mature enough to withhold consent or to realize the long-term consequences of their actions.

GROUP STUDY

The Spiritual Dimension: In the Old Testament, children were sacrificed to the god Molech in the interest of personal prosperity for their parents. The gods of the sexual revolution are attempting to devour our children. How can we protect them?

Group Approach: How can the church enter this public debate more effectively and at an earlier stage in order to protect children? How can we avoid either assuming that the worst will never happen or that things are already too bad for us to do anything about?

Influencing Culture: Do you understand the links between mental, spiritual, and emotional illness in adults and the molestation of those individuals when they were children? Use these insights as you interact with and minister to these victims.

"GENERATION PRO-CHOICE"
The Battle for Their Hearts and Minds

January 22 is the anniversary of the tragic Supreme Court decision in *Roe v. Wade*. We all know what over thirty years of legalized abortion have meant to this country: the deaths of millions
of children and the remorse and pain of millions of mothers and
fathers. But they mean something else. An entire generation—
the survivors—has always known nothing but *Roe* as the law of
the land.

NARAL Pro-Choice America, one of the biggest abortion advocacy groups, isn't overlooking that fact. In fact, it has turned

it into a slick marketing strategy. One of its Web sites, "Generation Pro-Choice," is geared directly to the under-thirty generation.

This site greets young viewers with these words: "If you support access to birth control, sex education, and abortion, and you've never lived in a time when abortion was illegal—then congratulations, you are Generation Pro-Choice. And we need your help in getting other young people involved in the fight to protect the right to privacy and a woman's right to choose—or else, quite frankly, we're going to lose it."

Visitors to the site can select a "sassy e-mail card" with a prochoice message that they can send to their friends. They can write to an advice columnist to learn how to protect their rights or take the "Pro-Choice Personality Challenge" quiz or learn to "organize on campus." In short, they can learn all kinds of "fun and cool ways" to push for abortion and to recruit their friends.

It's a savvy move on NARAL's part. The generation that fought for legalized abortion won't always be with us. If the pro-abortion side doesn't win the hearts and minds of the next generation now, its cause could fail.

And it's not surprising that there's a whiff of desperation about NARAL's efforts. In *World* magazine, Lynn Vincent writes, "Teens, increasingly, just don't like abortion. In a Gallup poll, 72 percent of American teenagers agreed that abortion is morally wrong. One-third said abortion should be illegal in all circumstances, compared with 17 percent of adults." A good trend, but don't be complacent.

As Suzanne Eller, author of the forthcoming book *Real Teens,*

Real Issues, reminded *World*, people don't always realize that "this is one of the most intelligent generations ever." She says that teens and young adults appreciate being taken seriously and appealed to on important issues. So despite the hokey attempts to be hip, NARAL is striking the right chord by telling young people that they can make a difference and by emphasizing concepts such as "choice" and "sexual freedom."

The good news is that pro-life groups know how critical the battle is. If the March for Life follows the patterns of the past few years, it will be what one friend described as "a big youth rally." We are reaching this generation. We need to help educate them, including our own kids, on how to make their case. We need to educate kids as to how to fend off the NARAL kind of appeal and teach them the basics of human dignity while encouraging them to talk to their friends. After all, we were fighting for this generation's rights even before they were born. That's a claim NARAL can never make.

TRUTHS TO CONSIDER

Pro-abortion forces are worried because the younger generation is able to observe the downside of abortion and its effects and are becoming pro-life in increasing numbers.

NARAL emphasizes the right to privacy and the right to choose to this generation but ignores the right to life and the remorse and pain of those who have experienced abortions.

Ironically, the very generation that pro-abortion forces appeal to is the first generation they said we had a right to kill.

GROUP STUDY

The Spiritual Dimension: How does God feel about the weak and powerless? What did he do to protect them in the Old Testament? Research the stand of the early Christian church on the issue of abortion.

Group Approach: Many are giving up on the abortion fight, feeling that it's a lost cause. What can you do to get involved in the various branches of the pro-life movement? Can you encourage a mother to have her baby or contact your congressional representative regarding partial-birth abortion issues?

Influencing Culture: How can you reach those young people (not necessarily Christians) who haven't made up their minds about abortion and gently explain your pro-life stance? Can you help your kids to do the same?

OBVIOUS BUT FALSE

Common Views of Love and Courtship

Ask the typical college student what love is. That's a no-brainer—love is a romantic feeling, right? And what is the purpose of sex? Pleasure, of course. What else could it be?

In his new book, *Ask Me Anything: Provocative Answers for College Students*, University of Texas professor J. Budziszewski tells students that both of these obvious answers are dead wrong. Take the idea that love is a feeling. If that were really true, then how could people getting married promise to love each other until they are parted by death? Feelings come and go, and you can't promise a feeling. What you can promise is a commitment of the will to the good of the other person. And that's what love is.

And there's that other obvious-but-wrong answer that the purpose of sex is pleasure. "False," says Budziszewski. Of course, sex is pleasurable, but that doesn't make pleasure its purpose. The exercise of every natural power is pleasurable. Eating is pleasurable; taking a deep breath is pleasurable; flexing a muscle is pleasurable. Is the purpose of all those things also pleasure? Think what that would imply. If the purpose of eating were pleasure, then if it gave you more pleasure to eat, purge, and eat some more, you ought to do it. The reason you shouldn't is that the purpose of eating isn't pleasure but nutrition. In the same way, says Budziszewski, the purpose of our sexual powers isn't pleasure but procreation, or making families.

In a snappy dialogue format, Budziszewski takes up these and many similar questions. The first part of the book is what he calls "girl and guy stuff." What are "the moves" of courtship, and why are they so hard to figure out? Is "missionary dating" a good idea or a bad one? Does it matter who you live with? Why do so many people seem to be afraid of growing up? And here's an explosive one: I got my girlfriend pregnant—now what?

My favorite question is why "sowing your wild oats" never works out the way it's supposed to. Sexuality, Budziszewski says, is like duct tape. The first time you use it, it sticks you to whomever it touches. But just like that duct tape, if you rip it off and then touch it to someone else, it isn't as sticky as it was before. So what happens when you pull it loose from one partner after another? Budziszewski explains that you just don't stick anymore; your sexual partners seem like strangers, and you stop feeling anything.

I like that answer. Not only is it thoroughly biblical, but it honors our natural design—the way we are actually made to fit the world as it really is. If you want to learn more about how to explain the creational plan for love and courtship to the young people in your life, check out this wonderful new book: *Ask Me Anything: Provocative Answers for College Students.*

Don't forget. If we go against the way God designed us to live, we are cutting across the grain of the universe, and we're asking for trouble. All we have to do to live right is to get with the plan—his plan, that is.

TRUTHS TO CONSIDER

Engaging in premarital sexual activity is, among other factors, a contributor to depression among teens; it does not help them to achieve sexual fulfillment.

Sexual activity was not designed as recreation that exploits and damages a person; it is the ultimate act of self-giving, mutual enjoyment, and support in the loving and safe covenant of marriage.

There is a myth that experience with successive sexual partners improves sexual functioning. Instead, it erodes the trust and care that make sexual relationships deeply meaningful.

GROUP STUDY

The Spiritual Dimension: Have you hurt or exploited someone in the area of sexual intimacy or vice versa? What steps have you taken to make things right, find healing, and move on to greater sexual wholeness through God's power?

Group Approach: What can we say to children from youth to engagement age regarding God's design for the sacredness of sexual activity and why we find sexual joy and fulfillment only within marriage?

Influencing Culture: In our culture, people fear that abstinence means missing out on something fun and fulfilling. How can you point to the greater happiness, security, and worth enjoyed by those who wait?

MARRIAGE AND THE FAMILY

LIE 2

Marriage can be between any two people, and it lasts only as long as both are happy.

Underlying Worldview: Marriage is not a sacred lifetime covenant between a man and a woman but a contract between any two individuals that should be dissolved when mutual benefits seem to cease. "Family" can be defined as any intimate and loosely committed group of individuals.

To foster moral and social stability, Western civilization has granted a unique status and benefits to heterosexual marriage and family relationships. These privileges are now under assault, primarily by those with limitless sexual and material demands. The roles and sexual orientations of the partners in marriage and family relationships are becoming interchangeable. This results in a movement toward gay marriage and adoption, increasing singleness and single-parent families, children born out of wedlock, and divorce.

Divorce rates have increased dramatically under this scenario, but the government doesn't do much to help. In a selection on divorce within this chapter, Jesse Ventura, ex-wrestler and former governor of Minnesota, says that premarital classes sponsored by the government would be "an insult to every free-thinking American's intelligence." Often, leaders in our culture don't even see the magnitude of the problems within our families.

Marriage is increasingly viewed as a negotiable contract, a perspective that feeds into our obsession with careers and materialism. Marriage is seen as a transaction and relationships as commodities. The need for more status and more stuff allows for less quality time with our spouses and kids. This is illustrated in this chapter by a reference to the movie *Elf*, in which a workaholic father (played by James Caan) is too busy to spend quality time with his son. When work beckons on Christmas Eve, he's faced with a choice between work and family.

More than thirty years ago, Betty Friedan, one of the founders of the feminist movement, wrote a book called *The Feminine Mystique*, which helped to send women into the workplace in droves. The negative effects are felt today by children and also by wives who experience a profound discontent with being absent from their main role as parents. Ironically, another selection deals with a homosexual parent who chooses to stay at home while the other parent is the breadwinner—right priorities but wrong values.

Increasingly, the state considers education to be the territory of government. Despite deterioration in our government-run educational system, parents are pressured to abdicate responsibility and play less of a guiding role in their children's education and formation. A Christian worldview sees both marriage and family as divinely ordained institutions that mirror the relationship among members of the Trinity. Married couples express this love in sacred covenant before God; they procreate and nurture children who mirror themselves. We need to allow God's radiant glory to be seen through our faithful commitments and our sacrificial love to our spouses and children. We also need to pursue the greater joy and fulfillment to be found in the quality time we gain as we put possessions and prestige in their proper place.

THE DIVORCE DISASTER

A State of Marital Emergency

"[It's] an insult to every free-thinking American's intelligence." That's what Gov. Jesse Ventura thinks of a Minnesota law designed to reduce divorce. The law was written to let couples take fifty dollars off the cost of a marriage license if they completed a premarital class. But Ventura vetoed it, claiming that government has no business getting into the marriage-counseling business.

Well, Ventura is wrong. Given the damage divorce causes society—in welfare and crime costs alone—government should do everything it can to help encourage strong marriages.

Consider that today, more than half of all marriages end in divorce. People who divorce are more likely to die from stroke, heart disease, cancer, and hypertension. Kids from broken homes are more likely to fail in school, abuse drugs and alcohol, commit crimes, and have children out of wedlock. In fact, Wade Horn, president of the National Fatherhood Initiative, says that children who grow up outside of a two-parent home "do worse on just about every measure of child well-being."

The evidence is clear. The cost of marital failure is paid by all of society, not just the couple whose marriage is shattered. And yet, as Oklahoma Gov. Frank Keating put it, it's easier to get out of a marriage than a Tupperware contract.

The good news is that state lawmakers are going all out to promote marriage-saving programs endorsed by the church—programs that have a proven track record.

My friend Mike McManus, who runs a ministry called Marriage Savers, says that lawmakers "are beginning to see that [saving marriages] is important not just for the individuals involved, but for the economy." That's why it makes sense "politically as well as sociologically to reduce the carnage of divorce," McManus says.

In Arkansas, Gov. Mike Huckabee has declared "a state of marital emergency." He wants to give state tax credits to couples who participate in premarital counseling. In Oklahoma, Gov. Keating has redirected $10 million in federal welfare funds to programs promoting marriage.

Florida passed the very law that Jesse Ventura rejected. It offers a discounted price for marriage licenses to couples who have completed premarital counseling. And Floridians are not waiting for kids to get engaged before preparing them for marriage. Florida teenagers can't graduate from high school without taking a class on marriage and family.

Some two dozen other states are also designing laws to make it harder to get a divorce.

Well, this is all good news—but critics have lost no time in beating up on these laws. For instance, the Freedom from Religion Foundation attacked a Wisconsin law that created a state marriage policy coordinator. The foundation claimed that paying a state official to help churches design community premarital counseling policies violates the separation of church and state. Sadly, a federal court agreed—and overturned the law.

You and I have to work with our own state legislators to create lawsuit-proof laws that encourage couples to think twice before tying the knot—and then make it harder to untie it, especially when children are involved.

Minnesotans, I hope, will agree that Jesse Ventura is dead wrong. The real insult to our intelligence is not premarital counseling but continuing to ignore the marital breakdown that's devastating American society. That's why fighting divorce with all the weapons the state has is a smart thing to do.

TRUTHS TO CONSIDER

Divorce has unrecognized effects on our society and economy in the areas of education, crime, drugs, disease, and emotional damage.

Our country has reached a state of marital emergency in which marriage is trivialized. Preparation and commitment are seriously lacking, but government and church now have an opportunity to revive and support the institution.

As the church, we cannot ignore this breakdown. We have tools to help provide the answers and the power to reinvigorate marriages.

GROUP STUDY

The Spiritual Dimension: The apostle Paul talks about total self-sacrifice and surrender within marriage. Where do you stand in this regard? Renew your commitment to be like Christ as it applies to your marriage.

Group Approach: Could you as church members find a younger couple that needs mentoring and encouragement? Could you find an older couple from whom to receive wisdom and guidance as you enter new stages of marriage?

Influencing Culture: Here are two ways to make a positive impact with your marriage. Love one another in little ways that your friends and neighbors will notice. Come alongside a married couple with a different worldview who needs your unconditional friendship.

LIFE BEYOND THE CUBICLE
Where Do Our Priorities Lie?

There is a scene in the movie *Elf*—a great family film sure to become a holiday classic—that should be familiar to many American families. When the father, played by James Caan, arrives late to dinner, he doesn't stop moving. Instead, he fills his plate while telling his wife and son that he'll be eating in his bedroom because he's very busy and has brought home a pile of work he has to do.

The film comes to a climax when the son arrives at his father's office, where he's working late on Christmas Eve of all nights, and the father has to decide between his job and his family.

Work or family. That's a decision moms and dads face every day. Americans pride themselves on a strong work ethic, but that ethic has disintegrated into a contest for who can work the most.

Columnist Amy Joyce of the *Washington Post* has been following the lives of eighty-hour-a-week Washingtonians. Recently, Joyce wrote about Lisa, whose father worked long hours and died before he could pursue any of his dreams and hobbies. This left Lisa "with strong feelings regarding the importance of maintaining a work-life balance." Then there's Kate, who has found a good balance. "Work will come and go," she reasons. "But there is only one life."

Similar thinking is going on in New York City. Recently in the *New York Times Magazine,* Lisa Belkin traced the lives of eight highly successful women who "had it all"—and found it all unsatisfying.

These eight women had Princeton degrees and Harvard and Columbia law degrees. "They chose husbands who could keep up with them" and "waited to have children because work was too exciting." The feminist dream? Not exactly. "I don't want to be on the fast track leading to a partnership at a prestigious law firm," said Katherine Brokaw, who left the workplace to stay home with her three children. "Some people define that as success. I don't," said Vicky McElhaney Benedict, another successful lawyer who quit to stay home with her children. "This is what I was meant to do. . . . I like life's rhythms when I'm nurturing a child."

In one sense, feminism has had a positive effect, argues Belkin. Capable female employees are coveted for their talents, but in a backlash against the feminist ideal, they're also more willing to leave, generally claiming family obligations. The "glass ceiling" was not the problem; it was their deep-down desire to be mothers. Many companies are recognizing the need to eliminate the dilemma of deciding between work and family by granting extended leave and, in some cases, sabbaticals. That, in turn, has had a positive impact on fathers who have taken advantage of this benefit and are able to manage their schedules around their family life, reversing the "absentee father" model.

This plainly illustrates the natural order of the way God created us. We're wired for work, of course, to be productive, but we're also created to have children and raise them. Women wanting to be home with their children are a good sign, not only of biology, but of moral disposition. It's a good sign, as well, that more and more women are discovering the lies of feminism. What really matters are those moments with the family—not reaching the next rung on the corporate ladder.

TRUTHS TO CONSIDER

Many women who have risen to the top in the marketplace find the rewards to be incomplete and unsatisfying, even with all the perks and recognition.

The moments with the family spent in nurturing, training, and intimacy matter more at a deep level than the next plaudit on the job.

There are creative ways to be productive in a dual-career relationship so that neither spouse has to be an absentee at home.

GROUP STUDY

The Spiritual Dimension: Search the book of Ecclesiastes and discover what the writer has to say about the vanity of toil under the sun. How do you keep the bigger perspective in mind and put the Kingdom of God and your family first?

Group Approach: How can you and others in your group better balance work and family by both providing well and spending quality time together? Compare notes with others, hold one another accountable, and keep each other in prayer.

Influencing Culture: Quality time is a felt need in our culture. How can we encourage this positive stay-at-home trend by arguing effectively that we are most fulfilled when giving time and love, rather than things, to our families?

"THE PROBLEM"
The New Female Phenomenon

In 1963, Betty Friedan wrote a book about "the problem that has no name," referring to the alienation and meaninglessness experienced by housewives. The book was called *The Feminine Mystique* and is credited with igniting the modern feminist movement and helping to drive millions of women out of their homes and into the workplace.

A generation of women later, Danielle Crittenden has written a book about what she calls "The Problem," but it's precisely opposite to the problem Friedan identified. It's the misery today's working mothers feel about leaving their children every day.

As Crittenden writes in her book *What Our Mothers Didn't Tell Us*, young women today are told to fit motherhood into their careers and are warned against letting motherhood "define them." But many women are surprised to discover that they like being mothers. Until you are holding your baby in your arms, Crittenden says, "You can't know how you're going to feel when you become a mother. This is motherhood's greatest joy and darkest secret. Suddenly, you can't stop thinking about your child."

The intense mother-child bond is usually ignored by our policy makers. "In all the policy discussion of the problems faced by working mothers," Crittenden says, the fact that "we love our children more than anything else and want to be with them as much as we possibly can . . . goes unmentioned." Instead, feminists try to convince mothers that "such feelings are imposed upon us by a sexist society." They dismiss full-time motherhood as "a servile and ultimately dangerous state for women to succumb to," Crittenden notes.

So-called solutions such as cheaper child care or family leave acts don't help. They aggravate the problem, Crittenden says, because they're based upon the wrong assumption "that a mother wants and needs more help being in the workforce away from her children, not less."

Even if every mother had Mary Poppins as a nanny, Crittenden asserts, she would still harbor "the agonizing suspicion that what her child needs most is *her*."

That assertion, by the way, is backed up by polls showing that a majority of mothers say they'd prefer to stay home with their children if they could.

That innate desire is backed up by Scripture, where some of the most striking images depicting God's nurturing concern for his people are those of mothering. For example, we read in Isaiah 66:13 that "As a mother comforts her child, so I will comfort you." And 1 Thessalonians 2:7 says, "We were . . . like a mother caring for her little children."

Danielle Crittenden is right. Instead of trying to find ways to make it easier for mothers to leave their children, we ought to help them find ways to stay home with them, if that's what they want to do. We should support changes in the tax code that would allow families to keep more of a father's income, so mothers are not forced into the workplace while their children are still in diapers. And we should encourage businesses to offer flextime and home-based work.

As we celebrate Mother's Day, we should commit ourselves to helping mothers who *must* work to find ways to spend more time with their kids. At the same time, we must remind mothers who choose to care for their own children that doing so does not put them in a "servile and dangerous state," as the feminists claim. Instead, motherhood is a sacred trust from God.

TRUTHS TO CONSIDER

There is really no surrogate for a mother's care for her child that can provide the holistic growth the child needs.

Many working mothers are not looking for better child support benefits, but for more time with their children, even though feminists say that these feelings are imposed by a sexist society intent on their subjugation.

We need to support measures that encourage women to stay at home, rather than laws that encourage them to stay away in order to further their careers and make more money.

GROUP STUDY

The Spiritual Dimension: Though we need to provide materially for our children, we also need to nurture their deeper needs. Do you trust God to help supply your financial needs as you concentrate more on nurturing your children in other ways?

Group Approach: Do whatever you can to advise or provide practical help to support stay-at-home mothers or those who are scaling back their workload to spend more time with their kids.

Influencing Culture: What can you do to support the deepest feelings of those mothers who want to stay at home with their children but are being overly influenced by feminist propaganda?

WARD AND WARD CLEAVER
The New Stay-at-Home Parent

Two successful working parents, one a corporate lawyer and the other an anesthesiologist, were faced with a decision. One needed to stay home to care for their newly adopted infant son. And so the lawyer gave up power lunches for peanut butter sandwiches, a high-paying job for one with no financial compensation. That story is similar to that of many married couples, in which one parent—usually Mom—decides to leave the workplace to care for the kids. But this isn't the story about a mom and a dad. It's the story of two dads, Jamie McConnell and his partner, Bill Atmore.

New York Times reporter Ginia Bellafante reported stories of several homosexual couples in which one decided to be a stay-at-home parent while the other worked to provide for everyone. "To some gay men," Bellafante writes, "the idea of entrusting the care of a hard-won child to someone else seems to defeat the purpose of parenthood."

And so Ray Friedmann left an accounting job, Bernie Cummings left a public relations management position, and a handful of others also left their careers to be stay-at-home parents. Their decisions reflect a growing trend among homosexual couples.

According to the 2000 census, there were sixty thousand male couple households with children and close to ninety-six thousand female couple households with children. Gary Gates of the Urban Institute noted that of almost ten thousand same-sex couples with children randomly selected by the Census Bureau, 26 percent of male couples included a stay-at-home parent.

"That staying at home constitutes the just and noble course of parenthood was a sentiment echoed again and again in more than a dozen interviews with gay fathers," writes Bellafante. And "because gay men are liberated from the cultural expectations and pressures that women face to balance work and family life, they may approach raising children with a greater sense of freedom and choice," writes Bellafante.

After the so-called sexual revolution, we've gone through the looking glass, and nothing is as it should be. Gender roles have been turned upside down and shaken, with resulting absurdities. It's okay, even laudable, for a gay father to stay home, but it's not okay for a heterosexual mother. Her duty is to climb the corporate ladder in the name of women's rights and equality—forgetting about her children's needs.

This phenomenon, strange as it is, nonetheless shows that God's design for us is right. When same-sex couples try to work out ideal roles as parents, the picture ends up looking (almost) like God's intention—one to nurture and one to provide. Children need the connection of a parent at home, and so these homosexual couples try to imitate the ideal situation for raising children. The problem is that they can't.

Some children of homosexual parents may turn out all right. But as with children of single parents—despite the heroic job that many single parents do—they know they've missed a crucial element in their lives. Mothers and fathers, filling their distinct roles, shape our identity.

Homosexuals have fought hard for the right to parenthood, but no one has a "right" to put kids in an artificial family. The homosexual's "right" is one thing, but what about the rights of the child who, I believe, deserves nothing short of God's real and enduring design for the family, with a male father and a female mother?

TRUTHS TO CONSIDER

Even with the best nurture and provision, no child will ever have the ideal experience in a gay parental or family environment, because God intended for parents to be a man and a woman.

A gay man or lesbian woman can never play the role of the opposite gender parent; this will only cause gender confusion in the child.

Inevitable ironies arise when we upset God's design for the family. Heterosexual women are expected to leave home and climb the corporate ladder, while gay men may seek to redress the female absence by providing the nurture of stay-at-home care.

GROUP STUDY

The Spiritual Dimension: What are your challenges in providing the right amount of training and nurture to your children? For those without children, where does personal advancement supersede building relationships?

Group Approach: How can we encourage a better use of time or resources for proper parental nurture and training so that our children can avoid some of the broken family situations that many people have suffered in the past?

Influencing Culture: Gay adoption is at best counterproductive. How can we encourage more heterosexual adoptions or foster care in our church and community?

FAMILY VALUES ON HBO?

Truth from Unexpected Sources

I don't watch the HBO series *Sex and the City*—that graphic television show depicting the supposedly glamorous sexual escapades of four single women in New York. And enough people have told me about it that I'm glad I don't watch it.

Recently, in the excellent English magazine *The Spectator*, writer Mary Kenny made an unusual observation: "*Sex and the City* means family values" read the title of her article. You've got to be kidding, right? Explicit sex, graphic language, glamorized promiscuity—where do "family values" fit in there?

Well, the truth we can't not know, to borrow the title of J. Budziszewski's recent book, can pop up in unexpected places— particularly the truth about human nature. We're made for one another, and men and women were created with certain roles. When we flout them, the way we're made will always reassert itself.

For example, the fact that homosexuals desire marriage actually betrays the lifestyle they extol. Of course they want to marry and have children—they're human, and that's the way God made us. But two "married" homosexuals can't do that, which is why marriage and homosexuality can never go together. Gay "marriage" has always got to be a counterfeit, and gays know it.

"The 'forces of conservatism' always win in the end," writes Mary Kenny, "because it is the natural order." Though moral Darwinists would say otherwise, humans weren't meant to jump from mate to mate or juggle multiple partners because sex is not a recreational act. It is not, says Kenny, that "brash, competitive, and indeed consumerist" activity depicted on *Sex and the City*. Rather, she goes on to say, it's one that "evokes in human beings something both animal and transcendental."

Exactly. Sex is a procreational act, carrying the weight of life-bearing potential. And it works to promote spousal unity. It's not meant to fulfill selfish desires, and if used for that end, it is ultimately unsatisfying.

So when we see Samantha, the most uninhibited character in the show, hopping from one sexual partner's bed to the next, writes Kenny, we cringe. Nobody applauds such self-deprecation. Then there's Miranda, the lawyer who is now a single mother, finding fulfillment in motherhood and wanting to cut back on her work to be with her child. She yearns for her child's father and for the stability and commitment of marriage.

Charlotte, the erstwhile WASP who always wanted marriage, converts to Judaism for her husband. And finally, Carrie, the center of the show, sums up the futility of the sexually "liberated" single life when she remarks to a friend, "I'm lonely. I'm really lonely." Later, at Charlotte's wedding, Carrie tells her, "I wish I had a man strong enough to catch me when I stumble."

Two are better than one, as Ecclesiastes says. We weren't meant to be alone or to give ourselves away to just anyone and everyone. The way that *Sex and the City* is ending up illustrates this truth. It tried to portray the glamour of the sexual libertine lifestyle, but it doesn't work—even on TV.

Sooner or later human nature—as created by God—kicks in. And apparently the writers of *Sex and the City* have found that out.

TRUTHS TO CONSIDER

One element contributing to the increase in singleness is a worldview of autonomy and self-centeredness that ends in rampant divorce or in reluctance to marry at all.

Some unmarried people want to build society by having the benefits of the selfless commitment of marriage but not the responsibilities or the moral commitments.

The church should support singles in every possible way so that they do not feel excluded from life in the body of Christ. Singles should also see married life modeled with joy and integrity in the church.

GROUP STUDY

The Spiritual Dimension: Give thanks to God that although all of us seek autonomy in our unredeemed natures, God has put a new spirit in us that seeks him first and depends on him to guide our lives in his way.

Group Approach: The church has marginalized singles in a number of ways. How can we be more inclusive, utilize their gifts, and support those who seek the married state?

Influencing Culture: How can we reach others with the message that the loss of lifelong faithfulness to a partner and the loss of parents for an individual child cannot be replicated either by a "tribe" mentality or by the "liberated" single lifestyle that many now espouse?

DECEPTIVE RHETORIC

Marriage and the Language of the Market

Abortion-rights groups ran an advertisement in several newspapers featuring pictures of automatic and manual transmissions. The caption read, "Everybody Likes Choice."

Comparing automobile purchases to the most important moral issue of our time may seem absurd. But, as attendees at our recent "Christians in the Marketplace" conference learned, enemies of the traditional family often appropriate the language of the marketplace.

As economist and author Jennifer Roback Morse told attendees, the assault on marriage "uses the rhetoric and language" of choice and the marketplace. It does so for the same reasons that pro-abortion forces use this rhetoric: It's "very seductive."

The goal of what Roback Morse calls the "lifestyle left" is to create "perfectly autonomous persons who are not connected to each other in any permanent way." As a result of this "deconstruction of the family," the state will enjoy more power.

Of course, putting it in these terms does not make it very salable. So, instead, the "lifestyle left" has repackaged their arguments in terms that Americans find more agreeable, using the language of the market.

Thus, marriage has ceased to be a covenant or a solemn vow and become a "contract." This rhetorical shift has led Americans to see marriage as a voluntary agreement between two adults. If marriage is a contract, then the parties are free to negotiate the terms of their agreement, enforce those terms, and terminate the agreement whenever they choose.

It's easy to see how this shift has damaged the family. Not only has it opened the door to "no-fault" divorce, but it has done the same for cohabitation and same-sex unions. If marriage is simply a contract, then it's impossible to limit the terms of that contract to one man and one woman in a lifelong committed relationship. Instead, anything goes.

There are other critical ways in which viewing marriage as a contract hurts families. This view "undermines the basis of generosity and self-giving" so essential to family life. On a construction site, a welder can tell the foreman, "It's not my job" if he's asked to do some carpentry. The same response by a husband to a request by his wife is a sign of a dysfunctional marriage.

In other words, there are no job descriptions in marriage. Yet, this is precisely where the "marriage as contract" rhetoric, and the worldview it produces, is leading us. Instead of seeing marriage and family as a joint effort lived out before God and the community, people see it as a "deal." And, as with all deals, the name of the game is to make sure that you get the best of the bargain.

This deceptive use of market language is almost as destructive for marriage as it has been for the unborn and their mothers. In both cases, it has provided people with a cover for acting selfishly, without regard for how their actions affect others.

TRUTHS TO CONSIDER

Those from an alternative worldview state serious moral issues as choices in the marketplace, where we have power and freedom; they thus shift the appeal to our autonomy and personal benefit.

When marriage is managed by a marketplace mentality, we view it as a contract instead of as a covenant, making sure that we do only the minimum necessary for our role and that we don't get cheated out of our rights and privileges.

Our marriage relationships do not derive from the marketplace but are designed by God as presented in his Word; they thrive on submission, sacrifice, and unconditional love.

GROUP STUDY

The Spiritual Dimension: How many times have we regarded God as a commodity? Have we tried to barter or bargain to get what we want? Do we prefer our own choices to his?

Group Approach: Do we measure our relationships among fellow believers according to who gets the most out of it or whether it was a good "investment" with recognition included? Why is this the wrong approach?

Influencing Culture: Can you effectively point out that reducing relationships to the level of commodities diminishes the value of the person? It also reduces opportunities for deeper fulfillment than anything money can buy, so that even on its own terms, the contract mentality shortchanges itself.

SEVEN BRIDES FOR TWO BROTHERS

Marriage and Foolish Consistency

After the Massachusetts Supreme Court's Goodridge ruling that created a "right" to same-sex "marriage," critics warned that the next logical step was polygamy. Once you decide that marriage shouldn't be limited to one man and one woman, there is no logically consistent reason to draw a line excluding polygamy.

Same-sex "marriage" advocates and their allies predictably labeled such arguments as "fear-mongering" and "implausible." As predicted, however, events are proving them wrong.

Tom Green thinks that the time has come to challenge the ban on polygamy. Three years ago, a Utah jury found him guilty on four counts of bigamy for being married to five women at the same time. He was sentenced to twenty-five years in prison.

Green's lawyers are preparing to petition the U.S. Supreme Court to review his case. If the Court agrees to hear his appeal, it will have to revisit an 1878 decision that allowed the states to criminalize polygamy.

Even if you dismiss Green as a crank and believe that the Court won't agree to hear his case, there is still growing support for Green and his position. In a *USA Today* article (October 4, 2004), Jonathan Turley, a professor at George Washington University Law School, calls laws against polygamy "hypocritical."

Turley notes that today "individuals have a recognized constitutional right to engage in any form of consensual sexual relationship with any number of partners." They "can live with multiple partners" and "sire children from different partners." The only thing prohibited under the law is marrying them all at the same time.

For Turley, our culture's unwillingness to take that final step is hypocritical. Prejudice, rather than a coherent principle, lies behind the criminalization of polygamy. And so, he says, it's up to the courts to protect "the least popular and least powerful," such as polygamists.

I could not disagree more with Turley, but that doesn't stop me from admitting that in many important respects, his argument is actually stronger than the one for same-sex "marriage." After all, while same-sex "marriage" is unprecedented in human history, polygamy is both ancient and, until recently, was widespread. While children are, at best, an afterthought in same-sex households, countless children have been successfully raised in polygamous households.

This makes it very likely that some judge somewhere is going to conclude that as with same-sex "marriage," the prohibition against polygamy is discriminatory and thus unconstitutional. Cases such as Goodridge and the Supreme Court's Lawrence decision have made traditional moral standards an unacceptable basis for legislation.

Some Christian conservatives, such as Congressman Chris Cox (R-CA), who wrote a widely publicized article in the *Wall Street Journal*, say that amending the Constitution is not a good idea. Please!

There is no other way to stop the deconstruction of marriage than to take the courts out of the equation. Turley is absolutely correct when he writes that people will not vote to legalize polygamy any more than same-sex "marriage." Writing the principle, therefore, of "one man and one woman" into the Constitution is the only way to keep judges from stripping the protection of law from traditional marriage.

TRUTHS REVEALED

Marriage can be defined as the union of spouses in an organic, procreative relationship, something that homosexual couples by their very nature are not capable of. By allowing homosexual "marriage," we put the family as well as the institution of marriage in danger, thus jeopardizing the very survival of civilized society.

We are defending marriage from a Christian point of view, but virtually every society and religion supports the institution of traditional marriage.

Although neither is desirable, it makes as much sense to support polygamy as it does to legalize same-sex "marriage."

GROUP STUDY

The Spiritual Dimension: Read the first chapter of Romans, and observe the relationship between legitimizing homosexuality and the final decay of a culture. In what less visible or controversial ways do you skew the parameters of divinely instituted traditional marriage?

Group Approach: Work with those who agree with you to support state and national legislation that defends heterosexual marriages. How do you evaluate the viability of polygamy in this context?

Influencing Culture: If gay "marriages" are legalized, it is inevitable that the concept of marriage will be expanded to include other combinations beyond gay couples. How can you communicate the ways in which the structure of society will suffer as a result?

THE TWO-INCOME TRAP

Mortgaging the Future for the Kids

It is said that when looking for a new home, the three rules are "loca-tion, location, location." But Harvard law professor Elizabeth Warren believes that should be changed to "schools, schools, schools."

In their book *The Two-Income Trap: Why Middle-Class Mothers and Fathers Are Going Broke*, Professor Warren and her daughter, Amelia Warren Tyagi, explain why "people who consistently rank in the worst financial trouble are united by one surprising charac-teristic. They are parents with children at home."

According to Warren and Warren Tyagi's research, even though today's two-income families earn 75 percent more than their single-income counterparts did a generation ago, they actually have less to spend. And it's not because these families are buying vacation homes or wide-screen TVs. It's because, in many cases, they must mortgage the future to purchase what they want most: good schools for their kids. In fact, the authors found school quality to be the most influential factor affecting housing prices. "Bad schools impose indirect—but huge—costs on millions of middle-class families. In their desperate rush to save their children from failing schools, families are literally spending themselves into bankruptcy."

Although today the majority of mothers work outside the home, the authors remind us that wasn't the case only a generation ago. When mothers did work, their income was for "extras," not for "necessities" like housing. But as families moved to the suburbs in search of safe streets and successful schools, the resulting "bidding war" created a situation where Mom's income was no longer a "luxury" but a necessity.

"Schools in middle-class neighborhoods may be labeled 'public,'" say the authors, "but parents have paid for tuition by purchasing a $175,000 home within a carefully selected school district."

Freeing parents from this trap begins with giving parents a choice. The authors' recommendation is a fully funded voucher system that would enable parents of children in poorly performing schools to send their kids to the school of their choice.

Opponents argue that vouchers drain needed funds away from the public schools. So Warren and Warren Tyagi suggest another school choice alternative: a voucher plan that would still give parents a choice but keep the tax dollars inside the public school system. Under their plan, which mirrors successful magnet school programs, parents would choose from among the public schools in a given area. This would prevent families from having to make the choice between a good school and an affordable home. They could have both.

The authors conclude, "By selecting where to send their children (and where to spend their vouchers), parents would take control over schools' tax dollars, making them the de facto owners of those schools. . . . Parents' competitive energies could be channeled toward signing up early or improving their children's qualifications for a certain school, not in bankrupting themselves to buy homes they cannot afford." And schools would be competing for students, which would significantly raise school standards.

Of course, the importance of this proposal is that it comes, not from the "big, bad Religious Right" that always talks about vouchers, but from a straight-thinking Harvard law professor. It makes good sense to me.

TRUTHS TO CONSIDER

Substandard school systems place a heavy financial burden on parents who want their children to get a good education, because they have to buy a home in an expensive neighborhood with a quality school system.

This creates a trap. Parents have to spend less time with their children and more time working in order to grant them a better education, when it is the responsibility of all schools to better utilize tax dollars to increase quality for those who pay for them.

A voucher system would keep tax dollars in the public system but allow parents a choice. This would give parents control over their own tax dollars, allow them to live in less expensive areas, and motivate all schools to improve.

GROUP STUDY

The Spiritual Dimension: Are you being led by the Spirit in the difficult area of providing the opportunities your children need to use their gifts, but not at the expense of quality time and training? Continue to seek God for balance.

Group Approach: The Christian/home/public dilemma regarding schools for our children rages on amid the different challenges and circumstances we all face. How can we better help one another with advice, encouragement, and even financial support?

Influencing Culture: This is an excellent way to get people from a different worldview to work together to improve the public school system. As a first step, they can demonstrate the value of vouchers. Find ways to work with individuals and with local and national government to advocate for choice and demand quality for dollars spent.

CHILDREN OF THE STATE?

Ending Educational Coercion

A band of civil rights groups raised legal eyebrows, announcing plans to sue California for failing to provide the "bare essentials" of a public education. Space shortages, poor materials, and unqualified teachers led some, including the ACLU, to say, "Enough is enough."

Their lawsuit was filed on behalf of seventy students from two dozen public schools, hoping to make the state pay for its failures. By pricking political consciences, the activists expected a payoff in the form of more tax dollars for public education.

Well, when it comes to identifying government's failed policies, for once the ACLU was on the right side. Policy makers on both sides of the issue were finally admitting the need for education reform. But the issue here isn't just propping up the public schools, but making sure that all our kids have a chance for a quality education.

What the public school lobby would really like to do is to keep parents out of it altogether. The teachers' unions don't want parents looking over their shoulders, and they seem to feel that winning court battles like this one will give them the money to fix the system—a system that in many cases is broken beyond repair.

You see, the only fix that makes sense for the long term is to give parents options, such as school choice and vouchers, so they can make their own decisions—an option that, not surprisingly, terrifies the teachers' unions.

A student's mother got on the local school board's curriculum committee after objecting to the evolutionist curriculum her daughter was being forced to learn.

Soon after she joined the curriculum committee, she discovered that most teachers aren't giving homework anymore. When pressed for reasons, one teacher said, in so many words, "Homework gets parents involved in the process, and we think education ought to be left to the professionals." In other words, educators don't want parents looking over their shoulders.

Outrageous. The Department of Education's own literature says that "three decades of research have shown that parental participation in schooling improves student learning." All the research shows that when moms and dads take an active role in their kids' education—helping with homework, attending special events and extracurricular activities—performance improves dramatically. But teachers also know that parents often don't approve of today's trendy curricula, so to keep them out of it, teachers don't give homework or otherwise involve parents.

This is one more reason why vouchers are so important. The solution to the problem is to empower parents to make their own decisions, through vouchers, through working with the schools, and through more active involvement in curriculum decisions.

Voucher opponents will be demanding more money for failing public schools, while parents will be looking for solutions that really work. But this is an issue that concerns all of us.

Over seventy-five years ago, the Supreme Court said that "the child is not the mere creature of the State," and that's a lesson the opponents of school choice need to learn. Our kids deserve the best that all of us, including parents, can give them and not merely what's convenient for teachers.

TRUTHS TO CONSIDER

Our public education system has declined to the point that in some places, facilities, materials, credentials, and curricula are inadequate to facilitate the learning process.

Educators do not want parents involved in the educational process because they will criticize overall standards and the content of curricula. Parents are also reluctant to agree that they have secondary authority in the educational sphere.

Educational vouchers are one way to provide parents with a choice for quality education. They can also give parents leverage in providing the quality that their children deserve and that their taxes have paid for.

GROUP STUDY

The Spiritual Dimension: Do you—above all things—train up your children in the ways of the Lord, providing a Christian perspective in whatever they learn?

Group Approach: What can you do to be more responsibly involved in your child's education? Can you improve in your personal interaction, in your relationship with the school, and in advocating for better standards?

Influencing Culture: How can we make it clear that choice in education is a tide that raises all boats and that we shouldn't have to pay twice for an education (public and private), especially when the local public system may be substandard?

IT DOESN'T ADD UP

When Two plus One Equals Too Many

A two-year-old boy in Ontario, Canada, may soon have three legal parents. His mother's lesbian partner is petitioning for legal recognition as his second mother. The boy's father, described as "a good friend of the couple," supports the two women in their quest. According to one newspaper, "Rather than replacing a parent, which adoption does, the family is seeking to 'add a parent.'"

Grace Kerr, a lawyer for the mother's partner, has stated, "We've got a loving circle of family, and they have done everything society could hope for in terms of providing for the child and would just like legal recognition. They are saying that, in their family, there is room for three parents."

The case has not received much attention yet from the media, but it should. If family court judge David Aston rules in favor of the petition—and he has said that he "can't imagine a stronger case"—the implications for families everywhere are staggering. After emphasizing that this case is about just one group of people trying to establish themselves as a family, Kerr then changed her tune. "The declaration of motherhood which we are seeking could set a precedent that would expand the number of people who will be able to seek relief as a mom or dad under the law," she said. In other words, she is recognizing that you can't change the legal status of one family without affecting all others.

Over the past few years, we have seen the devastating effects on families—and on society in general—when a parent is subtracted from a child's life. So what happens if we go beyond divorce and decide that a parent is someone who can be added to a family at will? Throwing one more parent into the mix certainly doesn't mean more love and attention for the child. As writer Stanley Kurtz points out in *National Review Online*, it could have just the opposite effect. "Once parental responsibilities are parceled out to more than two people," he writes, "it becomes that much easier for any one parent to shirk his or her responsibilities." To alter the parental role in this way cheapens the parent-child bond. Kurtz might have added that when relationships among adults are ill-defined and lacking in commitment, they, too, become easier to break, further destabilizing the child's world and undermining trust and confidence. Adding parents by court order is altogether different from the role of extended families, by the way. The involvement of grandparents, aunts, uncles, and cousins can be healthy because it's a natural arrangement that adds stability for parents.

Research shows that children of divorce have a harder time building lasting families of their own when they reach adulthood. Imagine what would happen to children raised in a group situation like this, where "parents" can be added—and probably subtracted—at will.

No family is perfect, and I know that single moms and dads today do a heroic job. But the family built on a commitment of a man and a woman to each other and to their own biological or adopted children is still the soundest and most stable model. The weaknesses inherent in the counterfeits only demonstrate the strengths of the original, designed by the Creator to provide the healthiest environment for parents and children alike. When it comes to parenting, "the more the merrier" just doesn't apply.

TRUTHS TO CONSIDER

Same-sex couples further the trend of separation between marriage and parenting. A legal move to add a parent will not reverse this.

Where children are caught in the breakup and re-formation of family structures, it is very difficult for adults to consider what is in the best interests of the children rather than just their own agenda.

One of the goals of those in favor of gay "marriage" is to further weaken heterosexual marriages so that there will be no qualitative distinction. When we undermine the unique purpose of heterosexual marriage, we contribute to the moral breakdown of society through the weakened bonds of family members.

GROUP STUDY

The Spiritual Dimension: How are your daily decisions affected by the realization that your family is a divinely appointed spiritual entity that aids each individual family member in becoming what God intended?

Group Approach: How can you as a small group or church support people from broken heterosexual marriages while reinforcing the reality that marriage is sacred?

Influencing Culture: What do your friends and neighbors see in your marriage and family life that draws them to Christ and his ways?

NEW PALTZ FOLLIES

Lawlessness and Democracy

A New York State judge issued a temporary restraining order that barred the mayor of New Paltz from performing same-sex "marriages." In his order, Judge Vincent Bradley said that Mayor Jason West had "[ignored] the oath of office that he took to uphold the law."

On that same day, New York governor George Pataki promised that the state government was prepared to crack down on any local official who issued marriage licenses to same-sex couples.

While this is good news and a step in the right direction in New York, we still have a long way to go in opposing a campaign that undermines the rule of law. Across the country, lawlessness continues to break out. Local governments in California, Oregon, and New Mexico have pledged to continue what they call a campaign of civil disobedience.

In evaluating their claim, the first thing we need to remember is that each of these municipalities and counties is part of a larger political entity, the state. States such as California contain communities with different cultural perspectives; people in Fresno, for instance, may not see the world as people in L.A. or San Francisco do.

Because the number of legislative representatives from L.A. and San Francisco exceeds the number from a smaller city such as Fresno, residents of Fresno are undoubtedly subject to laws that they themselves would not have enacted. But no one thinks that this gives the people of Fresno the right to disregard state laws they don't like. Instead they have the right to try, through democratic means, to change the law. What's true for Fresno is equally true in San Francisco. Remember that in California, the people voted overwhelmingly in favor of a referendum establishing that marriage is a union of one man and one woman.

What about civil disobedience? In Christian thought, the civil authorities are due our obedience, but that duty isn't absolute. The state may not command what God has prohibited, nor can it act arbitrarily or capriciously. But biblically there are no grounds here for disobedience.

It also needs to be noted that in a democratic polity such as ours, civil disobedience is always a last resort. Those who believe that the law is in error have the obligation to work through the democratic process before resorting to civil disobedience. That hasn't happened in San Francisco or New Paltz or anywhere else.

On the contrary, city officials are simply attempting to circumvent the democratic process altogether.

Their claim to moral kinship with the civil rights movement is spurious. African-Americans were shut out of the democratic process, and civil disobedience was one of the few options available to them. The same cannot be said of gay Americans, who are heavily involved in politics.

What's happening isn't a blow for freedom but a reckless disregard for law. This disregard should trouble every American, regardless of his or her opinion about same-sex "marriage," because lawlessness leads to tyranny. The rule of law is the most fundamental principle of free societies (which came, incidentally, from a Christian influence in the Reformation).

We don't get to pick which laws we'll obey. Those who try to do so are a threat to the rule of law that has made our way of life and freedom possible in the first place.

TRUTHS TO CONSIDER

The only laws we can disobey are those clearly prohibited by God because his moral law supersedes the laws of men; otherwise, the rule of law is undermined.

Offering marriage licenses to same-sex couples breaks both God's laws and the laws of the state and is really an attempt to sidestep the democratic process.

Unlike African-Americans, gays have not been shut out of the democratic process, and thus the last resort of civil disobedience on their behalf doesn't apply.

GROUP STUDY

The Spiritual Dimension: How do you think that the Reformation, with its repudiation of spiritual and civil tyranny, fostered the rule of law as the bedrock of our own society?

Group Approach: Discuss subtle attempts to get beyond the rule of law in your own lives when it doesn't suit you or when you don't agree with the law but still find it's not in direct violation of God's law.

Influencing Culture: Demonstrate to those who agree with the actions of the mayor of New Paltz that if the same approach—that is, handing out illegal licenses to satisfy one's individual conscience—were applied to illegal handguns, for example, the result would be chaos and the rule of law would be superseded by personal preference.

SOCIETY AND TOLERATION

LIE 3

We'll live in harmony if we tolerate the beliefs of others.

Underlying Worldview: We tolerate all relativistic beliefs and behavior in an amoral world in which we band together to better achieve our own personal fulfillment.

Because good and evil are human inventions, according to a commonly held worldview, we have no higher authority and can, through moral relativism, pursue our own interests without consequences. Thus life becomes a matter of continually enhancing pleasures and minimizing pains. The values of materialism, personal freedom, and power snugly fit into this worldview, with an outcome of being able to use others for our personal advantage.

This section covers a wide variety of issues in our changing view of society. They include affluence, democracy, fashion, cyberculture, hedonism, and postmodernism. Pursuing and consuming wealth are paramount to living a meaningful existence, and the boundaries placed by "authoritative communities" such as the church or the family no longer apply. New types of communities spring up, advocating agendas that empower individual autonomy. Among them are gays, feminists, and postmodern academicians.

Our children are increasingly ignorant of our historical roots in the Judeo-

Christian community and of the reasons why we owe a debt or duty to society. Ironically, individualism is disencouraged in terms of consumerism, where another false community is established in the form of "branding" for the sake of a superficial identity that is meant to multiply company profits.

Branding attempts to make a group conform to a product and a worldview. In the case of teenagers, Playboy now displays the rabbit logo on T-shirts for teenage girls. GapKids targets an even younger audience: preteens, with terry-cloth bikinis. Even preteens take their fashion cues from Britney Spears, who has gone far beyond the preteen scene to soft-core pornography.

This branding exploits even young children, who are a lucrative part of the market. Some products reflect the worst of a worldview that panders to the darkest desires of consumers. Even children are polluted with action figures, not of G.I. Joe, but of shock-rock star Eminem, accompanied by a dead woman in a trunk. Yet in the spirit of tolerance, one music critic calls Eminem "one of those charming rogues" on the pop culture scene.

Branding leads to mass culture, which leads to the "junk food" culture of the lowest common denominator. In the movie *L.A. Story*, actor Steve Martin appears with a helicopter displaying a giant hot dog, the symbol of a shallow, "junk food" popular consumer culture. In the same vein as *Playboy*, our "role models" who exhort us to the civic duty to vote are people such as Larry Flynt of *Hustler* magazine. In fact, anyone can qualify for fame in the present culture, as proven by the fact that far more students are familiar with the *American Idol* competition than with the political party of their state governor.

Progress in the cyberculture, with all its personal power and affluence, is ending not in greater fulfillment but in alienation. We as Christians have a great opportunity to display all the characteristics of a true community under God that the culture would like to possess. We can demonstrate loyalty, forgiveness, nurture, selflessness, provision, and true unity. These go far beyond the lie of superficial tolerance.

We can overcome the cynicism, alienation, and manipulation that others feel as a result of the false promises and expectations of a community based on a false worldview. Through the church, family, and service to our neighbors, let us provide alternatives that produce a just and merciful society, rather than mere toleration of evil.

REGAINING "HARD-NOSED TEACHINGS"

The Doctrine of Human Sin

Note: This commentary was delivered by Prison Fellowship President Mark Earley.

America was about to go to war—again—and liberal theologians were appalled. We are making a terrible mistake, they warned. We are demonizing the enemy and rushing to war. Oh, the president might claim that we're fighting for democracy, but in reality we're about to engage in a "clash of imperialisms." What Americans don't seem to realize, the clerics claimed, is that we ourselves are to blame for the evil acts of our enemies. As it turned out, the theologians were wrong—but many refused to admit it until World War II had been fought and won. Six decades later, as we fight the war on terror, Americans are hearing the same danger-ously wrongheaded rhetoric.

As Joe Loconte points out in his new book, *The End of Illusions*, if one studies the 1930s, one is struck by the familiarity of the modern debate over the war on terror. In the thirties, more than two hundred peace groups, deeply influenced by liberal theology, resisted giving military aid to those being destroying by Hitler's armies. Instead of demonizing Hitler, they said, we should address the "root causes" of Nazi aggression. And what were those causes? They claimed that the Treaty of Versailles had made Hitler "al-most inevitable." In other words, Hitler's bad behavior was all our fault. Sound familiar?

Even when the gathering storm had erupted into a hurricane of death and destruction, liberal theologians kept urging restraint. We ought to fight, not with weapons, but with peace summits and dialogue, they said. Worst of all, they refused to make moral dis-tinctions between the U.S. and Nazi Germany. The comments of minister John Haynes Holmes were typical, when he said, "If America goes into the war, it will not be for idealistic reasons but to serve her own imperialistic interests." If we won, he added, we would merely be replacing one tyranny with another.

Of course, in the wake of the Holocaust, the truth about the Nazis became clear. But given the evidence even before the war—Hitler's lies, Kristalnacht, and German tanks rumbling across Eu-rope—how could anyone believe that "dialogue" would do any good?

The answer, writes Loconte, was that "the latest fads in theol-ogy, psychology, and economics had flattened the Bible's hard-nosed teaching about evil and its deep link to human personality. . . . Indeed, the fatal flaw of liberal intellectuals was what the realists called 'the dogma of the natural goodness of man,'" Loconte says. This heresy assumes that "sin resides mostly in social and political institutions"; once man is freed from them through reform or revolution, he will "rise to new humanistic heights."

It took theologians such as Reinhold Niebuhr to attack this heresy and revive the scriptural definition of sin. Sin is humanity's rebellion against God and his laws. Hitler's rage and maniacal fury against the Jews could be stopped only through confrontation, Niebuhr asserted. Tragically, it took a world war to convince many Christians that Niebuhr was right. It is vitally important that modern Christians recall both the lessons of history and the lessons of Scripture. The line of good and evil runs through every human heart, and when it erupts into violence, it must be fought—not with well-meaning words but with force.

TRUTHS TO CONSIDER

No human beings are exempt from sinful tendencies. To recognize evil in the world is to recognize our own capacity for evil apart from God's sustaining help.

As our culture becomes more desensitized to evil, it is more important than ever for Christians to let redemption from that very evil be evident in their lives.

It is difficult to recognize and resist evil without adapting to it or feeling morally superior to others.

GROUP STUDY

The Spiritual Dimension: The early Christians in Rome were "resensitized" after being converted from a very decadent culture. What steps can you take to allow God to reset your moral gauge as our culture becomes darker and condones more evil?

Group Approach: How do you identify and resist evil without being drawn into the subtle belief that "might makes right"?

Influencing Culture: The evil in our world often seems overwhelming, and it is hard to believe that our actions make any difference. Identify a small, practical way in which you can name and act against evil within your personal life experience. What is the next step that you need to take?

NO ABSOLUTES WITHOUT ABSOLUTISM
True Truth

Have you ever tried to debate moral principles with someone who doesn't believe they exist? If you have, you know it's an exercise in frustration. In our anything-goes society, even mentioning that there might be such a thing as a moral absolute truth is a good way to get branded as intolerant, anachronistic, and a killjoy. And the more frustrated we get with this state of affairs, the more likely we are to turn the stereotype into a self-fulfilling prophecy. That is, our frustration can easily turn into anger, and our anger can begin to look very much like the arrogance that we're already accused of harboring.

The goal that Christians need to strive for, argues scholar Art Lindsley of the C. S. Lewis Institute, is "absolutes without absolutism." In his excellent book *True Truth: Defending Absolute Truth in a Relativistic World*, Lindsley writes, "Just as a need to relate truth to all areas of life does not make us relativists, so believing that there are some moral absolutes does not make us absolutists. . . . Absolutism might be defined as . . . a cluster of characteristics: arrogance, close-mindedness, intolerance, self-righteousness, bigotry, and the like." These are characteristics that many people already unfairly associate with Christianity, so these are characteristics that Christians need to work especially hard to avoid. After all, as Lindsley reminds us, the most fundamental doctrines of our faith— our fallen state and our desperate need for a Savior—are doctrines that make for humility, not pride.

At the same time, we still need to be able to talk about absolutes. An explanation of the Christian worldview makes no sense without them. So how do we do it? First, we can remember that believing in absolutes (i.e., moral truth that is binding on us) doesn't have to make us absolutists (i.e., closed-minded to other propositions).

Lindsley suggests that one of the best strategies is to turn the tables on relativists by pointing out the absolutism in their own thinking. As Lindsley writes, "Relativists consistently stand guilty of the philosophical sin of making exceptions to their own absolute rules." They claim that Christianity is a religion of intolerance, that Christians have committed abuses in the name of their faith, and that Christians shouldn't impose their values on others but leave them free to choose their own value systems. But where did they get their ideas of tolerance and justice—of right and wrong in general—if they genuinely don't believe in moral absolutes? Without such ideas, how can anyone formulate a meaningful system of values?

This kind of argument was effective with as brilliant a thinker as C. S. Lewis. Many years after his conversion, he wrote of his days as an atheist: "How had I got this idea of just and unjust? . . . A man does not call a line crooked unless he has some idea of a straight line."

If we're patient and persistent, it's not as hard as it might seem to make a relativist begin to see the truth about the "straight line." But we must never forget exactly who and what we're defending. Jesus was the embodiment of absolute truth but never an absolutist. And so as Art Lindsley puts it: "The defense of the Gospel is most effective when combined with the demeanor of Christ."

TRUTHS TO CONSIDER

Every philosophical or religious system has to have a starting point—a belief or set of beliefs that is considered reliable enough to build on.

For relativists, relativism is an absolute, and relativists implicitly advert to other absolutes when they make claims for justice and fairness.

Relativists, as much as those of any other worldview, need to be gently shown the weaknesses of their position and introduced to the source of all truth, Jesus Christ.

GROUP STUDY

The Spiritual Dimension: What worldviews make you rigid and defensive about your own beliefs? Where do you most need the example of Christ's compassion and grace in dealing with other people or in upholding your own faith and beliefs?

Group Approach: In what areas could the tables be turned on us for the ways in which we express our convictions? Are we intolerant of intolerance? Agree to help one another to detect and disarm such contradictions.

Influencing Culture: Can we express our beliefs firmly and clearly without taking responsibility for other people's beliefs and responses in a codependent way? We are responsible for sharing the gospel appropriately, but the outcome is not in our hands.

HOT DOG CITY
What's Wrong with Junk Culture?

One of the most famous scenes in film history is the opening shot in Fellini's *La Dolce Vita*. To symbolize Rome's historical significance, Fellini begins with a statue of Jesus sweeping across the skyline, hanging from a helicopter with outstretched arms.

Steve Martin liked it so much that he did a takeoff in *L.A. Story*. As the movie opens, we see something sweeping across the skyline, hanging from a helicopter. The camera zooms in and we see it is . . . a giant hot dog.

This is the perfect symbol for L.A., center of America's mass-produced, lowest-common-denominator popular culture.

In *All God's Children and Blue Suede Shoes*, Ken Myers says that "the challenge of living with popular culture" may be the most serious challenge facing Christians today. In some ways, it is even more difficult than the persecution Christians faced in earlier centuries. Of course, being thrown to lions is pretty gruesome, but at least it was an easily recognized threat. Popular culture is very subtle and can cause a gradual erosion of character that many Christians don't even recognize.

What do you mean, we don't recognize it? you may ask. Any Christian can tell you that the level of sex and violence has risen sharply in movies, rap music, and dime-store novels.

True enough, Myers says. But these are concerns about content; what we often overlook is form. The form of popular culture can shape the way in which we respond, regardless of the message. For comparison, consider the music and art of high culture. A classical poem or symphony has a complex structure that takes some effort to understand. It challenges the mind, and you have to work to appreciate it.

Harlequin romances, soap operas, and rock music don't require intellectual discipline. They're easy to understand, and they offer immediate gratification.

If anything, popular culture avoids making the audience work. It grabs our attention with catchy lines, loud music, and sensational visual effects, all designed to appeal to the senses and the emotions.

Over time, these things affect us. By focusing on immediate experience, pop culture discourages sustained attention. By angling for an emotional response, it discourages the use of our minds to analyze what we see and hear.

Pop culture is a bit like junk food. There's nothing inherently sinful about it, but too much of it can spoil our appetite for healthy food. Too much candy can ruin our taste for a fresh, crisp apple.

This is the principle that Paul lays down in 1 Corinthians 10:23, " 'Everything is permissible'—but not everything is beneficial." There's no harm in popular culture per se, but there is harm in making a steady diet of it. Constant consumption of movies, television, and rock music can encourage simplistic emotional responses to life instead of disciplined thought and analysis.

How can Christians survive in a junk-food culture—a culture aptly symbolized by a giant hot dog? By working to cultivate a taste for higher culture. As families, we ought to delve into good literature and listen to classical music.

Learn to love the things that feed the mind—and the soul.

TRUTHS TO CONSIDER

The offerings of popular culture may be more of a challenge to Christians than direct antagonism. In offering immediate gratification, they discourage critical thinking and intellectual effort.

Christians are rightfully concerned about the content of sex and violence, but the forms in popular culture also have a degenerate effect on our minds and emotions. They overpower us and discourage us from focusing on higher forms that contain more developed structures.

Though much in higher culture is permissible, not everything is beneficial. Thus, for the sake of our souls, we need to cultivate a taste for the finer creations of culture, especially those works whose excellence have stood the test of time.

GROUP STUDY

The Spiritual Dimension: Has too much popular fare affected your attention span? Not only higher culture, but Bible reading, Sunday school, sermons, and times of prayer can be shortchanged. Talk it over with God, and ask him to give you a hunger to pray and to do the hard work of studying the Scriptures.

Group Approach: Get together with others to analyze a film or book in popular culture, then compare it with a similar medium in higher culture. How do both form and content differ in quality and in their effects on your mind and soul?

Influencing Culture: Can you find a work of art that is excellent in form and content and has a strong Christian worldview? Offer to share it with someone from a different background. Perhaps even something as overt as Mel Gibson's *The Passion of the Christ* would work.

IMAGE IS EVERYTHING

Losing Our Identity at the Shopping Mall

Is shopping for school with your teenage daughter a challenge? If it is, you're not alone. The skimpy clothing popular among young girls has led some public schools to move to uniforms. Not a bad idea.

What's behind the push to dress provocatively? One clue observed by Alissa Quart in her book *Branded: The Buying and Selling of Teenagers* is that "youth is nothing less than a metaphor for change." That is, kids are trying to establish their identities.

Marketers cash in on this search for self by selling "image" to youth—and increasingly, that image is sexual. We've seen this in

Abercrombie & Fitch's thong underwear for seven-year-olds as well as in the company's depictions of bare-chested young males with provocative expressions in its advertising. And Playboy sells clothing for teenagers.

But it's not just the sexual image that many of these companies push on teens; the idea that they can acquire an identity through brands is the real threat to impressionable youth. Quart quotes Rabbi Jeffrey Salkin, who decries the increase in materialism in bar and bat mitzvahs, saying, "Conspicuous consumption with these events teaches the children that spending and having [are] more important than being." For many young people today, spending and having are synonymous with being. And having brand names, in their minds, is what makes them "cool."

"Cool is essential in establishing a brand identity," notes Ken Myers of Mars Hill Audio, "especially with teenagers, whose purchases tend to be more desperately linked with the establishment of an identity than are those of adults."

"The term *brand*," says Quart, "suggests both the ubiquity of logos in today's teen dreams and the extreme way these brands define teen identities." It's true—it's hard to turn your head in public without seeing brand names on posters, billboards, or the sides of buses. And this affects young people profoundly.

"One thing that's so compelling and strange about the [increase] in marketing to kids," says Quart, "is how much these practices have taken advantage of organic things that already exist in childhood and adolescence: the desire to communicate [opinions], . . . the sense of lack of identity, changing bodies and burgeoning sexuality, a desire to emulate adult culture."

Manufacturers and advertisers are participating in the phenomenon of "kids getting older younger," and in the process, imagination has been lost. Kids used to play with stuffed animals and other toys; now they take fashion cues from Britney Spears and play brand-name-laden video games. "The kind of imaginary world kids make up with their toys," said Myers, "is a zone in which they're really defining themselves." Now, they're being defined by marketers.

"As Lionel Trilling wrote thirty years ago, authenticity is an even more 'strenuous moral experience' than sincerity. [Brand-name products] aim to harness teens' desire for an ideal . . . world and give them a branded one instead," writes Quart. Our job, of course, is to teach our kids and grandkids to find their identity in themselves as God made them, rather than being swayed by brands and commercialized images—because in allowing themselves to be "branded," they not only lose money, they lose their true identity.

TRUTHS TO CONSIDER

The teenage years are a vulnerable time of discovering true identity, so advertisers take advantage of this to sell teenagers an image that conforms to worldly values.

Clothes and other products appeal to the need to cope with emerging sexuality and changing bodies. In being "branded," young people can escape the need to seek a legitimate identity.

A teen's true identity is found in Christ. We can encourage teens to resist losing that identity to pressures that conform them to a lifestyle that is not authentically theirs.

GROUP STUDY

The Spiritual Dimension: Teens are being exposed to more and more explicit material at an earlier age, making it harder for them to resist sin. Have your standards declined in what you allow yourself to view or in what image you project with your clothing and lifestyle?

Group Approach: How can we challenge our teens to evaluate the brands they are identifying with in light of their own Christian commitment? How can we avoid being overly legalistic while looking for consistency in Christian witness?

Influencing Culture: Can we point out the damage that "kids getting older younger" does to children and teens too immature to handle it? Christian teens should provide an example of a healthier, age-appropriate growth to adulthood.

NEVER TOO YOUNG

Teaching Your Kids about Civic Duty

Every October, Americans become immersed in all things Halloween. We spend nearly $7 billion annually on what is, at best, parties and, at worst, occultism. Then a few days later we breeze right by a truly important date: Election Day.

A report found that young people ages fifteen to twenty-six "don't understand the ideals of citizenship; they are disengaged from the political process; they lack the knowledge necessary for effective self-government; and they have limited appreciation of American democracy."

The study shows that only 66 percent of this age group believes it is necessary to vote in order to be a good citizen, compared with 83 percent of Americans over age twenty-six. But here's a telling example of the problem: Eighty percent of those under age twenty-six know who won the last *American Idol* competition on TV, but fewer than half know the party of their state's governor.

We know that young people who have taken a civics course are two to three times more likely to vote, follow government news, and contact public officials about issues that concern them. Yet while thirty-nine states require a course in civics or government in order to graduate from high school, there's still a great deal of apathy among young people. A new publication from the Thomas B. Fordham Foundation sheds some light. The collection of essays titled *Where Did Social Studies Go Wrong?* addresses the dumbing down of civics education.

Today, social studies theorists seek to create social activists, not informed citizens. In their minds, students don't need to know facts to "be effective change-agents; they're taught that facts are a matter of opinion," writes Brendan Miniter in the *Wall Street Journal*. And so today's young Americans, increasingly ignorant of their history and their government, are less engaged civically.

Part of the solution, of course, is to teach students that there is truth, that facts have an objective basis and are not mere opinions. You can do that if you get the local paper this week, sit down with your children, and point out what issues are at stake in the news. Talk about those issues—whether they are religious freedom in schools, abortion, or the war in Iraq—and discuss where you stand. Then find out what the candidates are saying and decide together which ones are the best choices on the slate.

A national survey released last year found that "whether or not parents discuss politics with their kids, take their kids with them to vote, and vote regularly is highly correlated with whether their kids engage in political life." If you don't engage them, somebody else will try to. The ACLU conducted a campus tour across America to reach young voters. And it featured, among other speakers, pornographer Larry Flynt.

Students who aren't educated in civics are susceptible to distortions of the facts or the current wind or fad of opinion. We need to counteract that with our children, teaching them about objective truth and their duty as citizens. It's the only way we can ensure that truth remains at the center of the public square.

TRUTHS TO CONSIDER

Today's young people are apathetic and have not been adequately taught the facts about our political process. Thus, they lack the knowledge necessary for effective self-government within an informed democratic process.

The ACLU and others are not interested in helping young people to learn the facts; they use ignorance of important facts to create social activists for their liberal causes.

Christians can regain lost ground through adequate civics education that teaches truth as well as by getting involved in worthy civic and political causes.

GROUP STUDY

The Spiritual Dimension: What were the key components of the Christian vision of the Founding Fathers that helped support our democratic process?

Group Approach: What can you do with your family and/or fellow believers to grow in knowledge of the political process and to get involved with those who support a Christian worldview?

Influencing Culture: We need to communicate to politically conservative candidates for public office our sense that their spiritual vision is important to their political objectives if we are to retain the values we all long to keep in place.

MULTIPLYING LIKE RABBITS

Fashion's Assault on Our Children

My daughter Emily was shopping in a swimwear store when she came across something that absolutely horrified her. Featured on the front of shirts clearly marketed to teenage girls was a rabbit head—the Playboy logo. While incidents like this no longer shock most of us, the fact is that in the past decade there have been unprecedented efforts to sexualize our children.

The marketing of sex to kids is nothing new; I've addressed the issue many times. But these efforts are increasing, and they're aimed where many kids are most vulnerable—fashion.

The *Washington Post* reported that GapKids sells terry-cloth bikinis for preteens, and Sears carries in its girls' section "metallic-looking bras and bikini underpants labeled 'Girl Identity.'" In Canada, the *Ottawa Citizen* reported that a seven-year-old girl accessed a hard-core pornography site by typing in the Internet address printed on her T-shirt. And Abercrombie & Fitch has been in hot water—again—for selling thong underwear to girls as young as seven.

This blatant pitch to kids underscores the problems facing parents these days.

First, this sexual imagery is aimed directly at kids, bypassing parental authority and protection. PBS's *Frontline* exposed the advertising world's efforts to create and sell to a parallel culture for youth.

And why not? According to Michael Wood, vice president of Teenage Research Unlimited, a company that studies teenage trends, girls aged twelve to eighteen currently spend more than $37 billion on clothes. With money like that, it is easy to see why companies such as Playboy that have always put the bottom line before responsibility are willing to exploit our kids for profit.

Playboy isn't even hiding the fact that it is marketing to teens. Helen Isaacson, president of the company's product marketing, told the *Wall Street Journal*, "We need to develop a buzz in the younger market and then move up."

This is why Playboy's marketing is so despicable. This debate is not simply about the appropriateness of certain clothing. Playboy is not just selling a bathing suit; it's selling an entire lifestyle that revolves around sex without consequences and is devoid of emotion and meaning—and it's selling this to kids.

This is nothing more than grooming young girls to be the sexual objects young men want them to be, and it's done under the guise of playfulness and fun.

Believers understand that the divorce of sexuality from the Christian ideals of fidelity, selflessness, and sacrifice has resulted in many of our culture's woes. We also know that Playboy is not selling fun to our kids but poison.

When kids believe the messages about sexuality embodied in the logos on skimpy outfits, they are internalizing patterns of thinking and behavior that will make it difficult for them to build lasting relationships; they are setting themselves and others up for a lifetime of suffering.

If we don't reverse these trends, our culture's woes will not only continue—they will multiply like rabbits.

TRUTHS TO CONSIDER

Playboy's logo for kids isn't just about fashion; it's selling the idea of sex without consequences with the motivation of selfish pleasure.

Advertisers are selling an entire lifestyle, that of an older generation who has made wrong choices and suffered the consequences. They are unleashing it not only on teenagers (see "Image Is Everything," p. 127), but on our innocent and unprotected children.

Sexual concepts at this age are disconnected from faithfulness, sacrifice, and true personhood; advertisers make young girls into objects of pleasure for the purpose of profit.

GROUP STUDY

The Spiritual Dimension: Jesus said that if we even look at a person with lust in our hearts we are committing adultery. Where might the playboy image be lodged as a result of the culture's influence? How can we deal in a victorious way with these subtle temptations?

Group Approach: How can you work together to stop buying products that implicitly sell immoral and addictive lifestyles? How can you make this clear to the company or retailer in a respectful but straightforward way, giving it an opportunity to change?

Influencing Culture: Parents wonder at teenage pregnancy, depression, and lack of responsibility. Can you make a link between the lifestyle lies that advertisers project and the resulting negative consequences among young people?

BANKRUPT AT AGE TWENTY-FIVE

Marketing to Teens, Tweens, and Kids

King Edward VIII of England quipped, "The thing that impresses me most about America is the way parents obey their children." That was almost one hundred years ago, but it certainly applies to today's culture.

Nowhere is this more true than in spending patterns. Many parents these days try to overcome emotional bankruptcy with stuff. On Mars Hill Audio, Ken Myers quoted one marketing researcher who described it as "guilt money." Parents say, "Here's the credit card. Why don't you go online and buy something, because I can't spend time with you."

The results? In 2002 alone, teens spent $100 billion. On top of that, they got their parents to spend an additional $50 billion on them. Over the past couple of days, we've been addressing how the alcohol industry targets kids and how popular movies send the message that having material goods is the ultimate virtue. No wonder advertisements skew young. That's where the money is. Marketers know it, and the results are disastrous.

In her book, *Branded: The Buying and Selling of Teenagers*, Alissa Quart writes that "those under twenty-five are now the fastest-growing group filing for bankruptcy." Nevertheless, "financial-services companies now create teenage-oriented credit and cash cards." There is even a debit card for kids that parents can fund through an advance from their own credit cards.

Marketers take advantage of this cash-rich audience. Teen magazines now appeal to tweens, those between the ages of ten and fourteen. The Cartoon Network airs commercials for MTV, a music channel for older teens and adults, during cartoons for seven- to eleven-year-olds. In *Branded*, Quart documents how marketers specifically target kids, tweens, and teens—even at their schools—through "sponsored" field trips and school events such as "Coke Day."

Marketers "acknowledge they have an easier time reaching teens because of the teens' increasingly bleak and atrophied familial relationships," writes Quart. "With parents out of the house, the social force of school and that world's currency—the in group's favorite commodities—now has a greater importance to teens than ever before."

She goes on to say that "teenagers have come to feel that consumer goods are their friends—and that the companies selling products to them are trusted allies. After all, they inquire after the kids' opinions with all the solicitude of an ideal parent."

We do our kids a terrible disservice when we teach them to fill their emotional needs with material goods and when we don't teach them how to just say no. Judith Martin, better known as Miss Manners, extols the authoritarianism of a parent's saying "because I say so." Responding to parents who question expressing their opinion to their children, she wonders "how the non-judgmentalists expect their children to develop judgment without having observed the process." Well said, Miss Manners.

TRUTHS TO CONSIDER

Wealth can be personified as a spiritual power. As we inordinately pursue it, it takes control and masters us.

A society is in decline when it defines worth mainly in terms of market value and minimizes the value of relationships and service to God and others.

As Christians, we need to guard against the negative effects of prosperity on others and on our children. We need to employ God's power to defeat the power of mammon.

GROUP STUDY

The Spiritual Dimension: Are we pursuing the benefits of more and more material things (avarice), or are we storing our treasures in heaven? What do you struggle with in the area of worldly security? This may not be material.

Group Approach: Do we handle our money and other resources in ways that help our children to recognize genuine values and set appropriate boundaries on their spending?

Influencing Culture: How do we demonstrate that the abundant life that God gives us is not dependent on material wealth? Are we generous in sharing our resources with others, especially those in need?

ACEH AND THE ABYSS
The Fog of Despair

"One death is a tragedy," said Joseph Stalin. "A million is a statistic." He was wrong. No decent person can help feeling overwhelmed by the enormity of the suffering caused by the tsunami on December 26, 2004. The thousands of dead aren't statistics; they are people made in the image of God, victims of a catastrophe that has spurred the world to action and left many in a state of despair.

One of these despairing people is David Brooks of the *New York Times.* In his New Year's Day column, he called the world's generosity "amazing" while wondering if this response was a "self-enveloping fog to obscure our view of the abyss." The abyss he's referring to is the sense that nature, contrary to what the Romantics have told us, is neither "a nurse [nor] a friend."

On the contrary, the events of late December remind us that for all of our technological prowess, we are subject to the natural elements, not their master.

Unlike premoderns who lived with this knowledge, Brooks finds himself unable to take comfort from biblical faith. The events in South Asia have left him thinking that instead of an active, albeit mysterious, God, there is only "nature's awful lottery." That being the case, we should mourn not only for the dead but also for "those of us who have no explanation," wrote Brooks, with reference to himself.

There is, however, a Christian response to Brooks's despair. Theologian David B. Hart wrote in the *Wall Street Journal* that we live in "the long melancholy aftermath of a primordial catastrophe"—the Fall, something we humans brought upon ourselves when God gave us a free will and we chose to go our way, not his. As a result of this catastrophe, ours is a "broken and wounded world." The "universe languishes in bondage to 'powers' and 'principalities'—spiritual and terrestrial—alien to God."

We see evidence of the Fall all around us, not only in disasters of the elements, but also in illness and death. Though you don't have to be a Christian to know that something has gone terribly wrong, you do have to be a Christian to understand God's remedy. In his incarnation, passion, and resurrection, God's Son judges and rescues creation "from the torments of fallen nature."

Now "all creation groans in anguished anticipation of the day when God's glory will transfigure all things" (Romans 8:21-22, paraphrased).

Until then, Hart says, we are "to hate death and waste and the imbecile forces of chance that shatter living souls"—not in despair, like Brooks and others, but in hope.

Hard to believe? Of course it is, even for some Christians. But we continue to live by faith. Until the day that Christ returns and our faith is completely vindicated, we are to cling to this gospel and preach it. Its truth and the acts of kindness and mercy it inspires are the only alternatives to the abyss of despair.

Christians now have an opportunity to help the victims of the tsunami, the suffering masses in Asia and the confused and despairing masses on every continent. We can uniquely offer hope to all victims.

TRUTHS TO CONSIDER

Disasters such as the tsunami create high drama out of the reality that most of the world's people lack the basic necessities of life while many Americans have more than they need.

We need to be sensitive to the impact of tragedies and natural disasters on those who do not share our faith and our hope. They also need our compassionate care.

Large-scale disasters destroy our illusions of being in control of our own lives and of the natural world. They challenge us to renew our trust and our dependence on God.

GROUP STUDY

The Spiritual Dimension: Jesus tells us to be alert, to be ready for greater challenges and tribulations. How can you prepare spiritually for a time of trial as massive change takes its toll? Ask God to make you aware of such opportunities.

Group Approach: Discuss your feelings about the distribution of the world's resources and opportunities and what you believe your role in this should be. Read and discuss a book such as *Poverty of Spirit* by Johannes Baptist Metz for some new ideas.

Influencing Culture: Find a reliable news source for staying informed about the tsunami or other disasters. Identify an agency through which your group can make contributions. Help an individual, a family, or a particular project so that your efforts are concrete and practical, not just abstract and overwhelming.

NO CONSERVATIVES NEED SIGN UP

Postmodernism and Academic Freedom

Undergraduates at the University of California at Berkeley look-ing to fulfill their requirement in writing and composition have several options—if they're liberal, that is. The instructor teaching "The Politics and Poetics of the Palestinian Resistance" makes it very clear that conservatives are not welcome in his class. Accord-ing to the course description, the subject matter is the culture and "poetry of resistance" published by Palestinians under the "brutal Israeli military occupation of Palestine." In case you missed the in-structor's drift, the last line of the description makes it clear. It states, "Conservative thinkers are encouraged to seek other sections." This blatant example of prejudice and disregard for academic freedom is especially ironic because Berkeley touts itself as the cradle of the free speech movement.

As soon as word spread about this "encouragement," university officials found themselves in the midst of a public relations disaster. UC chancellor Robert Berdahl criticized the English department for a "failure of oversight." He promised that the course would be monitored to prevent what he called "indoctrination."

While that's good to hear, the fact remains that this kind of discrimination against students with conservative and Christian worldviews is commonplace on college campuses. A women's studies seminar at the University of South Carolina requires prospective students to agree to certain propositions before they are allowed to participate in class.

They must agree that "racism, classism, sexism, heterosexism, and other institutionalized forms of oppression exist." In addition, students must also agree that "we are all systematically taught misinformation about our own group and about members of other groups."

Students who wish to take issue with these ideas, or even want evidence for these propositions, aren't welcome. Some professors have banned men from women's studies classes altogether on the theory that the presence of a single male would stifle the discussion.

Christians need to understand that there is something else going on besides the obvious violation of academic freedom. The indoctrination and political correctness we're witnessing on college campuses is the product of a postmodern worldview that dominates our universities.

The postmodern worldview denies that there is such a thing as truth—historical, moral, or otherwise. It denies that truth exists independently of our perspectives and interests.

This being the case, the truth of any given statement is merely a function of power. It is something that is imposed on another person or group, not something that is discerned or discovered.

In a worldview where no truth is recognized but only power, hearing opposing points of view is unnecessary, since teaching is no longer about the exchange of ideas. The goal is to impose the instructor's views on the students—in other words, to indoctrinate them.

Academic freedom is only possible when you believe that there's such a thing as truth. If you don't, no amount of oversight over class descriptions will change what goes on inside our classrooms.

TRUTHS TO CONSIDER

Postmodern educators think that they can impose indoctrination because without objective truth the free exchange of ideas to find it is unnecessary.

Forms of oppression and abuses of power do exist as the postmodernist posits, but they are part of our fallen nature in rebellion against God and can only be overcome by subjection to his absolute truth.

We need to protect our own academic freedom and that of our opponents, or our ability to speak truth in the marketplace will be severely curtailed.

GROUP STUDY

The Spiritual Dimension: Our fallen condition lends itself to oppressing those who are weaker than or different from us. Where do we need to repent of bias based on class, gender, or race, and how can we find grace and guidance to overcome these sins?

Group Approach: Find a solid overview of postmodernism and explore how it penetrates all of our cultural institutions. What old apologetic approaches do we need to abandon in order to combat these ideas and practices?

Influencing Culture: How can we make our voices heard in academia, not to impose our views but to provide an intelligent and cogent alternative to the lies of postmodernism?

AN INERT GRAY BLUR

Depressed in the Midst of Plenty

The years following World War II saw unprecedented progress in Western standards of living. The average American and Western European was wealthier and healthier than all but a handful of the people who had ever lived. That same period saw even greater growth in the incidence of clinical depression among the same population. As Gregg Easterbrook tells us in *The Progress Paradox: How Life Gets Better While People Feel Worse*, there has been as much as a "ten-fold increase in unipolar depression in industrial nations [in] the postwar era."

Some of this is the result of better diagnosis. Still, it's a shocking increase and on the surface, seems contradictory until you understand the role that beliefs and worldviews play in shaping how we feel about our lives. According to Martin Seligman of the University of Pennsylvania, much of the increase in depression can be attributed to the effects of ideas and beliefs that have taken hold in our culture. One of these is individualism, seeing all of life through the self. Previous emphasis on family, faith, and community "allowed individuals to view their private setbacks within a larger context." But now, in the age of the self, our setbacks take on "enormous importance."

Another mistaken idea that contributes to depression is the "postwar teaching of victimology and helplessness." "Intellectuals, politicians, tort lawyers, and the media" have worked to identify and designate new classes of victims. As Seligman notes, more and more Americans identify themselves as victims of one sort or another. The result is a sense of helplessness. Americans, especially the young, claim to have less and less control over their lives at the same time that they enjoy unprecedented personal freedom. And our mistaken beliefs aren't limited to our ideas about ourselves. For many years, astrophysicists have theorized that one day the universe will cease expanding, decay into an "inert gray blur," and extinguish all existence. This theory was cited by writer Thomas Pynchon and others as proof that life is meaningless.

As it turns out, those astrophysicists were probably wrong, but that hasn't stopped writers and philosophers from continuing to proclaim the meaninglessness of life. Easterbrook notes that the period of increased depression was one in which most

Western Europeans and many Americans "lost their belief in higher powers or a higher purpose." They took their cues from people such as Nobel Prize–winning biologist Jacques Monod, who wrote that "man knows at last that he is alone in the universe's unfeeling immensity, out of which he emerged only by chance."

Philosophical materialism, disguised as scientific fact, has contributed to the depression that has gripped the West. The irony is that the damage described by Easterbrook is largely self-inflicted. The West embraced these destructive ideas as it looked for alternatives to the Western Christian tradition. It believed that rejecting this tradition led to freedom. Instead, of course, it led to despair.

As it turns out, prosperity is no substitute for what Christianity gave the West—a sense of purpose that begins with understanding who "we"—and not just "I"—really are.

TRUTHS TO CONSIDER

Affluence does not buy happiness, especially without the spiritual, cultural, and moral foundations of a Christian worldview to accompany it.

Our gratitude toward God and others for what we do have will alleviate our discontent and allow us to focus on helping those less fortunate than we are.

We are much better off than previous generations and have more resources at our disposal; we should shake off our discontent and use these benefits for the Kingdom of God.

GROUP STUDY

The Spiritual Dimension: How have improved health care, lei-
sure, and technology lessened your perceived need for God? Allow
the Holy Spirit through prayer to show you what areas may stand
in his way. Everything you have is a gift from him.

Group Approach: How might you practice gratitude for what God
has given you? How can you live more simply and generously with
what you have?

Influencing Culture: How can you better communicate to others
that the source of your happiness is a love relationship with God
and others? How do you demonstrate your lack of dependence on
material goods?

"YOU CAN'T HUG A COMPUTER"

The Problem with "Virtual Parenting"

What if you could be with your child even when you were away from your child? Technology is making this idea a reality. More and more parents who have to be away for extended periods of time are using Internet hookups, webcams, and microphones to spend so-called face-to-face time with their kids.

Something like this could perhaps be a godsend for military parents or parents in prison, but like so much technology, this innovation has its darker side. In many divorce cases, it's being used as a substitute for personal parental time with a child. The nicknames given to this trend say it all—nicknames such as "virtual visitation" or "virtual parent-time." And the courts are getting on board.

A court allowed Paul Cleri's ex-wife to move out of state with their three children as long as Cleri could visit them—virtually, that is, twice a week. Cleri is appealing the decision. His ex-wife's lawyer called virtual visitation "one step away from being there," but Cleri told the *Washington Post*, "I don't view virtual visitation as a practical alternative to physical contact. You can't hug a computer."

However, many other so-called virtual parents think virtual visitation is a lifesaver. Some have promoted legislation in their states to let divorced parents supplement their visitation time in just this way. A host of Web sites such as Distanceparent.org and books such as *Moms over Miles* help parents set up "distance parenting plans" and suggest activities parents and kids can do by webcam. Yet even many virtual-visitation advocates recognize its limitations. A site called InternetVisitation.org emphasizes, "Virtual Visitation should *never* be used to replace or substitute for in-person or face-to-face visits with your children." The trouble is, that's exactly what it's being used for. David Levy of the Children's Rights Council told the *Post*, "Some parents are encouraged to allow a move-away on the promise that there will be e-mail and phone contact, and now webcam access."

Even Jim Buie, author of several books and articles about the advantages of virtual visitation, is ambivalent about his own experience with his son, whose mother took him to live five hundred miles away. On his Web site, Buie wrote, "When I look at Matthew's life as a whole, I see some unmet needs. For me to try and fill them via e-mail, online chats, telephone conversations, monthly visits, on holidays, and during the summer is unrealistic." Correct.

That's why, despite the good intentions of a lot of these parents, I think it's dangerous for virtual-visitation rights to be used in custody cases. Divorce is traumatic enough for kids. Anything that encourages courts to let one parent move away from the kids or take them away from their other parent does more harm than good. It's just a new attempt to prove old myths that have already been discredited—that is, that "quality time" is more important than "quantity time," that only one parent is really necessary, and so on. Instead of buying into such fairy tales, the courts—and the families involved—need to make every effort to ensure that kids grow up near Mom and Dad. A virtual parent, no matter how loving, is no substitute for the real thing.

TRUTHS TO CONSIDER

Beyond using technology to help us become more organized and efficient, we often expect technology to explain the meaning of our lives and facilitate our relationships.

We easily come to believe that our relationships should also be organized and efficient. We give and receive emotional fast food that is high in overhead and low in nurture and substance.

Long-distance parental relationships are like artificial limbs—they are valuable when needed but are never preferable to the real thing.

GROUP STUDY

The Spiritual Dimension: In what ways have you idolized the technology you use? How have you "worshipped" expediency over quality, participated in immoral content, or put technology ahead of family or spiritual life?

Group Approach: The world is hungry for community, preeminently in the form of sound parenting and family life, yet the church is especially weak at promoting Christian ideas about community. How can we prevent technological expediency from eclipsing true relational values?

Influencing Culture: How can we enhance parenting skills in our churches and communities? What classes can we offer, or in what ways can we come alongside struggling parents to support and encourage them?

AN UNSTABLE BALANCE

Wanting It Both Ways

For nearly a decade, the Institute for Advanced Studies in Culture, an excellent group on the University of Virginia campus headed by respected Christian sociologist James Davison Hunter, has been conducting a "Survey of American Political Culture." This survey measures changes in the "ideals, beliefs, [and] values" that "bind [Americans] together and direct their common actions."

What emerges from the latest installment of the survey is a portrait of a culture that wants to have it both ways and doesn't understand why that's not possible. According to the survey, "most Americans seek some balance or tension between commonality and diversity." They want a shared moral consensus as well as the freedom to choose their own values. For example, 60 percent of respondents envisioned a future where "Americans will be more unified in their moral commitments." Seventy-one percent saw Americans as becoming more, not less, religious. And an overwhelming number aspired to an America where the "lines between good and bad will be firmer" and to a society where people "stand strongly behind their personal convictions."

That sounds good. At the same time, 60 percent of the respondents said that in the future, "American families will take many forms." That's right—60 percent do not support the most important moral commitment to the traditional family. And the respondents' ideas about a more religious America did not include Christianity, the religious tradition that created our way of life. Three-quarters of them preferred a "mix of people of many faiths."

The survey results may seem schizophrenic, but they are understandable. They illustrate Americans' confusion over what it takes to make a good society. Take the attitudes toward religion. The results reflect a shift away from traditional religion, such as Christianity, to what Americans have come to vaguely call "spirituality." This shift enables people to enjoy the emotional and psychological benefits of religion without any restrictions on personal freedom.

The problem is that there is no evidence that this kind of religion can build the kind of society for which the respondents yearn. On the contrary, the "firm line" they desire between good and evil comes from people who subordinate their own opinions and desires to the requirements of their faith. As Hunter points out, this submission and accountability to religious tradition is the real source of morality. Similarly, the authority of the family to teach and reinforce moral standards is undermined by the insistence that this can take any form they choose. Like religion, the family's power to teach is rooted in the belief that it is the individual that must conform to its requirements and not the other way around. This binding of conscience is where the power to "stand strongly" comes from.

Thus, a future in which religion and the traditional family play less of a role is a future in which moral commonality is less, not more, likely. Postmodern thinking may promise moral freedom, but it produces moral chaos.

TRUTHS TO CONSIDER

It is no less true for adults than for children that we absorb the values of those we love and spend time with. If we want to have clear, godly values, we must spend time with God and learn to love his ways.

Wanting to have everything "both ways" is often a sign of insecurity. We don't really know what we want, we are afraid to express it, or we are afraid of missing out on the good things in life.

We don't often trust God or our own true desires enough to discover the abundant life that God desires to give us.

GROUP STUDY

The Spiritual Dimension: Are there significant areas in which you feel ambivalent, ambiguous, or conflicted in what you want or feel you should do? God is not the author of confusion. You can ask him to heal you and clarify your thinking in these areas.

Group Approach: In what ways do we persuade ourselves and teach our children that we can "have things both ways"? What needs to change for us to be of one heart and mind in our Christian lives?

Influencing Culture: Character is still applauded in our culture for the good results it brings in our lives. Can you persuade others that character is related to authoritative community with moral foundations? How do you model a life of character in the public sphere?

BIGOT BUSTERS
Shooting Down Democracy

A young woman in Washington decided to sign a petition to put a measure on the ballot in her state that would bar special rights for gays. But as she approached a booth set up at a neighborhood store, she was suddenly surrounded by a hostile gang of young men.

"Nazi!" they screamed at her. "Hate monger! Bigot!"

The frightened woman backed away. In fact, she was so intimidated that she never did sign the ballot petition.

It's all part of a new strategy by militant homosexuals to overpower their opponents. They form aggressive groups dubbed

"Bigot Busters" to intimidate voters. Election officials believe their techniques of harassment have effectively kept initiatives to bar special gay rights off the ballot in several states.

It's become a cliché to say that America is embroiled in a culture war. But if the Bigot Busters continue to have their way, the biggest prisoner of war will be democracy itself. As America loses its moral consensus, radicals on both the left and the right have given up trying to argue their cases rationally. Instead, they're turning to force and even to violence.

This dangerous new trend is explored in James Davison Hunter's book entitled *Before the Shooting Begins*. Can democracy survive, Hunter asks, when citizens no longer share a moral consensus? After all, when there's no common moral framework, discussion itself becomes impossible.

Rational discourse is displaced by force and violence.

Consider the hottest issues of our day. Animal-rights activists have broken into laboratories and destroyed years' worth of research. Gay-rights activists have invaded churches and desecrated their altars. Pro-lifers have actually shot and killed abortionists, and abortion supporters are shooting back.

Is there a way to stave off social chaos? Can we reconstruct a common moral framework for our society? The first step is to understand why that framework was lost in the first place. As Hunter points out, the culprit is a completely privatized view of truth and values.

In his own interviews with people on the subject of abortion, Hunter found almost no one who could give rational, well-thought-out reasons for his or her views. The average American falls back on "That's just the way I feel."

But if truth is merely private, then trying to convince others of one's opinion is seen as a power play—an attempt to impose one's private morality onto someone else. And once people make up their minds that it is merely a power issue, then why even bother trying to persuade others?

The only thing left is force.

That's why the watershed issue of our day is truth—the biblical teaching that truth is not private but transcendent and deeply rooted in ultimate reality. When radicals such as the Bigot Busters try to strong-arm the democratic process, we need to do more than complain to election officials. Christians must boldly cultivate a biblical worldview, dismantling the postmodern notion that truth is whatever "feels right."

If we do not, then the culture war will inevitably degenerate into an all-out shooting war. And the casualty will be America's democratic freedom.

TRUTHS TO CONSIDER

Some believe that we have no common moral framework in which to converse in the marketplace of ideas and thus have concluded that we can't achieve our objectives through rational persuasion.

We also have trouble rationally explaining our ideas because of the postmodern idea that truth resides in the individual rather than in universals. Thus we are drawn into power plays with our foes.

Our entire democratic system will be damaged if we cannot find a way to constructively dialogue and accept the processes of resolution that this system entails, always respecting others' rights and freedoms.

GROUP STUDY

The Spiritual Dimension: How do you treat others in relationships when you disagree or are angry over something? Are you a person who hears the other side and goes through a process of accommodation and reconciliation to preserve fellowship?

Group Approach: Can you clearly articulate your positions on some of the major, highly polarized cultural issues? Work out with others in your church some positions that are clear and logical in a spirit of love and understanding toward other positions.

Influencing Culture: Can you explain how both intimidation and ill-defined beliefs create a lose-lose situation for everyone as we attempt to work through various cultural issues? Take an issue and work with others who have a different view to at least come to a place of better understanding.

RULES FOR A REASON
The World Rethinks Dating

The June 2003 issue of the *Washington Monthly* ran an intriguing article by journalist Elizabeth Austin titled "In Contempt of Courtship." Happily married herself, Austin nevertheless found it depressing to study today's dating habits. Everywhere she looked, from popular culture to real life, dating was portrayed as hard, boring, thankless work—more like "applying for a new job" than having fun. Many single people would rather sit home and watch a "reality" dating show than actually go on a date.

"When did we start to consider dating a synonym for hell?" Austin asks. "Wasn't the sexual revolution supposed to make court-ship more fun? Yet everywhere we look, we see single people bemoaning the loneliness, the despair, the just plain drudgery of dating."

This led Austin to an astonishing conclusion. Maybe the sex-ual revolution, far from being the solution to a problem, was ac-tually the cause of far bigger problems between men and women. Not that Austin believes in saving sex for marriage. In fact, she expresses some contempt for "those counter-feminist conservatives" who are old-fashioned enough to wait for the wedding.

But she has to admit that "the way it's been done lately, court-ship isn't any fun. That's because there is currently only one broadly accepted rule of courtship. . . . If either party declines sex on the Third Date, it's a clear sign that the relationship is going nowhere."

Austin thinks that when you get right down to it, that's a sad way to live. We agree. Imagine starting a sexual relationship that fizzles out after a few dates, and having to go back out and find someone else to start another one with—another one that will probably also fizzle out. No wonder people dread dating these days!

Even Austin, with her mockery of so-called "Rules girls," has to admit that she misses the days when single people took some time just to get to know each other, rather than treating each other as something to be used and thrown away. "After all," she writes, "in all forms of human behavior, there are rules." And they're not there just to keep us from having fun, as Austin's single friends are slowly and painfully learning. They're there to protect us. As

Wendy Shalit explains in her best-selling book, *A Return to Modesty*, we all know that we need rules, so much so that when we discard them, we end up longing to have them back and even trying to make up new ones.

Austin bases her argument "not on morality but on sheer utility." We Christians base ours on the fact that our loving Creator designed us for something much better than a string of broken relationships and unhappy memories. But it's interesting that we've both reached the same conclusion. If Elizabeth Austin follows her train of thought to its logical conclusion, she may learn something from those women she dismisses as hopelessly prim and proper. Their lives, after all, are demonstrating an important truth: God's Word isn't just a set of arbitrary rules; it's a guide to the way the world really works. And this is a great apologetic opportunity to point out to people what happens when they turn away from truth. They discover that their own way of life is simply irrational. It doesn't work, and it's not true.

TRUTHS TO CONSIDER

The alienation, guilt, and even drudgery of dating stems from having separated sex from its sacred qualities. Through indulgence, men and women use and then abandon their partners.

Rules in relationships are not there to prevent enjoyment but actually to enhance it by protecting us from the adverse consequences of violating God's laws.

We can guide others to see that the natural and logical consequences of their behavior point to the validity of God's laws.

GROUP STUDY

The Spiritual Dimension: How have the rules God has set in place for sexual intimacy blessed you in your own dating and marriage relationships? When has "utility" overcome the rules and caused you trouble?

Group Approach: How can we reach out, through mercy and guidance, to help restore those in the church who have been burned by "utilitarian" dating relationships?

Influencing Culture: We should reach out to those who believe that sexual intimacy helps us to discover whether a relationship has potential. We can show how this knowledge can be found through restraint that avoids the pain of premature sexual intimacy.

THE ARTS

LIE 4

Art should break traditional norms and challenge outworn beliefs.

Underlying Worldview: Because there is no ultimate good, art both replaces God and helps us to create and revere what is beautiful. It allows us to express our individuality and to challenge conventional norms, thus redefining reality.

Art (painting, film, literature) is used to mirror the worldview that I have described in the previous three sections. Even art that is beautiful and has a classic Christian origin can be enlisted for the purposes of other ideologies and reinterpreted to fit other worldviews. It can especially be used to downplay evil and make it seem acceptable. Influenced by the Romantic views of the nineteenth century, we can also deify art, putting our faith in humanity rather than in God. This Romantic-era experiment to deify art failed and so will the more extreme attempts to be critical of our Judeo-Christian tradition.

Because of the postmodern view that facts are subjective and because our culture is theologically ignorant, literary fiction can masquerade as fact to attack a Christian worldview. The best-selling *The Da Vinci Code* mixes fact with fiction to argue the case for an unorthodox view of Christ's life that cannot be substantiated historically. Art, speaking authoritatively as a substitute for religion, can catch us off guard, especially in a theologically ignorant culture.

Heaven can be given a completely different reality. The best-selling *Tuesdays with Morrie* presents a view of heaven that revolves around self-gratification rather than holiness. There is no mention of repentance, only of unconditional acceptance. Art can reinvent reality along the lines of its own wish-fulfillment and deceive us when our guard is down. Sexual freedom is boldly proclaimed, and sexual exploitation can even penetrate a high art form such as classical music by the ways that women artists are portrayed on CD covers. For example, classical violinist Lara St. John posed naked, with only her strategically placed violin to cover her.

In this section you'll also read examples of how art continues to serve a Christian worldview and to oppose the lies that create an independent set of moral values. Qualities such as heroism, self-sacrifice, redemption, humility, and godly devotion rise to the surface in film because people still identify with them. The Lord of the Rings films exhibit many Christian themes. John Rhys-Davies, who played the dwarf Gimli, says that our generation faces a moral crisis on par with the threat to civilization in Middle Earth. Yet in the final film, *The Return of the King*, we see the ultimate triumph of good over evil that is the Christian hope.

Other films reflecting a Christian worldview also bring a ray of hope in art's redemptive value. Roberto Benigni's *Life Is Beautiful* shows the comedy of hope even in the midst of the Holocaust, the event that was one of the greatest victories for God's spiritual enemies. Eternal things are greater than the evil that man can do, however, and God is present even in the midst of tragedy. *Gods and Generals* also depicts many of the virtues just mentioned. It demonstrates that even in the carnage of war, devout men have sought the will of God. *Saving Private Ryan* shows the extent to which fellow soldiers will go to save just one life and how each life should be lived to the fullest. Finally, *The Passion of the Christ* challenges culture by unsparingly depicting humanity's darker side while providing an answer that is shockingly and graphically portrayed.

Another selection tells us that we need guidelines as we view sinful behavior on film. Although we need to understand our culture in order to critique it, in challenging the lies found in art we also need to cultivate pure minds and hearts since God resides in us. We combat the lies as we support the arts rather than minimize them and as we support the creative integrity of our artists without bending them to our own needs.

MYTH MEETS REAL LIFE

The Lord of the Rings and the Present Crisis

The *Return of the King*, the final installment in Peter Jackson's adaptation of J. R. R. Tolkien's Lord of the Rings trilogy, has played in theaters across the country. At a press event in Los Angeles, the cast and crew reflected the friendships, camaraderie, and hardships experienced in making the films.

The film, of course, has a great message, but one cast member added a powerful—if politically incorrect—perspective of his own. He talked about how the crises and challenges depicted in Tolkien's mythical world might help us cope with those we confront in our world today.

John Rhys-Davies, who plays Gimli the dwarf, told writers that "the older I get, the more certain I am of the presence of evil" in the world. Such a declaration of itself sets Rhys-Davies apart from many in the entertainment industry. But the British actor didn't stop there. He said that Tolkien was saying that there are "times when a generation may be challenged. And if that generation does not rise to meet that challenge, you could lose an entire civilization."

According to Rhys-Davies, this message has "huge resonance for today." For someone who, as he put it, believes in "Judeo-Greek-Christian-Western civilization," recent developments, especially in Europe, are a "catastrophe."

The civilization that has given us "democracy, the equality of women, the abolition of slavery . . . and the right to true intellectual dissent" is under assault—specifically, Rhys-Davies noted, by radical Islam. Instead of resisting that assault, parts of the Western world—and here he's referring to Europe—are committing cultural suicide.

Rhys-Davies pointed to demographic trends in Europe where, in some cases, the majority of children being born are the children of Muslim immigrants. While it's politically incorrect to notice this, it's folly to ignore the cultural implications.

The actor also expressed his support for the war in Iraq. He called it "extraordinary" and called Americans "the most optimistic people in the whole . . . world." He noted that no one believed that Germany and Japan could become democracies after World War II. Now, we're trying to do the same in the Middle East.

These views don't exactly endear Rhys-Davies to many of his

fellow actors. As he puts it, he takes a "lot of stick" for his views. Still, the benefits of Western civilization are so great that the alternative isn't some multicultural paradise but darkness. In Tolkien's language, it's the Orcs, Uruk-hai, and Sauron.

These are strong but necessary words. Our culture is hesitant to use the word *evil* and refuses to recognize what's at stake even in places like Iraq. Nowhere is this refusal more blatant than in the industry of which Rhys-Davies is a part. Yet not a single one of Rhys-Davies's critics—those "giving him stick"—would dream of giving up the benefits of Western civilization. They're not willing to pay the price for its defense or even to acknowledge that it's under attack.

But that price must be paid. As the trailer for *The Return of the King* tells us, "There is no freedom without sacrifice." Tolkien understood that, and so does the man who brought his heroic dwarf to life on the big screen.

TRUTHS TO CONSIDER

Multiculturalism that will blend an Islamic worldview into Western civilization is a recipe for disaster. Many in Europe, where this trend is advancing, are not ready to admit to the danger.

We need to stand firm in the face of terror. If we won't pay the price to defend the values of our Western civilization, we don't deserve to keep them.

Tolkien has dramatically demonstrated that there is an immense price to pay when evil is on the rise and our very civilization is being threatened. When we have right on our side, we should fight, even if we risk losing.

GROUP STUDY

The Spiritual Dimension: In the midst of affirming and including all ethnic and racial groups and thus "being all things to all people," are you still able to recognize beliefs and practices that oppose God?

Group Approach: Talk and pray with others to determine areas in which you could sacrifice for the greater good and the preservation of Judeo-Christian values. Are we afraid to speak up for truth because we, too, like our brothers and sisters in the Third World might be persecuted?

Influencing Culture: Rather than crying "evil" to the culture, where can we contribute to the Christian worldview by stressing the great ideas and works of Western culture? Can we begin by reading a book or taking a course that demands our full intellectual participation?

A PASSION FOR GETTING IT RIGHT

The Power of the Image

Imagine, for a moment, that an Oscar-winning director such as Steven Spielberg or Roman Polanski announces that his next project will be an historical drama.

Now imagine that groups representing the people depicted in the film are demanding to see if the script meets with their approval. There's no way that any responsible director would give in to those demands. In refusing, he'd have the wholehearted support of what is often called "the creative community" and the First Amendment watchdogs.

The exception, of course, is if the history in question is the passion of our Lord, in which case, creative freedom is expected to take a back seat to the demands of political correctness.

That's what is happening with Mel Gibson's film *The Passion of the Christ*. *The Passion* tells the story of the twelve hours surrounding the Crucifixion. While *The Passion* is only the latest in a series of films about Jesus, it stands out for two reasons. First, it is unsparing and unsentimental. In Gibson's opinion, previous cinematic efforts have failed to capture the enormity of Jesus' suffering on our behalf.

In *The Passion*, the audience sees the full horror of those twelve hours on-screen. The film shows actor James Caviezel, who plays Jesus, covered in blood. Caviezel, a devout Catholic like Gibson, believes that the honest depiction of Jesus' agony will draw many to the truth.

A second way that *The Passion* stands out is that it is entirely in Aramaic and Latin, with no subtitles. Gibson is counting on the visuals and on the audience's basic familiarity with the story to allow him to go for the maximum in realism and authenticity.

This quest for fidelity has made some people nervous. Even without seeing the film, some Jewish and Catholic leaders have accused Gibson's film of fomenting "religious animosity" and even anti-Semitism. They have worried that the film might blame "the Jews" for Jesus' death. And they requested that a panel of scholars be allowed to review the script before the film's release.

Gibson's defenders included Archbishop Charles Chaput of Denver. He wrote that he found it "puzzling and disturbing that anyone would feel licensed to attack a film of sincere faith before it has even been released." He reminded Gibson's liberal critics that when *The Last Temptation of Christ*—an attack on the historical Jesus—came out, "movie critics piously lectured Catholics to be open-minded and tolerant. Surely that advice should apply equally for everyone."

The archbishop is right, but "tolerance," you see, is no longer a two-way street. It's a weapon to intimidate certain groups. As Gibson has learned, the list of groups definitely includes devout Christians. A film that unapologetically says that there is such a thing as Truth and that his name is Jesus Christ violates all the taboos our culture has embraced.

This opposition makes Gibson's commitment to making this film all the more admirable. He knows that there's something more important than the support of the "creative community." And that is doing justice to the price paid for our salvation.

TRUTHS TO CONSIDER

Many of the attacks on *The Passion* have been based on the aversion of its detractors to the message of the film rather than to intolerance within the message.

We have tended to gloss over the full extent of the suffering that Christ underwent on our behalf. This is a disservice to the gospel message that shortchanges the work of the Cross on behalf of humanity.

When we proclaim the truths of Christianity, our first obligation is faithfulness to the message, not catering to the sensitivities of others.

GROUP STUDY

The Spiritual Dimension: Reflect on the great price our Savior paid to redeem us from our sins. How can this give us a greater aversion to sin and a greater love for Christ?

Group Approach: Find some trustworthy resources that deal with the theology of redemption, and connect your experience of *The Passion* with all the doctrinal aspects of what God has done for you on the cross.

Influencing Culture: Watch the video version of *The Passion* with a friend who is a seeker. Discuss the meaning of the film in terms of your own experience, your friend's experience, and the orthodox teachings of the Christian faith.

REDEMPTIVE REALITY

Benigni's Life Is Beautiful

The stunning Italian film *Life Is Beautiful* is one of the most moving comedies you'll ever see. It was nominated in both the Best Film and the Best Foreign Film categories. What is even more unusual is that it illustrates the Christian truth that there are purposes and realities that transcend our sufferings.

Roberto Benigni, who wrote, directed, and stars in *Life Is Beautiful*, is a comic genius who has been called "the Italian Charlie Chaplin." But the subject of his movie, the Nazi Holocaust, is anything but funny.

Benigni's character, a sad-sack waiter named Guido, courts the affections of a local schoolteacher and through various hilarious adventures wins her heart. They marry and have a son.

Then things take a dark turn. Father and son, who are Jewish, are sent to a concentration camp. Guido, who's been irrepressibly joyful throughout, doesn't let even this monstrous turn of events get to him. To shield his son from the horrors they're going through, Guido concocts a wild story, telling the boy that the whole experience is really just an elaborate game. They'll have to play very, very hard to win, he says, but if they succeed, the boy will win a magnificent prize: a real tank!

It's a measure of the film's brilliance that the humor is never mawkish or inappropriate. Still, that hasn't stopped some movie critics from expressing horror at the idea of a comedy set in a concentration camp. Critics have called it "profoundly unsettling" and say that it "trivializes the Holocaust."

How is it that Benigni has dared to use humor in a film about the greatest evil of this century? He's done it by expressing the Christian idea that there's more to life than what we see.

In the scene in which the father is being led away to be killed, he spots his son and makes a funny face. The message is that there is something that triumphs even over death, some transcendent reality that even in this ultimate moment of gravity enables Guido to make his son laugh.

Most of our cultural leaders operate from a purely naturalistic perspective that claims that material existence is all there is. Since for them nothing transcends this world and its horrors, pretending that we can laugh even in the midst of the Holocaust is offensive and absurd.

But Scripture teaches that there are eternal things, and if we understand their value, we will not be cowed even by the most appalling earthly circumstances.

Benigni seems to understand this profound truth. Courage, self-sacrifice, and love are all part of being made in God's image and are more real than our sufferings. That's why, when faced with the horror of the Holocaust, Guido can still make us smile.

This subtitled Italian film features an innocent Jewish man in his thirties who ends up being killed. It is not the gospel story, but it does point to the gospel, because it's about how God's redemptive reality trumps the very worst this world has to offer—yes, even the Holocaust.

TRUTHS TO CONSIDER

Even in the worst circumstances in life, we should not let our spirits be vanquished. We should attempt to protect others rather than think primarily about ourselves.

Those with a naturalistic worldview cannot understand that no matter how dominant the forces of evil are at a given time, good will triumph in the end, even over death.

In times of suffering we are best able to display virtues that illustrate God's amazing grace.

GROUP STUDY

The Spiritual Dimension: When have you had to face overwhelming suffering or opposition, and what was your response? Do you believe that even if you failed, God can give you all you need the next time?

Group Approach: How can we work together to acquire a perspective of joy and even humor in difficult circumstances that will be a source of encouragement to the church and a witness to the world?

Influencing Culture: We are sometimes scorned by those who think that our beliefs are pie-in-the-sky. How can we point out the victory of Christians in difficult times when others may have failed?

A DEBT OF GRATITUDE
Saving Private Ryan

The *Boston Globe* calls it "the war movie to end all war movies." Others are saying that it's Steven Spielberg's masterwork. One critic says that it "leaves no doubt that [Spielberg] is film's premier image-maker of the last quarter-century."

The film is *Saving Private Ryan*, and what makes it so good is its brutally honest treatment of profound moral questions—questions that lead us to consider the infinite debt of gratitude each of us owes for our very life, a concept that is stunningly consistent with a Christian worldview.

How do we repay a debt like that?

The film opens with a harrowingly realistic reenactment of the D-day invasion of Normandy. We see the action through the eyes of Capt. John Miller, played by Tom Hanks. Following D-day, Miller learns that he is to lead a search party to find a certain Private Ryan, whose three brothers have just been killed in action. The last living son is to be sent home to his grieving mother.

But no sooner do Miller and his party begin their search for Ryan behind German lines than a startling Pandora's box of moral questions is opened. Why are all these men risking their lives to save one man? Don't they have mothers too? Are they just pawns in some cynical PR maneuver by the Pentagon?

As first one and then another of the soldiers in the rescue party is killed, the questioning intensifies. Just how much is one man's life worth?

The answer comes in a stunning scene at the end of the film. It's now 50 years later and Private Ryan is visiting the graves of the men who saved him, who literally gave their lives for his. "I lived my life the best I could," he says to their gravestones. "I hope in your eyes I've earned what you've done for me."

But we can see that he has gnawing doubts. Obviously distraught, Ryan turns to his wife: "Tell me I've led a good life," he implores. "Tell me I'm a good man."

"You are," she answers him.

But the answer is not convincing, and how could it be? Behind Ryan's question is the inescapable reality that however good he is and however much he has accomplished in his life, he can never, ever repay such a debt. It's a stunning moment, because we, too, think of our debt to the eighteen-year-old kids who jumped off those landing boats into a hail of bullets.

How do we repay a debt like that? We have to admit with humility that we cannot. We can only express our gratitude. Columnist George Will has called the film "a summons to gratitude" for the generation that died so we might live.

The parallel to the gospel is powerful. God gave his Son's life that we might live. How does one repay such a gift? Spielberg may not have intended to raise the parallel, but in such effectively portrayed reality, the gospel isn't hard to find.

This film is rated R for extreme violence. If you rent the film and watch it with your friends, bring that final scene to their attention. Ask them that question: "Just how much is one man's life worth?" And then tell them the answer. "It's worth the Son of God sacrificed on the Cross for us."

TRUTHS TO CONSIDER

In this film, we learn the great value we place on a human life, especially after Ryan's mother had given her other sons in the war for the price of freedom.

Just as Private Ryan was saved by the heroics of his comrades, we have all been blessed by those who have invested in us for our good. We should thank them and return their kindness.

The sacrifice of Christ on the cross was God's ultimate answer as to the worth of each human life. This should inspire us to lay down our lives for others, no matter how seemingly insignificant or even ungrateful they may be.

GROUP STUDY

The Spiritual Dimension: Jesus says that there is no greater love than for a person to lay down his life for a friend. You may have sacrificed for those dearest to you, but what about that one person you know who has needs that you don't have the time or inclination to deal with?

Group Approach: Who in your church is marginalized, weak, or undergoing trials? How can you band together to practice love for one another?

Influencing Culture: "See how they love one another!" How can this observation of ancient Roman culture be fulfilled today, as our culture observes us with fellow Christians and as we reach out to those who oppose us?

A RELIGION FOR HEROES

Gods and Generals

When actors or directors are asked what attracted them to a particular project, the answer is nearly always the same: the story. Whether or not it's true, it's the right answer. Love of stories is in our very nature as humans. The problem is that nearly all films leave out an important part of many good stories: the role of faith. A welcome exception to that rule is the film called *Gods and Generals*. It is written and directed by Ronald F. Maxwell and produced by Ted Turner. Yes, Ted Turner, the man who called Christianity a "religion for losers," has now produced a film that highlights strong and credible Christian faith.

The film is a prequel to the 1993 film *Gettysburg* and tells the story of the first two years of the Civil War. The first hint that the film deviates from Hollywood's usual treatment of faith can be found in the trailer that tells us, "They read the same Bible," and "They believed in the same God."

These believers were the men who fought the Civil War, and in particular, the central characters of the film: Confederate legends Robert E. Lee and "Stonewall" Jackson, and Union hero Joshua Lawrence Chamberlain.

While these men were on opposite sides of the war, one important thing they had in common was their Christian faith.

To their credit, the actors who portrayed these characters understood the centrality of their faith. Jeff Daniels, who plays Chamberlain, told writers that Chamberlain's faith was the most important thing in his life.

Stephen Lang, who portrays Jackson, went even further to say that his character's relationship with Christ was the lens through which he viewed the world—or as I'd put it, his worldview. In Lang's words, Jackson was an "Old Testament warrior with a New Testament theology."

A respect for history required that the characters' faith be an important part of *Gods and Generals*. And that's just what the producers depicted. To their credit, they did not caricature faith or portray it negatively.

This film shows the vital role that Christianity played in the lives of these men, and the audience can see how their decisions and their character were shaped by their beliefs.

Thus, when Jackson tells a minister that they will see each other again in heaven, it feels natural. It is what the audience comes to expect from Jackson. Similarly, when he and Lee speak of something as being God's will, there is not the slightest hint of irony or cynicism. We know and accept that this is what they believed.

The film accomplishes this without being preachy or leaving audiences with the feeling that they are being proselytized. Instead, they are entertained and left with something to think about.

I don't hesitate to criticize Hollywood studios for the garbage they often release. It is only fair, then, to thank them for movies that Christians can and should support.

So thanks to Warner Brothers and—I never thought I would say it—to Ted Turner for *Gods and Generals*, a film that in telling a good story remembers to include the most important part.

TRUTHS TO CONSIDER

The role of faith is a legitimate part of many stories, but it's often considered by producers of commercial films to be "a private matter" and thus irrelevant.

Films can incorporate the Christian faith in a way that is accurate and appropriate without becoming preachy, thus enhancing the entertainment and edification of their viewers.

The Christian faith has been a viable part of the lives of many of our great leaders, a fact that our popular culture tends to ignore or cover up.

GROUP STUDY

The Spiritual Dimension: How do you utilize your faith in the "battle situations" of your own life? Does it play a similar role as it did for Chamberlain and Lee in times of crises and danger?

Group Approach: What other great American men and women leaders do you know who had faith? What contribution did their faith make to their historical accomplishments?

Influencing Culture: Find ways to communicate how the faith of great American leaders was integral to their exploits, promoting the virtues necessary to accomplish their notable achievements.

AN EVERLASTING PLAYGROUND

Understanding the Nature of Heaven

Many people have worried that Mel Gibson's brutal film about the crucifixion of Christ will bring out the worst in all of us. *New York Times* columnist David Brooks is much more worried about Mitch Albom, the author whose sentimental story *The Five People You Meet in Heaven* has spent months on the best-seller lists. Albom, you may remember, wrote the runaway best seller *Tuesdays with Morrie*.

"While religious dogmatism is always a danger," Brooks writes, "it is less of a problem for us today than the soft-core spirituality that is its opposite. . . . We've got more to fear from the easygoing narcissism that is so much a part of the atmosphere nobody even thinks to protest or get angry about it." He's right.

As Albom's book demonstrates, this religious narcissism may show up most in our ideas about heaven. Rather than being a place where God is worshipped and glorified, Albom's heaven, according to Brooks, is for the most part "an excellent therapy session," in a place where people from our past can chat with us about the significance of our lives.

The therapeutic heaven isn't the only vision of the afterlife that we find tempting. As a book review in Slate.com points out, we also love the idea of a heaven in which we'll experience unbridled luxury. Writer Adam Kirsch explains that this idea has been around for centuries, but a number of new books take it to unprecedented levels. For instance, according to the inspirational book *A Travel Guide to Heaven,* heaven is all about "having fun" in "the ultimate playground, created purely for our enjoyment."

The therapeutic heaven and the luxurious heaven have in common "their refusal of transcendence," Kirsch writes. We tend to think of heaven as being all about us—the answer to all our questions, the end of all our sufferings, the beginning of endless fun and excitement, with what Kirsch calls a "cruise-director God" catering to our every whim.

God has promised that heaven will be a place of joy, where our tears will be wiped away forever, but in concentrating completely on these aspects, we've lost sight of what heaven is ultimately about. As Kirsch speculates on present theories about heaven, he says, "Instead of angelic choirs, it now seems . . . [that] we will be greeted in heaven by the sound of a billion voices, all talking about themselves." When you think about that, our self-centered visions of heaven start to look pretty awful.

Compare this with C. S. Lewis's vision of heaven in his book *The Great Divorce*, in which new arrivals must learn to want God more than they want their own sins, their own desires, or even their own beloved family members. Only then can they experience the joy that God has prepared for them.

As Lewis wrote elsewhere, "A ruthless, sleepless, unsmiling concentration upon self . . . is the mark of Hell," not of heaven, which is why the hellish violence of *The Passion of the Christ* paints a clearer picture of heaven—that is, of the cost to bring us there and who we should look forward to meeting when we get there—than all the syrupy therapeutic or luxury visions we can ever invent.

TRUTHS TO CONSIDER

Our culture's spiritual narcissism appears in a view of heaven that focuses on personal luxury and a preoccupation with what is important to us rather than on the rule of a Supreme Being.

In heaven, we will not have a "cruise-director God" who is there primarily to cater to all our desires and alleviate all our personal inconveniences.

Our focus in heaven will be to give all glory and praise to God as the center of existence, with a humble awareness of the supreme cost our Savior paid with his blood to get us there.

GROUP STUDY

The Spiritual Dimension: Does your life revolve around how your behavior here and now will impact your time in eternity? Unlike the present culture, do you have a holy fear of disappointing God by not taking eternity seriously enough?

Group Approach: Though God has won our salvation and we can't earn it by our works, our actions here will affect our time in eternity. How can we reintroduce this in a healthy way to motivate joy, confidence, and increased obedience?

Influencing Culture: The laws of reciprocity and natural consequences can be seen in nature and in human relationships. How can we emphasize that we will reap what we sow while showing the need for a Savior before we get to the next life?

THE DA VINCI CONSPIRACY

Distinguishing Fact from Fiction

A friend came to me outraged over Dan Brown's thriller *The Da Vinci Code*. He read the book, and though he found the story fascinating, it was filled, he said, with the historical distortions of an anti-Christian—and specifically anti-Catholic—screed. Don't worry, I told him—it will blow over like all fads. Besides, no thinking person will take it seriously.

Well, I was wrong. Since then, I've talked to a lot of people who have read the book. It confirms the unbelief of nonbelievers while it turns off honest seekers, and it has confused and disillusioned many Christians.

That's because, while Brown is skillful in creating suspense, breakneck pacing, and surprising twists, he also has a knack for playing fast and loose with the truth.

The Da Vinci Code begins with the murder of a museum curator. A Harvard professor and a French code breaker are called in to decipher a cryptic message that he wrote just before he died. They discover that he was protecting a powerful and dangerous secret.

So far, just your average thriller, right? We soon find out that the curator had evidence that could disprove the deity of Christ. Although the church has tried for centuries to suppress the evidence, great thinkers and artists have planted clues everywhere—in paintings by Da Vinci, the architecture of cathedrals, and even in Disney cartoons.

That sounds like a loony conspiracy theory, except that Brown props up his flimsy edifice with impressive-sounding, supposedly historical "facts." One of his characters even states, "The historical evidence supporting this [story] is substantial."

But it's not. Brown uses a combination of lies and half-truths founded on a skewed perspective of church history. In Brown's view, the heretics of the early church were the real truth tellers, and the church banned their doctrines because they threatened the church's power base.

Just in case readers go back to their Bibles to check facts, Brown has his characters claim that the Gospels aren't historically accurate. Instead, it's the Gnostic gospels—books discarded by the early church as unreliable—that tell the truth about Jesus.

As Dan Brown knows, an adventure story such as *The Da Vinci Code* is an ideal way to get past people's guard. Between trying to guess who the real villains are and trying to decode the various clues scattered through the book, who's going to notice that Brown's religious theories are as phony as a three-dollar bill?

Christians need to notice. And we need to do our research so that we can respond to the fabrications in *The Da Vinci Code*.

Even though Dan Brown knows the techniques of writing a best-selling thriller, he uses them to reach the most banal conclusions. He apparently thinks it's exciting to show Jesus as an ordinary human being with strong leanings toward goddess worship. But the biblical story of Jesus—God the Son coming to earth as a man to die and rise again for our salvation—is infinitely more exciting. If you know Christians who are reading the book, tell them to throw it away. If you have non-Christian friends who have read it, debunk *The Da Vinci Code*. Then tell them a much better story—and one that has the added advantage of being true.

TRUTHS TO CONSIDER

The thriller genre of fiction makes it easy to get away with half-truths, poor reasoning, and inadequate research in order to convince readers of a biased theological position.

Because of increasing biblical and theological ignorance, *The Da Vinci Code* portrays heretics as the truth tellers. The average reader is not aware of that fact.

Though the adventure story may be entertaining, the story of who Christ is in *The Da Vinci Code* is a lot less compelling than the biblical version.

GROUP STUDY

The Spiritual Dimension: This novel is a blatant example of resistance to the gospel. What other novels or works of art or entertainment might slip under your radar screen that would influence you negatively?

Group Approach: Have you given time to studying with others the basic heresies concerning Christ and the Gospels in order to combat the views found in this best seller? Knowing them will also help you to better understand true Christology.

Influencing Culture: Use this novel to discuss the historical claims of the Gospels and the person of Christ. Point out the lack of any substantiation for this book as other than pure fiction.

REAL ART

The Hope beyond Ground Zero

On February 4, 2003, the White House announced that New York artist Makoto Fujimura was appointed by President Bush to the National Council on the Arts for a six-year term. Perhaps it's the worldview behind his art that caught the president's attention. Working in his studio three blocks from Ground Zero, Fujimura was deeply affected by the horrific events of September 11, 2001, and it caused him to challenge the artistic community to see the reality of our broken state of existence. Fujimura says, "Art cannot be divorced from faith, for to do so is to literally close our eyes to that beauty of the dying sun setting all around us. Death spreads all over our lives, and therefore, faith must be given to see through the darkness, to see through the beauty of the valley of the shadow of death. . . . Everyone has a Ground Zero to face."

Reflecting on his own conversion, he said, "I remember how I used to look at the landscape every day on my way to work, not believing what I saw was true or able to trust my own vision. I realized after my conversion that there was reality [grounded in Christ that] I could trust, and that I could also trust what was inside of me to express it. Reality is the foundation of creativity, and any artist who is honest has to make that assumption." Coming from Japan with a Christian population of less than one percent, the worldview shift in his art was radically countercultural and obvious to both his admirers and his critics. For Fujimura, art can best be understood in the context of the Incarnation. In the Lord's Supper, ordinary substances become sacred. The immanent becomes transcendent. If God became man and humbled himself, this incarnational principle can be applied to every act of creativity, and therefore, the results of artistic creation can become sacred. This is the theological understanding that flows through Fujimura's work.

Fujimura works in Nihonga—a medieval Japanese technique of painting using minerals. His works are painted in layers of mineral paints that become transparent over time, revealing the layers below. When asked by art critic James Romaine how this technique relates to his faith, Fujimura said, "The underlying worldview of Japanese art is cyclical, and yet the technique lends itself to this notion that there is a beginning and an end." There is history and story in the painting as this handmade paint is applied to handmade paper. "There is this rich fabric of story being woven as you work. That is something that is very significant to me, as I am someone who has come to understand that my worldview is a premise that allows for these stories to come alive. That understanding of the world or of looking at yourself as having a history is very biblical. Because there is a beginning and an end, there is resolution; even in death itself, there is this purpose."

As a contemporary artist creatively embracing and painting his way through the wreckage of September 11, Fujimura is an example of a Christian effectively using art as a vehicle to show us reality— its depravity and brokenness, but also the hope of restoration that the Great Artist, incarnate in Christ, brings to all things.

TRUTHS TO CONSIDER

The arts can be beautiful and enriching, pointing us to God, or they can be manipulated and adapted for evil purposes. We will use and appreciate art based on our own moral and spiritual development and understanding.

Properly understood, the arts reflect God's glory. We are "subcreators" under God, with the ability to express the beauty of his creation.

Fujimura's technique of Nihonga provides a metaphor for Christian life. As we grow in Christ, the successive layers of our experience become increasingly transparent to reveal God at the center of our being.

GROUP STUDY

The Spiritual Dimension: What forms and individual works of art enhance you spiritually? How can you allow art to nourish your spiritual growth more deeply?

Group Approach: How can we better support Christian artists, who are frequently offered little affirmation in the church? We may also tend to denigrate the value of their art if it takes unfamiliar forms or challenges us in unexpected ways. How can we overcome this?

Influencing Culture: The culture has created stereotypes of Christians' relationship to the arts, which unfortunately are sometimes justified. How can we overcome the bias regarding prudery, lack of professional quality, and ignorance of artistic value, whether on the part of the artist or the consumer?

CLASSICALLY SEXY

Baring It All for Art?

A colleague of mine went shopping for CDs. He was greeted at the store by a life-size cutout of a beautiful young singer wearing a tight-fitting, low-cut dress.

The size and placement of the cutout made it hard not to look at it. Since he knew that the singer was all of sixteen, he left without buying anything.

Sadly, this kind of marketing is all too common in the pop music field. But my colleague was not shopping for popular music. He was in the classical section of the record store.

Here, too, instead of baring their souls for the sake of music, artists have taken to baring their skin for the sake of sales. Plunging necklines and even partial nudity have become common on classical CD covers.

Patrick Kavanaugh, the artistic director of the Masterworks Festival, wonders "why so many brilliant classical musicians have stooped to disrobing in order to sell Bach partitas." A case in point is violinist Lara St. John. The cover of her 1996 recording, *Bach: Works for Solo Violin*, features St. John naked, with only "her strategically placed violin to cover her."

While the cover created a ruckus, the CD sold "phenomenally well for a classical recording" and set a precedent that other record companies were prepared to follow.

Some people may dismiss concerns about low necklines on CD covers as prudery, but as Kavanaugh says, the real issue here may be "the future of classical music."

This "sex sells" approach diminishes and demeans the music. As John Kasica of the St. Louis Symphony told Kavanaugh, this approach "draws all your attention to the performers rather than to the music." It takes "away from the depth of the music itself" and turns artistry into a secondary concern.

As Kavanaugh points out, artists have been "practicing six to eight hours a day from the [age] of five." As if that weren't enough, now they have to look like centerfolds as well.

There is another way that this marketing diminishes the music. Violinist Lisa-Beth Lambert of the Philadelphia Orchestra says that selling a "spiritually uplifting product" through such "degrading means" is incongruent.

It is more than incongruent; it's disrespectful. Names such as

Bach, Beethoven, and Mozart are rightly regarded as synonymous with "genius." Their output represents high-water marks in Western civilization.

What Lambert calls the music's "spiritual uplift" is a function of how, in the creation of great art, man reflects his own creation in the image of God. It was through great music that C. S. Lewis first glimpsed the joy that led him to Christ.

Great music provides us with a glimpse of transcendence. It is a gift from God, which is why the Bach violin works that St. John played were signed "SDG"—*soli Deo gloria*—by their composer.

And it is why Christians should be outraged by this crass marketing approach—not only because it is another example of our culture's obsession with sex, but also because of our culture's inability to recognize what's worthwhile, trading the exhilaration of great music for the titillation of plunging necklines.

TRUTHS TO CONSIDER

Our preoccupation with sex and its link to selling unrelated products has plunged us to new lows with the exploitation of women artists associated with Western civilization's best music.

There is an inherent contradiction in trying to attract a new generation to the spiritual uplift of classical music by appealing to their baser nature through the lust of the eyes and the lust of the flesh.

We need to reassert the solid Christian values within the hearts of many composers and overcome the cheapening of their achievements by their present packaging.

GROUP STUDY

The Spiritual Dimension: When have you overindulged in lower forms of popular entertainment and not cultivated a taste for art and music that, as with the experience of C. S. Lewis, allows you to experience a joy that brings you closer to God?

Group Approach: Find books that allow you to better understand classical music and the composers and musicians involved. Go to concerts and borrow or buy CDs that will better allow you to experience the spiritual uplift of this music.

Influencing Culture: Share with others the connections between the music of their classical favorites and their Christian faith and values. Can you argue that without a Christian worldview, the quality of music would not be the same?

"EXIT JESUS"

God in the Public Square

A friend of mine recently installed voice-recognition software on his computer. Instead of keyboarding his thoughts, he now speaks them. He tested the software by saying a wide range of words and sentences and found that the software did reasonably well, even on technical vocabulary.

But then he spoke the word *exegesis*, meaning the explanation or elaboration of a biblical passage or other text. He nearly fell off his chair laughing when *exegesis* came up on the monitor screen as *exit Jesus*—a computer Freudian slip, but prophetic nonetheless.

Later that day, several news dispatches reminded him that there is a concerted effort to "exit Jesus" from public discourse. For example, Pastor Richard Parker was ready to deliver the customary invocation at the Warren County, Virginia, Board of Supervisors meeting. Just before he was to speak, the county attorney alerted him that he could say "Lord" or "God," but not "Jesus" in his prayer.

Pastor Parker walked out, rightly explaining that as a Christian pastor he would not pray if he had to "exit Jesus."

Hundreds of violations of religious freedom in the United States have been documented by a Texas-based group, the Liberty Legal Institute. On October 20, it presented the Senate Judiciary Subcommittee on the Constitution, Civil Rights, and Property with a fifty-one-page report titled, "Examples of Religious Hostility in the Public Square."

Here are a few examples: A Houston teacher trashed two students' Bibles, then marched the students to the principal's office and threatened to report their parents to Child Protective Services for allowing them to bring their Bibles to school. A ninth-grader got a zero on her research project because she chose Jesus as the topic, and her teacher refused to let her submit a substitute project. A St. Louis public school student was "caught" praying over his lunch. As punishment, he was lifted from his seat, reprimanded in front of classmates, and ordered never to pray in school again.

At a New Jersey veterans' cemetery, an honor-guard member was fired for telling a deceased veteran's family, "God bless you and this family." A Minnesota state employee was banned from parking in the state parking lot because his car had stickers saying, "God is a loving and caring God" and "God defines marriage as a union between a man and a woman."

McKinney, Texas, "has no problem with people meeting in their homes for football watch parties, birthday parties, or even commercial gatherings to sell Tupperware." But when a few couples gathered in a pastor's home, they were told, "The City prohibits a church meeting in a home unless the home sits on at least two acres." And on it goes, for fifty-one well-documented pages.

Make no mistake—well-financed organizations are working hard to expel Christianity from public discourse. If agitators try to do this in your city or school district, there are Christian attorneys and organizations that can help you. If we stay alert and resolute, our adversaries will not succeed in "exiting Jesus."

TRUTHS TO CONSIDER

Those of other worldviews have said in past years that Christians have not allowed them to be heard, but now the opposite seems to be true.

Those who are suffering the natural consequences of forbidden sexual behavior are now blaming those who hold Christian beliefs for their diseases—a form of scapegoating similar to what Jews have experienced through the ages.

People who insist on toleration and respect for all groups so that their deviant sexual behavior will be accepted should be exposed for hypocrisy when they tolerate anti-Christian bigotry.

GROUP STUDY

The Spiritual Dimension: When we view sacrilege and open slander of the Christian faith, we should pray for revival, since God has allowed this darkness in a nation where Christianity has had a strong influence.

Group Approach: What is our appropriate role as a church when people seek to silence us in a culture built on freedom of expression and respect for all groups?

Influencing Culture: It is increasingly costly to speak the truth in our culture. How can we do so with humility, compassion, and kindness to those who oppose us?

TO WATCH OR NOT TO WATCH

Should We View Sin On-Screen?

Christian film critic Denis Haack once deliberately decided to watch what many believers would consider to be a really bad movie. Why did he put himself through such an ordeal? He had noticed that the kids in his church were talking excitedly about a film they'd seen called *Reality Bites*. So Haack decided to go see the movie himself—just so he'd know what influences were at work on the kids.

Haack didn't like much of what he saw. *Reality Bites* portrays a group of college graduates trying to make sense of their lives in the postmodern world. Searching for love, they move from one sexual relationship to another. Immorality is often depicted in a way that makes sin appear attractive and even compelling.

Bad film, like bad literature, encourages viewers to identify with evil characters and draws them into a vicarious experience of sexual fantasies, dreams of wealth and power, or dark obsessions with violence.

Certainly, reveling in vicarious sin has no place in a Christian's life. But as Haack's story illustrates, there may be good reasons for going to see films that we would normally avoid. As Haack puts it, "Watching *Reality Bites* helped me understand more clearly some of the pressures young believers face as part of a generation being molded by pop culture."

After viewing the film, Haack could help teens understand how *Reality Bites* stacks up against biblical reality. He discussed with them the nature of sin and the true results of immoral behavior.

The results of this discussion were wonderful. The teens discussed how they could share their new insights with their unsaved friends who had also seen *Reality Bites.*

Haack routinely watches teen films simply because the kids he works with watch them. There's a biblical precedent for what he is doing. When the apostle Paul traveled to Athens to witness to the Greeks, he quoted pagan Greek poets. What's interesting is that Paul quoted these poets approvingly and then applied what they said to God. Yet, as historian E. M. Blaiklock points out, these poets were not referring to the God of Scripture; they were referring to the Greek god Zeus. In effect, Paul made use of the "pop culture" of the ancient world—in Greek poetry—as a means of explaining the gospel to his Athenian audience.

And that's what you and I may sometimes be called to do. Of course, we would normally prefer to keep clear of movies that offer positive—and sometimes graphic—portrayals of sin. But as Denis Haack says, "The question we should ask is this: Will this film help me understand something about life and culture that will allow me to live more faithfully as a follower of Christ?"

For better or for worse, movies are part of our culture. But if we have the proper tools, we can even take films that portray a nonbiblical worldview and use them to glorify Christ.

TRUTHS TO CONSIDER

At times we need to observe sin in order to discern the motives and struggles of those involved. This is not to indulge ourselves but to show that we understand what the individual is dealing with when we offer a solution.

The apostle Paul used illustrations from ancient Greek popular culture to reach that culture. We can do likewise in our own culture.

We can benefit from learning what traps to avoid as well as from recognizing the redemptive qualities in works of popular culture, but we should never be deceived into practicing the sin that is portrayed.

GROUP STUDY

The Spiritual Dimension: How do you handle the balance between being wise as a serpent and innocent as a dove, as Jesus put it? How can you deal with the images and attitudes that Satan will play back to tempt and harass you?

Group Approach: Share with others your own boundaries in this area and hear their wisdom. Every one of us has different "sin tolerance" levels. We need to make sure that we don't cause a weaker brother or sister to stumble by what we participate in.

Influencing Culture: How can we be like Paul in identifying with some things in popular culture that are important to those with a different worldview? Can we use those things in a positive way to point them in the right direction?

THE DANGERS OF READING

Dickens and the Social Order

Note: This commentary was delivered by Prison Fellowship President Mark Earley.

When you hear the name Charles Dickens, what comes to mind? *A Christmas Carol?* Sentimental tales of poor but loving families, or helpless orphans saved by wealthy benefactors? All of those impressions are accurate, but there's a lot more to Dickens than that. In fact, there's a lot more to this great novelist than many literary critics have been able to see. Author, editor, and critic Myron Magnet suggests that this is because so many readers and critics bring their own preconceptions to their reading of Dickens (and many other authors). As Professor Lilia Melani of Brooklyn College summarizes, "Because of Dickens's moral outrage and his attacks on society's institutions and values, later critics, who were often Marxists, hailed him variously as subversive, rebellious, and even revolutionary."

But in a provocative book that has recently been reissued titled *Dickens and the Social Order*, Magnet makes the point that Charles Dickens—the passionate reformer and champion of the downtrodden, a man usually hailed by modern liberals as one of their own—was actually more of a traditionalist than many people realize. With his emphasis on the reality of fallen human nature and the importance of families, Dickens echoed themes we have found to be very important in keeping children out of a life of crime. For example, Dickens lived in an age when many philosophers and writers promoted the inherent goodness of human beings, especially human beings unspoiled by civilization. But Dickens was completely unconvinced by that utopian idea. In an essay that could be described only as politically incorrect today, he wrote bluntly, "I have not the least belief in the Noble Savage. I consider him a prodigious nuisance, and an enormous superstition. . . . If we have anything to learn from the Noble Savage, it is what to avoid."

While Dickens had his doubts about civilized society, he viewed it as vastly preferable to the alternative. That has left some critics wondering whether Dickens was actually attacking fallen human nature rather than society. That suggests that Dickens—radical as he was in some ways—would have very little in common with reformers today who operate by putting all the blame for society's ills on someone else. Magnet also demonstrates that Dickens's attitude toward human nature is at the root of his strong belief in the need for families. In *Barnaby Rudge*, for example, the fatherless, untaught, and undisciplined characters are naturally inclined toward villainy, not saintliness. They have, as Magnet puts it, "undeveloped or defective souls" and "built-in . . . aggressiveness." This illustrates why even imperfect families play a vital role in restraining the young from giving in to their worst impulses and in teaching them to function in society.

In short, Magnet makes a strong case that radical critics who have seen in Dickens a reflection of their own political views have missed a great deal of what he had to say. This shows the trap that even the most intelligent and educated readers can fall into. It takes more than intelligence to be a good reader—it also takes discernment, humility, and a willingness to listen to other people, beginning with the author. Without those qualities, reading can be downright dangerous.

TRUTHS TO CONSIDER

Being a good reader requires many of the same traits as being a good listener. Otherwise we may simply impose our own ideas on a book and never understand what the author is actually saying.

Charles Dickens seems like a radical or liberal writer because he is passionate about the right of all people to enjoy the benefits of traditional values. He does not sentimentalize human nature or protect the vested interests of a few people at the expense of the poor and marginalized.

We shouldn't be hesitant about creating stories and images that will flesh out our Christian beliefs and demonstrate the power of a Christian worldview to a post-Christian culture.

GROUP STUDY

The Spiritual Dimension: Go back to the parables of Jesus and notice how he uses images and stories to convey spiritual truths that go beyond mere abstract concepts. How can you use images and symbols in your own life to convey a deeper and wiser grasp of truth?

Group Approach: Choose a novel to read and discuss. See if you can identify the worldview that underlies the story.

Influencing Culture: Encourage artists within your congregation to create music, visual art, theater, and stories that portray the truth of their worldview while maintaining the integrity of their unique creative abilities. Perform or display their work.

A TRIUMPHANT RETURN
The Return of the King

After seven years in the making, the final film of the Lord of the Rings trilogy, *The Return of the King*, is now in video format. The good news is that, like the other Lord of the Rings films, it was worth the wait. The better news is that, even more than the earlier films in this trilogy, what we see on-screen respects the Christian faith of the book's author, J. R. R. Tolkien.

Tolkien wrote that Lord of the Rings is a "fundamentally religious and Catholic work, unconsciously so at first but consciously in the revision." Director Peter Jackson and screenwriters Philippa

Boyens and Fran Walsh knew this, so they consciously honored what was important to Tolkien. Many of his beliefs thus come through on-screen.

What sets Lord of the Rings apart from other stories about good versus evil, aside from its extraordinarily imaginative treatment, is how Christian truth is portrayed in a way that confounds the wisdom of the world. While the great and powerful play a role in defeating evil, in the end, it's the humble and unremarkable hobbits that save the day.

This paradox of the weak shaming the wise and the mighty is most prominent in *The Return of the King*, in both the book and the film. At the end, the hero of the third film isn't Aragon, the king-to-be, or even Frodo, the ring bearer. It's Samwise Gamgee, a gardener who is arguably the humblest of the four hobbits.

Time after time, when it appears that the quest to destroy the Ring of Power is about to fail, Sam somehow summons up the will to go on and, most important, takes Frodo with him. The cinematic Sam mirrors what Tolkien wrote in his book: "His will was set and only death would break it."

Tolkien's faith also comes through in an exchange between another hobbit, Pippin, and Gandalf the wizard. Hours before a battle in which he is sure he will die, Pippin tells Gandalf that he "never thought it would end like this."

Gandalf replies, "End? No, the journey doesn't end here. There's another path we all must take. The gray rain curtain of this world rolls back, and it will change to the silver clouds, and then you see it."

When Pippin asks, "See what?" Gandalf replies, "White shores and beyond, a far green country under a swift sunrise." Gandalf's words, with a vivid picture of heaven, comfort Pippin as he contemplates battle and possible death.

According to screenwriters Boyens and Walsh, *The Return of the King* is about faith in the need for good to oppose evil, faith in those who join you in that struggle, and faith in a higher power that will ensure the eventual triumph of good.

It was considered unlikely that Tolkien's masterpiece could be brought to the screen in a way that would do the story justice—and even less likely that it would honor Tolkien's faith. But that is what this film does. That makes *The Return of the King* an easy film to recommend. A great book has become a great film precisely because its makers remembered what the author thought was most important—the truths of a Christian worldview.

TRUTHS TO CONSIDER

Though *The Lord of the Rings* is in the genre of fantasy, it is structured within a Christian cosmology and reflects the truths of a Christian worldview.

The story dramatizes the overturn of the wisdom of the world, depicting those who are small and humble, rather than the great and powerful, as overcoming evil.

Great books have a greater chance of becoming great films when the producers choose to be faithful to the text, and Christians have much to gain from a cultural standpoint by reading and viewing them.

GROUP STUDY

The Spiritual Dimension: How can heaven be a great comfort to you when you are faced with great adversity?

Group Approach: Read a book from The Lord of the Rings series again or for the first time, or better yet, read it to your children. Write out what it means to you in a journal.

Influencing Culture: Get some books that deal with Tolkien's Christian worldview in his fiction and then interact with movie and fantasy buffs, expressing your insights and graciously receiving theirs.

CHRISTIANS IN CULTURE

LIE 5

Christian beliefs are a private matter.

Underlying Worldview: The Christian faith should remain private and internal. It should not be applied to culture because of its absolutist, intolerant message and its history of oppressing those who disagree.

Christianity, it is said, is at the root of much that is wrong with our society, including racism, sexism, and homophobia. According to this way of thinking, the only way forward is to be set free from the repressive constraints of Christian values and to move toward self-realization and autonomy. In the pluralistic melting pot of American culture, biblically applied Christianity is not given a voice because it supposedly excludes other voices. Even though this would also be true of the Muslim faith, it is not considered to be in the same category.

According to the culture, being a Christian also disqualifies one from total objectivity in everything from law to coaching in sports, especially if one applies Christian values in those situations. Separation of church and state is invoked as meaning complete exclusion of God from the public square, but it doesn't exclude the state from transgressing on private religious convictions. Thus, for example, according to law, contraceptives must now be included in prescription drug packages in a Catholic parachurch organization.

Our fault in leaving this lie unchallenged can be seen in how ethics is taught in the marketplace. Because there are no absolute values, ethics becomes what is pragmatic in achieving success, as long as the behavior can be rationalized. This is strikingly illustrated in this chapter in the case of the Abercrombie & Fitch boycott. When young people were depicted without clothing in sexual poses and even in group sex shots, thousands in the Christian community made their voices heard through a boycott. The retailer swiftly rescinded the catalog, though it did not admit the true reason for this.

Christians need to radically live out the Christian ethic, which can't help but challenge other ethical systems. Positive examples include conservative trends in social issues among Christian young people and the faith-based movement that enlists government support of Christian ministries to the community. Erika Harold, crowned Miss America in 2002, is an example of an effective young person. Her platform issue was teenage sexual abstinence, which was not approved by the official Miss America committee. Nonetheless, she adamantly held her ground amid hostile pressures.

The temptation to mimic the culture, or to sell out, leads to compromise, denigration of the gospel, and a poor witness. The slogan "What Would Jesus Drive?" used to sell Toyotas is an apt illustration. What is even worse is Christians copying consumer products. Substituting J. Christ for the J. Crew brand on a T-shirt in Christian gift stores only exploits the worldly product with a cheap imitation. On the other hand, not all T-shirt messages are tacky. One young person's emblazoned message about abortion took courage and spoke truth: "You will not silence my message. You will not mock my God. You will stop killing my generation." Christian beliefs penetrate every area, and we should banish the lie that they are private. We need to know the difference between when we're called to confront, when to forgive, or both. We need wisdom to know what to say and how to say it.

There are many ways of being persuasive as we present our worldview to our culture and counteract its lies. The best way is to live out the message of the gospel by liberating others from the powers of deception and sin. Robert Webber, author of *The Younger Evangelicals*, states that we should change our world, "not by power politics, but by a presence of humble servanthood." Younger evangelicals want to rebuild communities and meet the needs of those who have no advocate: the poor, the homeless, and prisoners. It's a vision that Christians should embrace regardless of their age.

ABERCROMBIE & FLINCH

A Boycott That Worked

If you went into your local shopping mall in the Christmas season of 2003, you'd find something missing from the counter at Abercrombie & Fitch, the clothing store that uses pornography to sell clothing to kids. The Christmas edition of its quarterly magazine was gone. Although the company won't admit it, economic pressure from thousands of citizens is almost certainly the reason that it pulled the *Christmas Field Guide* from all 651 stores. The issue featured pictures of naked male and female models in sexual poses, including group sex. Advice from a so-called "sexpert" urged kids to get as much sexual experience as they can in college—including "sex for three."

How this came about is an interesting story. Joe Gibbs, former coach of the Washington Redskins and now a NASCAR owner, called me; he was absolutely outraged over the Abercrombie & Fitch catalog. He also called my friend Jim Dobson. Jim got on the air immediately for his radio show and urged listeners to call Abercrombie and say that they were boycotting their products. Groups such as the American Decency Association and the National Coalition for the Protection of Children and Families joined in.

The result? The day before Thanksgiving, my colleague Anne Morse went into an Abercrombie store in Bethesda, Maryland. As Morse wrote on *National Review Online*, when she asked for a copy of the quarterly, she was told by a manager that all Abercrombie stores had been ordered the day before to stop selling the quarterly. No reason was given for the decision, the manager said.

Morse called Abercrombie's national headquarters in Ohio. Abercrombie CEO Mike Jeffries was not available, but an employee told Morse that Abercrombie stores were being boycotted all over the country. He said that the company had been receiving three hundred calls per hour from citizens who were angry about its catalog exposing kids to pornography.

Who, Morse wanted to know, was behind the boycott effort?

"Ever hear of Dr. Dobson?" the young man replied.

Morse then called the company's ordering number and asked if she could buy a copy of the quarterly over the phone. No, she was told; from now on, the quarterly would be available only to people with existing subscriptions.

Morse's article was posted online on Monday morning, and by Monday afternoon, Abercrombie executives were denying everything. Yes, they had yanked the Christmas quarterly right at the start of the Christmas shopping season—but no, the boycotts had nothing to do with it. They denied that the company had been receiving calls from the public. Hampton Carney, a spokesman for the company, told reporters that Abercrombie simply needed the counter space for a new perfume display.

Sure they did. They not only peddle porn—they don't tell the truth.

Abercrombie says that the spring issue of the quarterly will be just as it has always been, so pro-family groups will continue this boycott because this is a fight we must win. Christians are called to be salt and light—and that means protecting kids from sexual sewage and from lifestyle advice that could destroy them.

TRUTHS TO CONSIDER

Sexual experience before marriage, such as in the college years, does not prepare one for a mature sexual relationship in marriage but actually harms the wholeness and integrity of marital sex.

Christian organizations can lead the way in boycotting morally harmful products; this is an effective way to stop the proliferation of sexually explicit material that will be injurious to consumers, especially children.

Companies that exploit sex for their own profit probably can't be trusted to tell the truth about their motivations or actions.

GROUP STUDY

The Spiritual Dimension: The Bible tells us to be modest in our dress and behavior. Perhaps we may not be guilty in the area of sexuality, but what about vanity or other anti-Christian values that might determine what we own?

Group Approach: It's not possible to boycott everyone or to stop investing in all these products, but how can we as a church keep abreast of what various companies do in their advertising or be aware of products that demand a similar response?

Influencing Culture: How can you explain to those who take a different view that boycotts and other such actions are not taken merely to exercise power in the marketplace or to curb the free expression of others?

SUV SPIRITUALITY

Jesus behind the Wheel?

In November 2002, there were two well-publicized attempts to link the name of Jesus to people's car-buying decisions. Though these efforts were well intentioned, they raise serious questions.

At that time, "Come Together and Worship" toured the country featuring prominent Christian singers and speakers and distributing Christian literature at each event.

I know the people appearing in the tour—they are good friends of mine—and they have the best of intentions. The problem was with the tour's sponsor, Chevrolet. Chevy's goal was to help evangelicals to see Chevy's cars and trucks as part of what it means to be an American evangelical. A Chevy spokesman was unabashed in saying that this was not about religion. "It's about selling cars," he said.

This isn't the only attempt to draw a link between faith and driving habits. In response to news about the concert tour, a group called the Evangelical Environmental Network (EEN) announced a campaign to convince Christians to drive more fuel-efficient cars rather than, for example, Chevy Suburbans.

The EEN argued that this was a moral and spiritual issue involving stewardship of the environment and love of neighbor. Fair enough—we have to be good stewards. But what got people's attention was the way it summed up its argument in its advertising. "What Would Jesus Drive?" was emblazoned across the top of the ad. In case you had trouble answering that question, the motto was imposed across a picture of a Toyota Prius, a fuel-efficient, gas-electric hybrid.

EEN took a full-page ad in *Christianity Today* to ask that question, and their television ads were to be broadcast in the South and the Midwest.

Scarcely had the "What Would Jesus Drive?" campaign been announced than jokes about what our Lord would do in other circumstances began popping up. They became a staple on late-night television, in editorial cartoons, and on the Internet. The effect thus far has not led people to rethink what they drive but has only resulted in turning the Lord into a cartoon character.

These seemingly opposite efforts raise the same serious questions about the line between commerce and the gospel. And they are hardly the only examples of a troubled mingling of faith and commerce. A recent article in the *Weekly Standard* described the "flourishing market" in Christian merchandise such as T-shirts and trinkets.

Increasingly, every secular market niche has a Christian counterpart. It's difficult to escape the conclusion that religion is often being put to the service of commerce, rather than the other way around.

That's why Christians need to be vigilant, not only because we risk profaning what is sacred, but because we also run the risk of detracting from the message—as we've seen with "What Would Jesus Drive?"

I'm not suggesting that I have the answers to these questions, which go far beyond these two examples. Often I've had to swallow hard at the commercial exhibits of T-shirts and trinkets at Christian conventions and at the sponsorship of worship concerts. Without criticizing those involved in these cases, I'm suggesting that we think seriously and carefully about the dangers of tying the gospel to American commercial enterprises.

What would Jesus drive? I don't know. The only thing the Bible tells us is that he drove the money changers out of the Temple.

TRUTHS TO CONSIDER

In popular culture, sexuality is used to influence the buying decisions of consumers. We must guard against using religion in the same way.

Using the value of the Christian faith for the purpose of making more money can be sacrilegious; it trivializes and degrades the sacredness of our faith.

Discretion and wisdom are needed because potential revenue for the Kingdom's purposes may need to be refused in order to maintain the sanctity of the Lord's name and message.

GROUP STUDY

The Spiritual Dimension: What fads or trends in the Christian marketplace have influenced you because of their marketing tactics? How does the Holy Spirit want you to guard against this?

Group Approach: Take inventory of the products you buy, whether commercial or spiritual. What is the motivation behind your purchases—are they brand or image driven, are they self-oriented, or are you acting under the lordship of Christ?

Influencing Culture: How can you so represent the life and message of Christ that the culture will see this not as just another product to be sold for personal enhancement but as a reflection of the Savior?

SLOTHFULLY TACKY
The Scandal of Christian Merchandise

Two conservative journals have discovered what most of us already know: There is a lot of junk out there being marketed to Christians.

Nearly everyone agrees that a lot of this stuff is cringe-inducing and only confirms people's worst stereotypes of Christians. What they do not agree on is what we should do about it. Any answer to that question must start with remembering the place of beauty in a truly Christian worldview.

An article about what is euphemistically called "Christian

merchandise" appeared in the *Weekly Standard* magazine. In it, writer Stephen Bates gave readers a sense of just how much stuff is included in that category and how tasteless some of it can be.

Christian merchandise, he wrote, is more than books and music. It's outerwear, underwear, food, knickknacks, and even rubber duckies that say "Depend on Christ the King." Instead of well-known brand names such as J. Crew and Fruit of the Loom, this stuff is branded with Christian substitutes such as "J. Christ" and "Fruit of the Spirit."

Neither Bates nor Jeremy Lott, who wrote about the subject for *Reason* magazine, uses these lapses in taste as an excuse to bash Christians. Lott writes that these often-tacky artifacts "can embody real meaning for those who use them . . . [since] they reflect their values and beliefs."

That is true, but only up to a point. The problem with these "artifacts" is not that they are inconsistent with people's beliefs. It is that something vital is missing from those beliefs: an appreciation of taste and beauty.

You see, an appreciation of beauty is not optional for Christians. Pursuing beauty is as mandatory as the pursuit of truth and goodness, which is why aesthetics has historically been considered a branch of moral theology.

St. Augustine, Thomas Aquinas, and C. S. Lewis all wrote that beauty, like truth and goodness, has its origin in God's very nature. Aquinas said that beauty "participates in the divine brightness." Beauty gives us a glimpse of God's integrity, perfection, and majesty. Beauty points to the order and intelligence that sustains the universe.

And it points to the source of that intelligence and order. Augustine and Lewis both wrote of the role that their love of beauty had in their conversions. In his *Confessions*, Augustine exclaims, "Oh, Beauty, so old and so new! Too late have I loved thee!"

And in *Surprised by Joy*, Lewis describes the joy and longing he felt as a boy when he listened to Wagner. The feelings inspired by the music provided evidence of something truly awe inspiring that alone could fulfill his longing.

I spoke recently to the Christian Booksellers Association. It's an outstanding association that has greatly raised the professional standards of the publishing industry and of booksellers. I'm optimistic that we are going to make a real effort to raise the standards of what we offer to the world. As Christians, we can and should do better than the kind of stuff that makes us all cringe. An indifference to beauty, after all, is as foreign to the Christian worldview as indifference to truth or to goodness.

TRUTHS TO CONSIDER

Tacky knockoffs of worldly products and fads display laziness, exploitation, and a lack of craftsmanship and taste on the part of Christians.

We need to restore the proper cultivation and appreciation of beauty and creativity among Christians, rather than benefiting from the success of a secular product in a way that borders on trademark violation.

There is enough originality to go around in expressing our Christian faith. We need to ask God for the discipline and vision to remain relevant and compelling without looking like a poor imitation of the world.

GROUP STUDY

The Spiritual Dimension: How can you improve your aesthetic side so that you can better appreciate the Creator and express beauty in your life? Seek out an unfamiliar area in the arts and get acquainted with it.

Group Approach: Read an introductory book on Christian aesthetics and the need for beauty to accompany truth. Be willing, with a gentle and humble spirit, to critique Christian workmanship that falls short of standards that bring honor and glory to God.

Influencing Culture: Be willing to admit our errors and failures to those who criticize Christian merchandise. Seek out quality creations that demonstrate the beauty that God, who made us in his image and wants us to create.

HIT AND MISS
Miss America Follies

You would think that the people who run the Miss America pageant would be thrilled to have Erika Harold representing them. In contrast to the popular image of beauty queens as Malibu Barbies, Harold is a Phi Beta Kappa graduate of the University of Illinois, and she will attend Harvard Law School after her year as Miss America. Harold, who is proud of her multiracial heritage, is also a powerful symbol of the changing face of America.

Yet, if recent events are any indication, pageant officials probably can't wait for Erika's tenure as Miss America to be over. Why? Because she takes the "Miss" in "Miss America" a little too seriously for their taste.

Since 1990, Miss America contestants, along with contestants at affiliated state pageants, have been required to adopt what are known as "platform issues." In her successful campaign for Miss Illinois, Erika's platform issue was "Teenage Sexual Abstinence: Respect Yourself, Protect Yourself."

In addition, Erika, a committed Christian, has served as a representative for Project Reality, an Illinois-based abstinence education program.

So Erika's commitment to promoting abstinence was well-known to Miss America officials before she was crowned in Atlantic City in 2002.

Imagine her surprise when pageant officials began to pressure her not to talk about abstinence publicly. Then, just prior to her appearance at the National Press Club, those pressures became an order. Do not talk about abstinence, she was commanded.

To her credit, Erika refused to buckle under. She told reporters, "I will not be bullied. I've gone through enough adversity in my life to stand up for what I believe in."

While the furor and the negative publicity prompted pageant officials to reverse themselves—at least publicly—we're still left with a huge irony. As a representative of Concerned Women for America put it, Erika is "too wholesome" for the people who run Miss America.

It's ironic because, according to the representative, "the abstinence message and Miss America [should be] a perfect fit." The word *Miss* historically implies more than being unmarried. It carries "an image of purity and chastity."

Even worse is the hypocrisy and blatant double standard involved in this controversy. Pageant officials defended the contest's continuing relevance in a letter to the *Chicago Sun-Times*. In that letter, they cite Erika's multiracial background and her academic achievements as they write, "The most successful [pageant contestants] have the courage to take stands on controversial issues like gay rights, abortion, or the war against Iraq—questions many politicians duck every day. The contestants challenge others to stand up and speak out."

Yet they still tried to silence Erika for doing just that. Apparently, a stand is only courageous if it involves a position shared by pageant officials—and this seems to require a liberal bias.

Miss America's story is a cautionary tale about the obstacles Christians face in getting their message across, and as an example—thank you, Miss America—of the courage demanded of believers in the face of hostile pressures.

TRUTHS TO CONSIDER

Even Miss America today is supposed to stand for the opposite of what a young female's moral values were a few decades ago.

The hypocrisy of a double standard is clearly seen when the courage to stand up for controversial positions you believe in only applies to those with a liberal bias.

Christians can make a significant impact on the culture when put in positions of influence, whether at a local or a national level.

GROUP STUDY

The Spiritual Dimension: When have Christians, such as the apostle Paul, stood up for what they believed in and triumphed in the face of opposition? When have you had even a small opportunity to do the same?

Group Approach: What can be done in your church to expose the lies of the condom argument as opposed to abstinence in order to protect and inform our young people?

Influencing Culture: How can you more effectively share the abstinence rationale, not only as a health issue, but as preserving the future stability of marriage based on purity?

EXPELLING THE FOUNDERS

God and History in California

In the aftermath of the 2004 election, certain disappointed voters voiced their fear of an impending "theocracy"—a government takeover by "fundamentalists" and "extreme right-wing Christians." That fear, of course, is wholly unfounded, but news from Cupertino, California, raises the opposite concern.

Steven Williams teaches fifth grade at Stevens Creek School in this Silicon Valley city. Part of the curriculum is American history, but Williams has been prohibited by the school's principal, Patricia Vidmar, from using any historic materials mentioning God. That includes the Declaration of Independence, which refers to "Nature's God," "Creator," "Divine Providence," and the "Supreme Judge of the World."

Mr. Williams has sued the school, claiming religious discrimination and violation of free-speech rights. News reports indicate that he is a Christian.

One lawyer familiar with the case stated, "The district has chosen to censor men such as George Washington and documents like the Declaration of Independence. [Its] actions conflict with American beliefs and are completely unconstitutional."

According to various news sources, the principal started her crackdown on Williams last May by requiring him to submit all lesson plans and handouts for her approval. He claims that she systematically rejected any statements by American founders that mentioned God or religion. Included in the ban, according to Williams, "are excerpts from the Declaration of Independence, George Washington's journal, John Adams's diary, Samuel Adams's 'The Rights of the Colonists,' and William Penn's 'The Frame of Government of Pennsylvania.'"

Williams's attorney, Terry Thompson, notes that "Williams wants to teach his students the true history of our country. . . . He hands out a lot of material, and perhaps 5 to 10 percent refers to God and Christianity because that's what the founders wrote." The suit asserts that Principal Vidmar did not subject any other teacher to prescreening of lessons.

So far, the district has neither denied nor confirmed the allegations, but it hardly seems likely that Williams would make all this up. For decades, crusaders for secularization, aided by sympathetic courts, have worked diligently to remove all traces of religion from

America's public schools, even engaging in revisionism—the rewriting of history books.

Secularists view the public school as their exclusive domain in which no child should be exposed to a religious idea. Such a view is just censorship of Christians. There's nothing neutral about these acts of discrimination. They prescribe secularism as official doctrine.

And frankly, it makes me mad. When I went into the Marine Corps, I was ready to give my life for a country that, in the words of the Declaration, believes that "all men are created equal" and are "endowed by their Creator with certain unalienable rights." Words that for millions of Americans through the centuries have been worth dying for are certainly worth teaching to our young people.

TRUTHS TO CONSIDER

At this time in our country, Christians seem to be the only group that can be discriminated against with impunity.

We need to speak for justice without adopting the tactics of those who would invalidate and banish us.

We need to support one another in remaining strong and faithful under this kind of discrimination, while continuing to follow and explain our beliefs.

GROUP STUDY

The Spiritual Dimension: How often do you spend time in prayer asking God to strengthen your ability to stand firm as a Christian despite opposition and harassment?

Group Approach: How can you use the time with your group to continue to grow and be nurtured by God's Word, prayer, and Christian fellowship rather than be diverted into complaining about how you are mistreated? On the other hand, when you suffer injustice, can you speak frankly about your experience and find the support that you need?

Influencing Culture: In your particular life and circumstances, what does it mean to love those who persecute you, as Jesus said we should do? What response will be most effective in making the Christian message clear to those who oppose you?

THE CHURCH'S GREAT CHALLENGE

Christians in the Marketplace

Zogby International took a poll of American college seniors in which 97 percent said that they believed their professors had given them a good education in ethics. But when asked what those professors had taught them, 73 percent responded, "What is right and wrong depends on differences in individual values and cultural diversity." Only a quarter of them said they had learned that there are "clear and uniform standards of right and wrong."

Similarly, a reporter for *Forbes* magazine observed an ethics class at Harvard Business School in which the professor and students discussed case studies but avoided coming to any moral conclusions. Students were graded on how well they could logically defend their position, not on whether their position was actually defensible. The reporter wrote that students in this kind of class, rather than developing moral principles, merely "develop skills enabling them to rationalize anything short of cannibalism."

We've talked extensively about the importance of bringing Christian ethics into the business world.

Why do we spend so much time on this subject? Think of it this way: We spend a third of our lives in the workplace, exercising the talents, creativity, and energy given to us by God. For this very reason, the Reformer John Calvin believed that the first act of discipleship was a choice of vocation. The impact of our work on our lives and on the lives of those around us is huge, yet our churches spend less and less time teaching how to apply our Christian principles in the workplace. And at this time, the business world is in dire need of principled, ethical people.

The fact is that we are living in a postmodern age when people find it impossible to agree on standards of right and wrong. We can't even teach them. What disasters this leads to have been evident in the scandals rocking the business world in the past couple of years concerning Enron, WorldCom, and others. What people are just beginning to realize is that unethical behavior at these companies is simply the logical result of the moral relativism that permeates our culture.

The good news, as I have discovered, is that people who have been hurt by these economic scandals are willing, perhaps for the first time, to listen to biblical teaching on ethics. The church needs to be ready to meet that challenge. A recent poll by George Barna showed that 54 percent of people who called themselves born-again Christians do not believe in ultimate moral truth—without which, of course, there can be no ethics. But consider that for a moment. We say that we follow the One who is "the Way, the Truth, and the Life," and yet we can't bring ourselves to acknowledge that truth exists? No wonder we're having little impact on our culture!

If we truly believe in Christ and the Christian worldview that he taught, then we can't help but bring that worldview into every sphere of life—including, especially, the workplace. If churches are not teaching ethics and followers of Christ aren't setting an ethical example, who will?

TRUTHS TO CONSIDER

The beginning of true discipleship is in our choice of vocation, the place where our talents will have the greatest impact.

Business ethics today do not support an objective basis for truth but actually allow businesspeople to logically justify behavior that is utilitarian and motivated by self-interest.

The Christian worldview is not effectively penetrating business ethics because many of us don't wholeheartedly support absolute truth. We have the tools to be the leaders in ethics that are true and that work.

GROUP STUDY

The Spiritual Dimension: God expects you not only to adhere to the bare minimum but to go beyond the rules in letting your light shine in the business world. Would those who work with you judge your behavior as excellent in this regard?

Group Approach: Ethical behavior in a complex business situation is often challenging. What articles or books on ethics can you read and share that will bring greater light to the situations you face in the workplace?

Influencing Culture: The greatest way to influence the workplace is to connect solid ethics with success. How can you communicate, without seeming proud, that your ethics are a major part of what others value—the bottom line?

REBELS FOR LIFE

The New Sexual Revolution

Thousands of teenagers and young adults descend on Washington, D.C., every January, ignoring biting wind, rain, and mud. Coming from universities, high schools, and churches around the nation, they take red-eye bus rides, sleep in church basements, and forego showers to defend the lives of the unborn.

They sport pro-life paraphernalia, such as the popular black T-shirt with white lettering that says: "You will not silence my message. You will not mock my God. You will stop killing my generation."

Though journalists often ignore them, the numbers and ages of today's pro-life protesters have abortion supporters worried. And that's good news for Christians who work for a culture of life.

In a book from Loyola Press, *The New Faithful: Why Young Adults Are Embracing Christian Orthodoxy*, Colleen Carroll traces a grassroots movement among young people toward moral absolutes and Christian commitment. Carroll wrote *The New Faithful* after traveling the country on a Phillips Foundation journalism fellowship and interviewing more than five hundred young adults. Theirs is the story of a new generation of politically active, morally conservative young Americans who reject abortion and sexual license.

These are the young people who make virginity pledges by the thousands, pack Promise Keepers rallies and World Youth Day festivals, and swarm the National Mall each year to march for life.

Their convictions come from life-changing conversions. And their embrace of the gospel has led many of them to rebel against their elders by embracing traditional morality.

In *The New Faithful*, we read story after story of young men and women clamoring for strong moral teachings and committing themselves to lives of sexual integrity. At a sexual abstinence rally in Chicago, one beauty queen told her cheering young crowd that "the new sexual revolution is not being led by adults, but by young people. We are seeing a complete turnaround in young attitudes toward sex and relationships."

Pollsters are seeing it, too. UCLA's annual survey of college freshmen shows support for legal abortion steadily dropping since 1990. Back then, 65 percent of incoming freshmen said that abortion should be legal. In 1999, 53 percent thought so. And Gallup polls taken in October 2000 found that 40 percent of eighteen- to twenty-nine-year-olds think that abortion rights should be more restricted. In fact, the under-thirty crowd leads the nation in anti-abortion sentiment.

What's more, a growing number of young adults reject the pop culture slogan "If it feels good, do it." In 1998, the UCLA survey found approval of promiscuity at a twenty-five-year low, with only 40 percent of students approving of casual sex, down from a 1987 high of 52 percent.

Of course, not every young American embraces chastity or rejects abortion. And those who do so are fighting an uphill battle against a culture that mocks their deepest convictions. But as these new faithful find in Christianity the courage to go against the grain, more of their peers may follow suit.

I encourage you to read *The New Faithful* and to share it with young people you know who are struggling against sexual immorality and the culture of death. They need to know they're not alone and that America can be transformed by a generation marching for life.

TRUTHS TO CONSIDER

Contrary to cultural propaganda that says that young people are increasingly more liberal, there are optimistic signs that a backlash against moral decadence is leading to a more conservative approach to moral values.

These young people are not focused merely on their own spiritual well-being but are willing to be vocal about their beliefs and to challenge the culture.

Their sexual integrity and pro-life stance may help to turn the tide for all Christians in the future.

GROUP STUDY

The Spiritual Dimension: How effectively have you connected biblical truth with moral values for the young people with whom you come in contact? Do you live in a way that models these truths?

Group Approach: Generations in the church need to learn from each other's visions and experiences. Share your perspectives with younger or older members, and see what you have to give and receive.

Influencing Culture: Combat the idea that young people are naturally and increasingly liberal by sharing the ideas of young evangelicals. Perhaps this will give hope to those who think that the negative effects in society will only increase with the passing years.

LOOKING FOR REASONS
Disaster and a Prophetic Voice

Thinking of the terrorist attacks in New York and Washington on September 11, 2001, I want to comment on the meaning of a prophetic response to this national disaster. Christians are called to speak prophetically to the world, calling for repentance.

The reaction of some evangelicals, however, was unfortunately to place the blame for the attacks on people in groups that have had a secularizing effect on American society. I don't associate myself with those comments, nor do I believe that most American Christians do. These remarks were ill-timed and inappropriate, as those who made them have, to their credit, acknowledged. They have apologized for them.

Though I believe that the dynamics of secularism have done immeasurable harm, it is unfair to associate this tragedy with those forces. Nor can we lay the blame at the feet of Arabs or Muslims in general, as some are wont to do.

The hijackers who crashed airplanes into the World Trade Center and the Pentagon were Muslim in name only. Several of them were involved in drunk driving and visiting strip bars, things no religious Muslim would ever do. In reality, they were anarchists seeking to destroy, destabilize, and make us slaves to fear.

But, you ask, aren't Christians supposed to be prophetic within the culture and point out sin? Of course, but there are biblical guidelines for doing so.

First, remember the words of the apostle Peter, "For the time has come for judgment, and it must begin with God's household" (1 Peter 4:17, NLT). The sins of Christians and of the church are our first order of business. Our materialism, pride, disunity, gossip, and lack of love are as much a cause for judgment as anyone else's behavior. To single out the transgressions of others while ignoring our own is to turn biblical teaching on its head.

Second, the biblical prophets who pronounced God's judgment upon the people were careful to count themselves among those being judged. When judgment came, they shared in the suffering of the people. Jeremiah wept and wrote laments when Jerusalem fell, Ezekiel went into exile, and Moses threw in his lot with the people when God told him of his intention to wipe out Israel and begin again with Moses. We always speak as fellow sinners, and we should be the first to repent.

Third, if we would be prophetic, we need to speak out for the right reasons—not to scapegoat, condemn, or denounce, but out of love for our neighbors. Rather than demonize others, we offer an alternative to destructive worldviews that have left many victims—including the victims of 9/11—in their wake.

Comments that sound self-righteous and point the finger at others make it hard for ordinary people to see how the Christian message differs from the condemning message of the hijackers. As Christians, we should be measured and balanced in all we say—a word of caution for all of us.

TRUTHS TO CONSIDER

As Christians, we are called to be prophetic, not to retreat from addressing evil. We are to call for repentance, especially amid signs of judgment.

As Christians, we need to include ourselves as sinners and to be very careful of where we point the finger of judgment, or we will further incriminate ourselves.

Since judgment begins with God's household, we should concentrate first on getting our own relationships right with him, even as we combat the evils of society.

GROUP STUDY

The Spiritual Dimension: Jesus tells us to get rid of the plank in our own eye before taking the speck out of our neighbor's eye. When have you judged a person or group, knowing you were guilty yourself, if perhaps in a different way?

Group Approach: Is our choice of prophetic words, examples, or reasoning balanced and adequately informed? If not, what can we do to improve our witness to God's standards?

Influencing Culture: Rather than changing tactics or refusing to admit our errors as we confront issues, how can we better admit mistakes without giving up our argument altogether? Find a past case in point where this may apply.

THE NEW COUNTERCULTURE
Younger Evangelicals and the Search for Purpose

The war in Iraq has sparked a renewed passion for activism among youth on both sides of the debate. But, as the *Wall Street Journal* put it, "This is not your father's protest generation."

The protesters of the sixties and early seventies shared a common countercultural vision of a new society with socialist values, sexual liberation, and the end of conventional ideals such as monogamy and the nuclear family.

In today's permissive culture, however, there is not much left to run counter to. "The counterculture of thirty years ago is the mainstream today," said New York State Supreme Court Justice Gustin Reichbach, who marched in 1968. "Our success shifted the parameters of what constitutes counterculture."

By contrast, today's antiwar protesters are not countercultural at all. The one common distinctive they share is fear. Paul Buhle of Brown University notes that a counterculture forms around a sense that "everything I've been told is a lie," and it extends to values about all of life—war, race, sexuality, and art. "So far," Buhle writes, "we've seen very little of that [today]. The only thing that unites people is fear of the consequences of war."

He's right. But while the current antiwar movement may not be motivated by a desire for a new counterculture, another group is. It's the group Professor Robert Webber calls the "younger evangelicals."

Rather than seeking a change of values in our culture, they personally want to live out of a different set of values. Webber notes in his latest book, *The Younger Evangelicals*, that they have a renewed understanding of living in the world without being part of it. "In a sense, they hold the world together," writes Webber. They view themselves as having "a redemptive, transformative place in the world."

The renewed activist spirit among youth is encouraging because the passion of these "younger evangelicals" is not motivated by antiwar fears but by hope in Jesus Christ. Webber believes that the war on terrorism will call them to clarify the differences between the church and the nation and their own place in both.

They understand that America is not the church. The nation's job is not to be identified as God's people but to promote the good and the well-being of its people while restraining evil. The church, on the other hand, is called to proclaim Jesus to the nation. It "does not 'have' a mission; it *is* mission." And though we are to be good citizens, we are citizens first of God's Kingdom.

"The Church, then, is a counterculture that has a different vision of the world than that of people who are not in the Church," writes Webber. He goes on to say that younger evangelicals can change their world through a worldview that works, "not by power politics, but by a presence of humble servanthood." They want to transform culture by rebuilding communities and meeting the needs of the least of us—the poor, homeless, prisoners, and children—who have no advocate.

Just as the sixties countercultural influence is still felt today, there is a great opportunity for today's younger evangelical countercultural influence to be felt tomorrow, and that should encourage us all.

TRUTHS TO CONSIDER

The negative consequences of the countercultural vision of the sixties, including socialist values and sexual liberation, have thwarted the goals of community, equality, personal freedom, and justice that were sought at that time.

Today's younger evangelicals have a social vision that is based on the person and teachings of Jesus Christ. They want to transform culture through servanthood instead of politics.

Ultimately, the issues of war, poverty, and discrimination can only be resolved through a counterculture that lives out the values of God's Kingdom.

GROUP STUDY

The Spiritual Dimension: Do you think the older generation of evangelicals is resistant to the hard work of serving the outcasts of society and merely focuses on the spiritual side of the gospel? How do you achieve a healthy balance?

Group Approach: How can you interact with and work alongside the younger generation and become involved in your church's efforts to serve the marginalized?

Influencing Culture: How can you demonstrate that efforts on behalf of the church and faith-based initiatives can better achieve some cultural goals?

PRISONERS' KIDS AND THE STATE OF THE UNION

A Faith-Based Solution

President Bush gave a magnificent and memorable challenge to the nation in a previous State of the Union Address. He defined the crisis of our day with a combination of plain talk and unforgettable rhetoric. He summoned the nation to rise to the challenges of foreign policy, the war against terrorism, and the domestic front.

I was especially thrilled that the president reaffirmed his commitment to faith-based solutions and specifically singled out the children of prisoners. I've talked with the president about Angel

Tree, and I know that reaching these kids is something about which he cares deeply.

Mark Earley, the president of Prison Fellowship, was at the White House when President Bush named Jim Towey to head the White House Office of Community and Faith-Based Initiatives. I know Towey well, having worked with him when he was an aide to former Senator Mark Hatfield. He's an able man with great experience who once worked for Mother Teresa and then as director of health and rehabilitative services in Florida.

The president spoke about having "faith in faith" in order to meet the needs of the country and especially to care for those with broken lives, such as the children of prisoners. After the meeting, Mark Earley was able to stay behind and talk with Jim Towey about what Prison Fellowship is already doing to meet the president's objectives.

We've had a historic opportunity with Angel Tree this year of reaching 615,000 kids. With the help of technology in matching churches and children by computer, we can greatly expand that number in the future.

And Angel Tree reaches far beyond Christmas.

In his address, the president said, "We need mentors to love children, especially children whose parents are in prison." Angel Tree mentoring kits will be sent out to all of our partner churches in February so that these kids can be mentored on a year-round basis. And in the summer, churches are sponsoring a prisoner's child with Rich and Helen DeVos scholarships to send them to summer camp. Four thousand went last year.

The president has issued a challenge, and Christians ought to support his faith-based efforts, particularly in Congress, which provides federal aid to certain ministries that might qualify. It's a signal to the nation that the answer to our social needs is not found in government but in the gospel. The president has stuck his neck out for us, and we've got to do our part to push his efforts forward.

Even more important, Bush has summoned the nation to restore what was once the great cardinal virtue of American life: a sense of civic responsibility. He also summoned us to compassion. But the church shouldn't need any special urging. The Bible, after all, calls us to do these things.

Because of the president's leadership, the eyes of the country are on armies of compassion. I say, staff them with the church. Let's let people see the life-changing power of the gospel. What a witness it can be to our nation and the world to see lives transformed! And a great place to start is with those million and a half children of inmates who are otherwise destined to a life of hopelessness and crime. So as the president said, Christians, "Let's roll."

TRUTHS TO CONSIDER

Faith-based solutions that apply biblical principles to social issues can help us meet the overwhelming challenges we face as a nation.

Faith-based initiatives combine the motivation of the true compassion of Jesus with an ability to work within existing cultural and political structures to achieve mercy and justice.

Whether government is a partner or not, churches need to once again assume their responsibility to reach out on behalf of the Kingdom of God to meet the needs of society and, through that witness, to bring others to Christ.

GROUP STUDY

The Spiritual Dimension: Do you think of the whole person when you minister to others, or do you have a spiritual/material dichotomy that may leave out practical needs?

Group Approach: What faith-based initiatives are you involved with as you reach out to individuals or support a worthwhile program? Can you articulate a clear "faith-based" purpose for meeting the needs of the whole person?

Influencing Culture: How can you explain to others how the "faith-based" dimension of outreach to the community usually provides for greater and longer-lasting results?

FAITHFUL UNTO DEATH

The Plight of Burmese Christians

About 250 years ago, Tibeto-Burman tribal groups settled in the hills where India, Bangladesh, and Burma meet. Since then, they have struggled to earn a living and maintain their cultural identity. In Burma, they're called the Chin. Since the turn of the twentieth century, they have been overwhelmingly Christian, around 90 percent. For many years, crosses dotted the mountaintops and villages in the Chins' homeland.

Not anymore. According to Benedict Rogers of Christian Solidarity Worldwide, these crosses are being torn down and replaced by Buddhist pagodas by order of the Burmese government. Just as the crosses once gave witness to the Christian faith of the Chin, their removal testifies to their persecution. As Rogers writes in the latest issue of *Crisis* magazine, to add insult to spiritual injury, the Chin are also forced to financially support Buddhist projects and festivals. And the Burmese government often denies faithful Christians privileges that it extends to others, such as education and exemption from forced labor. Christian children are often removed forcibly from their homes, never to be seen again.

Still, these practices pale before what some of the Chin and two other significantly Christian ethnic groups, the Lachin and Karen, suffer. The Burmese army tortures village leaders. Christian women are gang-raped and killed by soldiers, their mutilated bodies placed on display as a warning to others. But despite their suffering, Burmese Christians maintain what *Crisis* calls an "unbroken faith." After the Burmese army burned down one village, the Christians returned, rebuilt their church, and gathered for worship under a sign quoting Revelation 2:10 (KJV): "Be thou faithful unto death, and I will give thee a crown of life."

Their extraordinary circumstances have led to some extraordinary assistance, none more so than from a former Special Forces officer who attended Fuller Theological Seminary. Members of his group, the Free Burma Rangers, risk their lives by infiltrating Burmese territory to provide assistance to Burmese Christians.

Their missions, which sometimes bring them within inches of the Burmese army, provide medical care and spiritual sustenance to thousands of Christians across hundreds of miles. They also document the persecution of our Burmese brethren. But their valor will be for nothing if their documentation doesn't produce action, and that's where we come in. Christians in the West, and especially in the United States, need to see the plight of Burmese Christians as a matter of the highest concern. Although Burma is a pariah state, it is not immune to external pressure. This pressure is what has kept Burmese Nobel Peace Prize–winner Aung San Suu Kyi alive. The place to start, of course, is to become informed. Then share what you learn with your friends and in your churches. We've got to build a public backlash. While few of us are called to be God's commandos in the jungle, we're all called to help bear the burdens of our brothers and sisters, even if they are halfway around the world.

TRUTHS TO CONSIDER

Persecution of Christians is increasing around the world; it is worse than at any time in history, but many of us are not aware of this and thus do nothing about it.

Persecution takes many forms. We should petition our government to voice opposition to those governments who allow and foster it.

Prayer for our persecuted brothers and sisters is extremely important. Those who are persecuted can feel our prayers lightening their load.

GROUP STUDY

The Spiritual Dimension: Caring for persecuted Christians is one of the tasks most neglected by believers. How might you set up a reminder to pray daily for a specific person, group, or country?

Group Approach: If you are involved in prayer or Bible study groups, tell them about the needs of the persecuted church. Can you gather with one or two other people to pray in Christ's name on their behalf?

Influencing Culture: Help others to understand that the worldview of other religions or secular states excludes freedom of belief for Christians. Explain why our country, based on these freedoms, needs to protest these actions.

LOVING MONDAYS
Business as a Calling

Growing up in a churchgoing family, John Beckett sometimes wondered whether he ought to go into the ministry. Even though he wanted more than anything to go into business, he had an unsettled feeling that "ministry would somehow be the 'right' thing to do." But somehow, circumstances always seemed to guide him in other directions.

The question came once again after John became a successful businessman and was supporting a growing family. For a long time, he prayed about it. "After several months, and to my surprise," John writes in his excellent book, *Loving Monday*, "I sensed it was I who was being asked a very key question: Would I be willing to completely release my involvement in the company and follow a very different direction in life?"

Framed that way, the question was even more disturbing, as the unknown often is. But John couldn't shake the feeling that God was testing his motives, trying to get him to reveal where his heart and commitment really lay. Finally, he writes, "I responded to the query by making perhaps the most difficult decision I'd ever made—a decision to release to God my future and all that I owned, including the company."

Once he did that, John writes, "The wonderful irony is that in return came the unmistakable assurance that I was where I belonged—in business."

Many Christians, I suspect, are like John Beckett. They work hard to make money but do not feel fulfilled because of a vague sense of guilt. They think the only real way to serve Christ is to work for a church, a mission, or a Christian organization. But in a biblical worldview, there is no such dichotomy between the sacred and the secular.

As I have argued in *How Now Shall We Live?* all of life is to be under the lordship of Christ. Our gifts and inclinations come from our Creator, who has fitted each of us for the occupation in which we can serve him best. This means that not only ministry, but business, politics, the arts, science, health care, and hundreds of other areas are included.

Once we realize this, work can be a joy. We discover that we can use our work for God's glory. In his book, John Beckett lists a number of ways that we can use our work for God. As a business owner, he manufactures the best products he can. As the head of his company, he has written a mission statement that clearly reflects biblical principles. As an employer, he recognizes the worth and dignity of his employees, each one of whom is made in the image of God. That has led him to craft a generous maternity leave policy, to provide financial help to employees who have adopted children, to help employees further their education, and to find other ways to help them grow personally, professionally, and even spiritually.

Not all of us have the opportunity to affect as many people as John Beckett has, but each of us can find ways to serve God through the work he has given us. As John relates in *Loving Monday*, we can truly dedicate our occupations to God only when we realize that the work belongs to him and not to us. That ought to be obvious, but it is often forgotten in the busyness of our days. Thank you, John Beckett, for this important reminder.

TRUTHS TO CONSIDER

Working in the marketplace is no less important a calling than being involved in ministry. It can also achieve God's strategic purposes.

All of our secular efforts and interests can be used for God's glory as we use our gifts to pursue excellence in his name.

All of life is under the lordship of Christ; we should be salt and light in every sphere of culture.

GROUP STUDY

The Spiritual Dimension: What areas of our lives have we set apart as not being "spiritual"? How do we limit the lordship of

Christ by equating it with certain pursuits? How can we change this for the better?

Group Approach: How can you work with others in the church to better understand how to live out your faith in the marketplace? Perhaps you could start accountability groups, read select books, or bring in speakers?

Influencing Culture: Sometimes we hide our light under a bushel and don't connect our faith with what we do, so that others in the secular marketplace have no idea of our beliefs. How can you be a better witness by what you do and say?

A COMPASSIONATE LAW

Signing the Sudan Peace Act

In October 2002, an event of enormous symbolic importance oc-curred at the White House. The president signed the Sudan Peace Act into law. The radical Islamic government in Sudan has bombed, raped, murdered, and enslaved hundreds of thousands of Christians and animists of southern Sudan for nearly two decades. This bill is long overdue.

In the room for the signing were Mariam Bell, our Wilberforce Forum's director of public policy, and Jim Tonkowich, managing editor of BreakPoint, along with groups of people we've worked with for years to pass this legislation. There were representatives of evangelical groups, conservative Roman Catholics, the great fighter for human rights Michael Horowitz from Hudson Institute, some liberal groups such as the Congressional Black Caucus, and a number of Jewish groups as well.

This bill—a new law—is of huge significance for two reasons: First, in it the United States has, for the first time, taken a tough stand in defense of the persecuted Christians in the Sudan. Every six months, our government will decide whether the Khartoum government is negotiating in good faith with the Sudanese People's Liberation Movement in the south, and if not, the United States will seek an embargo against Khartoum. There is also $100 million in humanitarian aid and the stipulation that the secretary of state collect information about all war crimes, genocide, and crimes against humanity—such as slavery—committed by either side in the conflict. This law creates good reasons for both sides to quit the violent civil war and seek peace.

Second, the Sudan Peace Act is momentous because of the coalition that has come together to fight for the sanctity of life in the Sudan. The persecuted Sudanese are mostly Christians, and yet the coalition that pushed for the law was by no means all Christian. Passing the Sudan Peace Act is a grand example of how we are to bring Christian truth into the marketplace in this secular age.

Christians got involved in this issue because of the very core belief of our worldview that life—all life—is sacred. Other groups that favor abortion obviously don't agree with us. Yet in this case, we appealed to common standards of justice. Slavery, all sides believe, is wrong, and so is the persecution of blacks, who make up most of the Sudanese population. We made a good case for legislative action, and it produced a victory in defense of a central truth of our faith.

This is a great illustration of how Christians can make an appealing case in the public square and can advance Christian beliefs when we do so.

William Wilberforce did precisely the same thing in his struggle against slavery. He was motivated by his biblical worldview, but he brought others along with him who saw the injustice of slavery. He not only got legislation passed but made a tremendous witness for Christian views about human dignity. I don't think that it is a coincidence that Wilberforce's work against slavery coincided with the Wesleyan revivals in England.

The signing of the Sudan Peace Act into law is a moment of triumph to be savored. It's also an example of how to present and persuade others of a Christian point of view in the public square—an example we would do well to emulate.

TRUTHS TO CONSIDER

As with Wilberforce and Wesley, there is always the possibility that successes in the area of human rights can lead to spiritual revival.

There are still areas related to common standards of justice where we can work together with those who oppose us on other major cultural issues and obtain righteous results.

Some believe that nations will do what they wish regardless of how we respond, but embargoes and withholding of aid are often effective means for change.

GROUP STUDY

The Spiritual Dimension: The parable of the Good Samaritan exemplifies how we should treat those who are not of our class or ethnic origin. Our hearts should be moved by the suffering of those far away, especially when they are our brothers and sisters in Christ.

Group Approach: Discuss the nature of slavery in terms of what is enslaving those around you. What can you do to set them free through the power of Christ and through your responses as his servant to their bondage?

Influencing Culture: How can this new "Sudan" paradigm of working with other groups in the culture who are normally our adversaries be employed in other issues where the Christian worldview can have a positive impact?

SECTION SIX
_____

THE MEDIA

LIE 6

Entertainment is a vehicle to help us fulfill personal desires.

Underlying Worldview: We need larger doses of entertainment that break useless taboos, accompanied by advertising of products that stimulate our primary desire for self-fulfillment in the pleasures in life—sex, possessions, and power.

The media are the primary conduits of the destructive messages we have discussed in the sections on the person, the family, and society. They mold and dictate our views of what is acceptable in popular culture, and they shape reality to fit a Darwinist postmodern worldview. They manipulate us by emphasizing image over authenticity and self-indulgence over self-sacrifice, and they desensitize us to exploitative sex and violence.

Christians tend to focus on issues of sex and violence, or on pro-abortion and pro-homosexual stances in the media. In this section, we explore further concerns about how our children are seduced by harmful products, visual saturation that contributes to illiteracy, exploitative media celebrities, and the promotion of deviant lifestyles. Subtle virtues are being undermined, as best summarized by the stars of MTV in one of these selections. It doesn't even occur to these stars that the seven deadly sins, as they have been called since medieval times, constitute wrong behavior. Rapper Ice-T says that lust isn't a sin and that the whole list of the seven deadly sins is "dumb." Actress Kirstie Alley's comments reflect what is hardest for the MTV generation to grasp—that the wrong kind of pride is lethal. "I think some idiot made that up," she says.

These stars justify the sins of lust, pride, sloth, anger, and greed as normal to our human nature. And no wonder—these modes of behavior are consistently portrayed as both natural and desirable. In one sense, they are "normal" and "natural" to all of us as fallen creatures. Yet, Christians understand that these sins violate God's law, and only by God's saving power can we overcome them. According to lie #6, we should break cultural norms and satisfy our base desires. The media continue to break taboos because they think that this is liberation from bondage, but the reason these taboos are in place is because these behaviors actually lead to bondage. Janet Jackson bared her breast in front of the nation's largest TV audience at the Super Bowl. Though we are shocked the first time, we are desensitized for the next such occasion, and the media's worldview seeps into our souls. This is especially true when rules of decency are not enforced and the outrage subsides.

At the same time, the Christian worldview as presented on television is largely ignored or ridiculed. Even heaven, as portrayed there, is an extension of media reality! In movies such as *Meet Joe Black, City of Angels,* and *What Dreams May Come*, heaven is a benevolent afterlife in which God is conspicuously absent and a person is not held accountable for past behavior. Hollywood takes the life-after-death doctrine from Christianity but omits the fact that our choices on earth have consequences in heaven.

When visual images encompass our worldview, we experience a "dumbed down" society with intellectual amnesia. We lose any point of reference from the past and thus cannot learn its lessons. One example of ignorance is found in reactions to the film *The League of Extraordinary Gentlemen*. A major critic panned the film, scorning its "idiotic dialogue and general lunacy." But another film critic wondered if today's cultural illiterates would understand the characters' literary roots in Jules Verne's Captain Nemo (played by Sean Connery), H.

G. Wells's Invisible Man, and Oscar Wilde's Dorian Gray. Without that context, the dialogue is silly; with it, the movie is witty and creative.

The media create celebrities who become more popular and influential than our political leaders. Agricultural experts do not come to testify at a congressional hearing on a farm bill. Rather, three star celebrities who have played roles in agrarian movies show up—Jessica Lang, Sissy Spacek, and Sally Field. They carry more weight in terms of publicity.

Advertisers sell a worldview more than a product. In one commercial, Tommy Hilfiger has a unisex perfume worn by men and women with the exact same hair, clothes, and body types. The message is that men and women are interchangeable.

Others exploit those who offer the least resistance—our children. The figure of Joe Camel has seduced youngsters into thinking that smoking is cool. Magazines such as *Rolling Stone* and *People* have more than the average share of liquor and tobacco ads. Children are also featured as defying adults and as being more knowledgeable about products.

The media's exploitation of our base nature and its desires can best be seen in "reality TV." On *Temptation Island*, we are titillated as all of our fantasies of excitement and sex are fulfilled, knowing that this isn't scripted but is really happening. Good deeds and holiness are very boring by comparison.

So how do Christians respond? That can vary from unplugging the TV (instructions inside) to developing discernment as to what to watch and why, as found in the "Christians and Culture" section. The ability to project images and information is a gift from God that should be used for the message of the Kingdom and for his glory. Christians can also use it in a discerning manner to understand and participate in our culture. We need to pray for wisdom and boldness.

HIP VIEWS OF SIN

The Prophets of MTV

MTV has made a business of depicting lust, vanity, and violence, and thus of glorifying the very things that Christians re-
nounce as sin. Over a decade ago, MTV decided to tackle the
subject of sin. It was a special MTV news report called "The Seven
Deadly Sins" that featured interviews with pop celebrities and ordinary teens. They were asked to talk about the seven sins con-
demned by Christian tradition as the most dangerous: lust, pride,
anger, envy, sloth, greed, and gluttony.

The program was intended to show that people still grapple

with the same sins that have plagued human nature for millennia. But what it really showed was that modern young people are woefully ignorant of even the most basic moral categories.

Take lust. Rap star Ice-T glared into the MTV camera and said, "Lust isn't a sin. . . . These are all dumb." Not much moral enlightenment from that quarter.

One young man on the street seemed to think that sloth was a work break. "Sloth. . . . Sometimes it's good to sit back and give yourself personal time."

Anger didn't fare much better. "Kaboom! That's anger," said one not-so-articulate young woman.

The hardest sin for the MTV generation to grasp is pride. Actress Kirstie Alley would have none of it. "I don't think pride is a sin, and I think some idiot made that up," she snapped. "Who made these up anyway?"

When told that the seven deadly sins are a heritage of medieval theology, Alley showed a slight spark of contrition. She didn't mean "to knock monks or anything," she said. But really—the antiego thing didn't work for her.

That just about captures the tone of the whole program. No one seemed concerned about whether the seven deadly sins represented moral truth; the interviewee's only standard was whether or not something worked for them.

The predominant form of expression was the language of therapy, and concepts were judged against feelings of self-esteem. "Pride isn't a sin—you're supposed to feel good about yourself," one person said. Envy is wrong because it "makes you feel bad about yourself," said another.

Even the program narrator joined the chorus. "The seven

deadly sins are not evil acts," he said, "but rather universal human compulsions."

It's amazing that even in the context of talking about sin, there was not a word about moral responsibility, repentance, or objective standards of right and wrong. Moral reasoning was thoroughly replaced by psychotherapeutic jargon, and sin was only a sickness, a compulsion, an addiction.

The goal is not holiness but health. Of course, this failure of moral insight is not limited to the entertainment industry. If you listen closely, you'll hear the same language in serious news shows, best-selling books, and even Sunday morning sermons.

You and I may never watch MTV, but we are all affected by this degeneration of our moral discourse. Do you ever use the biblical vocabulary of sin, guilt, and repentance? If someone asked you to define the seven deadly sins, would you stumble over the answer?

MTV might just be giving us a clue about our own moral confusion. Are we also in need of serious moral reform?

TRUTHS TO CONSIDER

Leaders in popular culture don't look at sin in the light of moral truth but in terms of what works or doesn't work for them.

This worldview states that moral responsibility and guilt lie outside our choices—they relate to sickness or addictions. The goal in life becomes personal freedom and wholeness rather than holiness.

We need to use terms such as *repentance, guilt,* and *salvation* in relation to sin. We need to understand biblical and historical definitions of sin in order to combat its effects in our lives.

GROUP STUDY

The Spiritual Dimension: The Bible describes sin as slavery. Where in our lives are we not free in the grace of Jesus Christ? What sins do we particularly struggle with? Can we seek God's forgiveness, realizing that sin creates separation from him?

Group Approach: We have stressed forgiveness in the church to such an extent that we often fail to define sin well. Without a spirit of condemnation toward others, how can we realistically depict what is dishonoring to God so that we can be liberated from it?

Influencing Culture: Romans 1 states that we all know that there is a God and that we have offended him. How can we present both the love and the holiness of God in such a way that those of our culture will want to reconcile with him?

TV UNPLUGGED
Solving the Entertainment Dilemma

The story of Justin Timberlake ripping off part of Janet Jackson's bodice during the 2004 Super Bowl halftime show caused an uproar throughout the country. CBS apologized, but the raging debate continued. Most people had the innate sense that this was a watershed moment in the culture war.

Jackson, of course, was trying to jump-start her fading career. Timberlake had left his band and was trying to make it on his own. What do entertainers in that position want more than anything else? Publicity. And they got plenty of it.

But it wasn't just the bodice ripping. As FCC Chairman Michael Powell told *Good Morning, America*, "I personally was offended by the entire production."

As I thought about Powell's comment, I realized that our concerns go well beyond the Super Bowl fiasco. That's only the tip of the iceberg. I personally am offended by most of what I see on TV. I realize that it is an entertainment medium, and the industry considers that the nature of entertainment is to push the limits.

But, as Ken Myers wrote in his book *All God's Children and Blue Suede Shoes*, "television's role as an entertainment appliance presents at least two problems." First, access to televised entertainment is easy, and we humans have an endless hunger for entertainment—something to distract us in a fallen world. It pains me to see my own grandkids sitting zombielike, channel surfing and focused on nothing but fleeting images.

The second problem, says Myers, is that television is a visual and dramatic medium. "The dramatic images of television have much more power than anything that is said on the air," he writes. "Television doesn't have much power to encourage reflection." Television is a flood of sights and sounds that overwhelms everything else. The flow never stops, and we don't have time to think—at least not until someone's bra gets pulled off.

Yet as Myers notes, "Abstract ideas are . . . essential to the maintenance of the social order; freedom, justice, and duty, to name a few abstractions, can be illustrated in drama, but understanding the essence of them requires the analytic powers of language." He goes on to apply this to our faith, saying that drama and images can illustrate but cannot communicate "the essence of what God has revealed in propositions."

Now, I know some Christians who advocate that we just get rid of the problem. As the bumper sticker says, "Kill Your TV." Well, if you can't control it, that's good advice. But my suggestion is that you keep it for important things such as current events, sports, and good movies.

My advice is to unplug it. That way, if you want to watch, you'll have to get down on your hands and knees, reach behind the furniture, and plug it back in. The inconvenience may make you think twice. Plopping down in your favorite chair and flipping the remote will be a thing of the past. And every time you want to watch TV, you'll be forced to make a choice rather than going on autopilot.

While we need to protect ourselves and our kids from the overt problems with TV programming—sex, bad language, and violence—we need to be just as careful about the less obvious problems of a visual, image-driven medium. My solution: Unplug it.

TRUTHS TO CONSIDER

Television continues to push the limits of social acceptability, appealing to our fallen nature and its insatiable desire for entertainment that titillates us.

We don't have time to reflect on the constant barrage of images that assault us on TV in order to evaluate their substance and their implications in our lives.

We need to control our intake of television and to be more intentional about what we watch, making it difficult for sensory overload of unhealthy fare to occur.

GROUP STUDY

The Spiritual Dimension: Has television as an entertainment medium gotten in the way of your priorities in life? Ask God to show you the subtlety of the temptation.

Group Approach: With fellow believers, discuss ways to evaluate the content of the shows you're watching. Are the images and ideas worth your time and participation? What can you learn from the cultural worldview that television puts forward?

Influencing Culture: There is still a perceived need for some censorship of television programs aimed at young viewers. How can you work to maintain boundaries by appealing to nonprofit and government watchdogs?

MARKETING DEVIANT LIFESTYLES

Social Messages for Sale?

An Ikea furniture commercial portrays a young couple who look for all the world like newlyweds. They wander about the store, exchanging affectionate glances as they select furniture for their home.

The scene would be a cozy appeal to family life except for one detail: The couple is gay. The commercial is one example of how advertisers portray sinful behavior as perfectly normal.

Other ads flirt with substance abuse. Last year, *Newsweek* ran a series of articles highlighting what was then a new advertising trend—one it labeled as "heroin chic." These ads featured skeletal, sunken-eyed models who looked like heroin addicts. Ginna Marsdon of the Partnership for a Drug-Free America said the ads made lethal drugs look glamorous.

Other ads suggest that there's no real difference between the sexes. Perfume manufacturer Tommy Hilfiger has been advertising a unisex fragrance with male and female models all dressed identically and all sporting the same hairstyle. The underlying message seems to be that men and women are interchangeable.

Clearly, advertisers are selling social agendas along with their fragrances and furniture. This is not to say that advertisers are intentionally ideological in their ads. Most of them are simply pragmatists out to make a buck. They're trying to appeal to markets with high disposable incomes, such as gays and teenagers.

But going after the bottom line has turned corporations into agents of social radicalism. Ads that glamorize gay lifestyles and drug use have helped to normalize and spread deviant behaviors.

Harvey Cox, author of *The Secular City*, writes that Western culture used to look to God for its values. Today, we've lowered our sights to the purely pragmatic secular horizon. Today's secular urban man, Cox writes, is only interested in results. He has little interest in metaphysical considerations. The only question he asks is, "What works?"

The irony is that businesses have historically been a conservative force in society. With these ads, they've become a leading edge into perversity.

It's time for folks in business to realize that they're responsible not just for what they sell but also for how they sell it. Instead of focusing simply on what works, advertisers ought to consider the consequences of the images they're projecting into our minds and hearts. They are filling our eyes, ears, and imaginations with vivid images of sin that lower our resistance to immorality.

Ads that make sin look acceptable and even chic can lead to tragic consequences. Just ask the parents of teenagers who have died of a drug overdose. Ask anyone who has watched a loved one embrace the gay lifestyle, only to die an early death from AIDS.

You and I have a simple way of letting businesses know what we think of their ads: Boycott their products. If you hold stock in companies that sell unhealthy lifestyles along with their products, let them know why you object to these ads with an attitude.

TRUTHS TO CONSIDER

Advertisers don't necessarily mean to promote a worldview; they wish to increase their bottom line and think that what is trendy or on the edge might help to sell their products.

Business has historically been conservative, upholding traditional values for stability. Radical ads may now contribute toward the decay of the productive, healthy environment businesses thrive in.

As we see these ads indirectly promoting unhealthy lifestyles that are harmful to those we love, we need to confront these businesses with their social responsibilities.

GROUP STUDY

The Spiritual Dimension: Jesus said that what comes out of our heart defiles us. What comes out is a product of what goes in. Are the images of electronic or print advertising defiling our hearts and desensitizing us to what is morally objectionable? Take steps to avoid these temptations.

Group Approach: How can we reach out to those in the church who have been seduced by the more subtle images projected in mass advertising? Start with the material products we buy and go on to the subtle sins they produce, such as pride and greed. Why do we sometimes appear to be no different from the world?

Influencing Culture: Now move on to the further edge. Rather than just complaining to advertisers, what can you do to help those caught in sins such as adultery, homosexuality, or drug abuse because you hold a different worldview?

FIDELITY AND THE CREATIVE CLASS

An Impossible Goal

In a recent article in the *New York Times*, Caryn James discusses "one of the year's hottest topics" in movies and on TV—infidelity. Whether it's recent movies such as *Closer* and *Kinsey* or the hit television series *Desperate Housewives*, cheating on your mate and then telling him or her about it is the order of the day. While James does a good job in describing the phenomenon, her explanation comes up short. That's because she omits an important factor, which is the nature of our creative class. In both *Closer* and *Kinsey*, characters admit to infidelity, expecting that being honest will

somehow make up for their betrayal, and in both cases the be-
trayed party disabuses them of that notion. As Kinsey's wife tells
him, the traditional restraints against adultery "keep people from
hurting each other." The unfaithful character in *Desperate Housewives* was preparing to tell her husband when her confession was
interrupted by his arrest.

What's behind this sudden interest in infidelity? According to
James, it's a belief on the part of the filmmakers that "infidelity [is]
one more fact of life." In these movies, "monogamy has come to
seem an impossible goal; [thus] the new ideal is honesty about infidelity." In their estimation, filmmakers are portraying the world
as it really is.

There's another, albeit politically incorrect, explanation for
the increased onscreen depiction of infidelity. In an essay about
HBO's *Sex and the City*, Lee Siegel of the *New Republic* noted
that the show's creators were gay men. This led him to suspect
that the promiscuity on the part of the female characters was
really "an ingenious affirmation of a certain type of gay-male
sexuality," which is notoriously promiscuous. Siegel called the
popular show "the biggest hoax perpetrated on straight single
women in the history of entertainment." Single women who see
themselves in the relationships and anonymous sex portrayed
on the screen are actually watching a justification for the gay
men who produce the show. The same thing may be happening
in *Desperate Housewives*. As with *Sex and the City*, its creators
are also gay men. It's altogether likely that the show's misgiv-
ings about marriage and family life reflect the creators' own
concerns.

Now, no matter what you hear, there is no substantial evidence of a strong desire on the part of most gay men to marry and start families. Even advocates of same-sex "marriage" acknowledge that gay ideas about fidelity differ from those of heterosexuals. And so these ideas are finding their way onto the big and small screens. That's not to say there's a conspiracy or a deliberate agenda. But it does reflect a worldview that is much more prevalent among our edgy creative class than in the population at large.

And it is not just gay men. Writers such as Richard Florida have written about the link between creative people and indulgence in so-called "alternative lifestyles." This link makes socially liberal views on cultural matters such as same-sex "marriage" almost mandatory in Hollywood, so it shouldn't surprise anyone that "monogamy has come to seem an impossible goal" on TV and in the movies. But believing that life onscreen is just like real life would be the worst kind of hoax—self-deception.

TRUTHS TO CONSIDER

So-called honesty about extramarital affairs does not make them okay. Sexual betrayal is always destructive of all of the people involved.

Honesty is needed in marriage as a basis for trust. How can speaking to a spouse about betrayal be honest unless we are seeking forgiveness, reconciliation, and support for amending our actions?

We tend to judge people and things superficially, whereas God understands their underlying reality. We can ask God for the wisdom to discern the true nature of what we see and hear.

GROUP STUDY

The Spiritual Dimension: Ask God to show you ways in which you conceal your true nature or intentions when you speak or act. Pure motives and worthy goals don't need to be hidden.

Group Approach: How do you challenge and encourage others to grow in fidelity and integrity? Do you have access to men's or women's support groups when you need them? Would a person in your church who needed help have somewhere to go?

Influencing Culture: How can you show that the positive results others see in your life are based on the hope you have in eternal life through Jesus Christ?

OUR SHRINKING CULTURE
Movies and Cultural Literacy

Critics were very hard on the recent film *The League of Extraordinary Gentlemen*. Roger Ebert, citing the movie's "idiotic dialogue . . . and general lunacy," proclaimed, "What a mess!"

What a colleague of mine who saw the film found most troubling was not what happened on the screen but what was going on in the audience that illustrates our shrinking culture.

The League of Extraordinary Gentlemen is based on a comic book series of the same name. It is set in 1899, in an imaginary world where the great characters of nineteenth-century fiction are real. For example, you see Jules Verne's Captain Nemo interacting with H. G. Wells's Invisible Man and Oscar Wilde's Dorian Gray.

As a result, the film, like the comic book version, is filled with amusing allusions to nineteenth-century literature. At least, it would be amusing if the audience caught the references. In his review, Washington-area film critic Joe Barber wondered if the audience could be expected to be familiar with these books.

Judging by the showing my colleague attended, Barber's concerns are realistic. Early in the movie, Nemo introduces the others to his first mate, who tells them, "Call me Ishmael"—the first line from *Moby Dick*. The audience around my colleague had puzzled expressions on their faces. The joke, requiring cultural literacy, had flown right past them.

Historian E. D. Hirsch would not be surprised. In his great book, *Cultural Literacy*, Hirsch writes that American children, including those from affluent families, are not being taught "the basic information needed to thrive in the modern world." Not only do they not get references to classic literature, but words such as "carpetbagger," "Waterloo," and "Alamo" mean nothing to them.

It shouldn't surprise us, then, that this cultural illiteracy would be reflected in our popular entertainment. Forty years ago, *The Music Man* featured a song whose lyrics went, "I hope, and I pray, for a Hester to win just one more *A*." Most of the audience today would miss the reference to Nathaniel Hawthorne's *The Scarlet Letter* and the meaning of the lyrics that, in this case, glorify adultery.

To accommodate our illiteracy, this summer's fare is taken from comic books, television shows, video games, and even a themepark ride. As Thomas Hibbs of Baylor University has noted, movies, like the rest of popular culture, are being dumbed down by being entirely self-referential.

These pop-culture images are increasingly the only shared references in our culture. The participants on VH-1's *I Love the Eighties* know more about the hairstyles worn by musicians in that decade than they know about the Declaration of Independence or the great books of our history.

This glorifies the trivial and the fleeting; even more, it deprives us of the moral guidance and wisdom that only knowledge of our own heritage can provide.

TRUTHS TO CONSIDER

We are no longer connected to the values of Western civilization through the great classics and have no communal reference points beyond current popular culture.

Cultural illiteracy limits our horizons and choices so that we have the impression that today's values are the only ones that are relevant to how we live.

We can begin again to provide the moral guidance and wisdom consistent with Christianity by promoting classics of the Judeo-Christian tradition to our present culture.

GROUP STUDY

The Spiritual Dimension: Take advantage of the wealth of spiritual truth in literature and the arts, knowing that all truth is God's truth. Like Paul at Athens, use that knowledge to create a bridge to the Christian worldview for others.

Group Approach: Find a good book on the relationship between Christianity and literature, and identify some key themes that you and others might like to investigate.

Influencing Culture: Rather than communicating ethics or the gospel through the Bible, why not communicate through someone's favorite work of literature that reflects these values? Perhaps others have missed the connection.

STAR POWER AND SUFFERING CHILDREN

Exploiting Celebrity

Two-year-old Arya Eng is as cute as can be—and getting weaker every day. Arya has spinal muscular atrophy, which causes muscle weakness and can cause death in children.

Adam Cohen writes in the *New York Times* that Arya's mother, Loren Eng, has lobbied Congress for increased funding for spinal muscular atrophy research. Compared with similar diseases, she argues, research for her daughter's ailment is badly underfunded.

"Members of Congress," writes Cohen, "listen sympathetically, and then usually say the same thing: The best thing Mrs. Eng can do is to find a celebrity." Without a celebrity spokesperson such as Christopher Reeve, no one—apparently not even in Congress—is going to hear Loren Eng or Arya's cries for help.

Cohen points out what should be obvious. "There is something wrong with a system that favors sick people who have access to sitcom stars over those who don't."

I'll go even further. There is something wrong with a culture that elevates sitcom stars and other celebrities to the status of experts when they are not. Some years ago, congressional leaders were trying to get a farm bill passed but couldn't generate enough interest. So they called three witnesses before their committee— Hollywood stars Sissy Spacek, Jessica Lang, and Sally Field.

Now, why were they called to testify? None was an expert on farm policy. But each had played a farmer's wife in a recent hit movie. Their appearance in Congress was widely publicized, and the bill passed. No one cared what the secretary of agriculture or leading economists said about policy, but when Sissy Spacek testified, the hearing room was packed. It was the most pitiful example of celebrity worship I had seen until Adam Cohen pointed out this new low.

In Loren Eng's efforts to find a celebrity spokesperson for spinal muscular atrophy, she discovered what Cohen calls "the disease world's dirty secret." Far from altruistically supporting what they believe to be a good cause, many celebrities demand payment for their services, and the more well known the celebrity, the higher the fee. Mrs. Eng will probably need up-front cash to sign a celebrity to encourage Congress to fund the research that little Arya and children like her so desperately need. It's the cult of celebrity gone mad. And as I've been saying for years, we Christians are part of the problem. As I wrote in my book *The Body*, we often create our own superstars: "baby-faced World Series heroes, converted rock stars, and, yes, former White House aides who supposedly would have run over their own grandmothers," and we hold these people, not theologians and pastors, up as experts.

Americans are so dazzled by the big tube that anyone who is on it—for any reason (the person could be a rogue or a thief)—is rewarded. As someone once said, people are famous today for being famous. But celebrity for celebrity's sake is unhealthy.

There's nothing wrong with famous people standing up for what they believe. But when Congress and the culture elevate celebrities to the unwarranted status of experts, and when suffering children are held hostage to celebrity contracts, it's time to call a halt. We need to teach ourselves and our children to respect people—not because their faces are recognized but because of their abilities, accomplishments, and character.

TRUTHS TO CONSIDER

The pop-culture celebrity cult has elevated so-called stars to the status of experts, and the disadvantaged now need them for leverage in obtaining government help.

Based on a culture that values money above all, there is the scandal that these celebrities actually require cash up front to plead the cause of the disadvantaged.

Christians are also guilty of creating superstars whose fame helps accomplish their goals, as opposed to elevating humble pastors and theologians as role models.

GROUP STUDY

The Spiritual Dimension: Have you exalted people in the larger church because of their fame, books, conferences, or charisma? Has the spirit of pride entered your own world in the desire to be noticed or praised?

Group Approach: What can we do in our church to show appreciation for those spiritual leaders who have labored tirelessly and humbly with no thought of recognition? How can we also play down the celebrity cult of popular culture in our own lives?

Influencing Culture: How can we reeducate our society to value those who provide true service to others rather than just entertainment? Do we realize the serious limitations of entertainers who pose as experts in fields that are not their own?

IT'S ALL ABOUT PROFIT
Exploiting Kids for Cash

The story got only a brief mention in the *New York Times*—a three-paragraph article buried on an inside page. To me, it's a big story—and a disturbing one.

The article reported, "Magazines popular with teenagers like *People*, *Rolling Stone*, and *Sports Illustrated* tend to have more advertisements for liquor and beer than other magazines, and that suggests that the alcohol industry may be indirectly appealing to underage drinkers." A study published in the *Journal of the American Medical Association* showed that "for every million more readers ages 12 to 19, a magazine had 60 percent more advertisements for beer and distilled liquor."

I don't think it's a question of "indirectly" appealing to underage drinkers at all. I think the alcohol industry knows exactly what it's doing—just as the cigarette industry did with its now infamous Joe Camel image. Problem drinking doesn't usually begin in middle age. It's when you get a kid hooked at age sixteen that you've got him for life. And it's easier to get him hooked at an age when his paramount concern is to be "cool," to fit in with everyone else. In their relentless drive for more and more profits, both the alcohol and the magazine industries have completely forgotten their responsibility to society and to children.

Perhaps the saddest part of this story is that it has received so little attention. In an interview with PBS's *Frontline* a couple of years ago, Professor Mark Crispin Miller observed, "In a thoroughly commercialized environment, there is very little incentive to be careful of the sensibilities of particular segments of the audience. Thirty years ago, a certain kind of commercial approach to children would have been unthinkable. . . . [But] we're all far more jaded about advertising than we used to be. . . . So [advertisers] tend to do things that are more outrageous than anything they would have tried thirty years ago."

We're so "thoroughly commercialized"—so caught up in materialism—that we've forgotten that the most basic human instinct is to protect and guide our children. Greed seems to control the conversation, and even parents fail to weigh in on behalf of their kids.

You and I are not going to prevent magazines from printing beer and liquor ads or from using sex to sell beer, liquor, and just about anything else. And, since the ads are on billboards as well, we're not going to be able to prevent our kids from seeing them.

We can, however, prepare our kids by helping them to understand the worldview that underlies most advertising. It's a materialistic worldview that's selling hedonism. The company that makes the advertised product just wants our money and is willing to promise us any pleasure in order to get it.

There was a time when advertisers yielded to the opinions of parents, but no longer. Since kids have money, kids are the market, and the opinions of parents are less important.

This makes it all the more urgent to talk with your kids about advertising and the worldview behind it and to warn them where this kind of exploitation can lead. The really "cool" answer is to see through this advertising blitz and "just say no."

TRUTHS TO CONSIDER

Advertisers do not care whether they are corrupting young people before they are able to make healthy adult decisions about consumption; the advertisers care primarily about profits.

Our materialism and image consciousness have eclipsed our desire to protect and guide our children; we need to redress this balance.

Today, children have more money to spend, and thus parents have less of a say in what their kids do regarding harmful consumption.

GROUP STUDY

The Spiritual Dimension: As adults, we are also tempted by materialism and hedonism. How do ads for luxury products affect your walk with God?

Group Approach: How can you protect children close to you from the harmful lies of advertisers? What positive assets from the Christian worldview can you substitute to make commercial come-ons less attractive?

Influencing Culture: Many in secular culture are sympathetic to curbing the alcohol and tobacco industries' exploitation of children. How can we work alongside them even if we hold different underlying principles?

REALITY, OR SOMETHING LIKE IT

Reality TV and Boredom

Let's be honest. Why would anyone want to watch a race between a human and a giraffe or eavesdrop on a blind date between annoying strangers or listen to terrible singers wail like banshees?

That we do want to watch is unquestionable. So-called "reality TV" is changing the television business. The public has a seemingly insatiable appetite for these shows, and, as one network executive told the *New York Times,* "We've got a responsibility to satisfy that appetite."

As if what the networks are turning out weren't bad enough, Gloria Goodale reports in the *Christian Science Monitor* that the public bombards producers with new ideas. Favorites include people falling off buildings or out of airplanes, televised brawls in prisons, and street fights between homeless drunks—already an Internet favorite.

The producers have said no to these and other dangerous and degrading ideas, but how long will that last among people who think that they have "a responsibility to satisfy that appetite?" Goodale notes that when Natalka Znak first had the idea for *Temptation Island*—sexy singles romping in the tropics—she was told that it was over the top. Today, it's old hat.

The title of a new book by Richard Winter, a psychiatrist and associate professor of practical theology at Covenant Seminary, gives away his diagnosis for the sorry state of TV and why we watch it. The book is titled *Still Bored in a Culture of Entertainment.*

"When stimulation comes at us from every side," Winter writes, "we reach a point where we cannot respond with much depth to anything. Bombarded with so much that is exciting and demands our attention, we tend to become unable to discriminate and choose from among the many options. The result is that we shut down our attention to everything." That is, we get bored.

Overstimulated and bored, we start looking for anything that will give our jaded spirits a lift. Winter says that boredom explains the rise in extreme sports, risk taking, and sexual addiction. "The enticements to more exciting things have to get louder to catch our dulled attention," he writes. And so reality TV gets more risqué and more degrading by the day—a trend that shows no signs of abating.

Natalka Znak says that death is a line that no one will cross. I think she's wrong. Boredom will lead us right down the Roman road to the bloody lust of the Colosseum.

Richard Winter not only diagnoses the problem, he also offers a solution. We must recover a sense of passion and wonder. He notes that boredom is part of life in a fallen world. There are times when we will be bored. But engaging the world rather than passively watching it can mitigate much of our boredom.

He writes, "Finding interest and joy in life involves active engagement with the world. . . . The person who wants to be involved with life knows that it is necessary to move toward someone or something, to want to understand and know."

And engagement with the world—that is, wanting to understand and to know—is also central to developing a Christian worldview.

So if you're bored, read Richard Winter's book, *Still Bored in a Culture of Entertainment.* Your boredom can be a wake-up call, not only to reality TV, but also to pursuing passion, wonder, and a Christian worldview.

TRUTHS TO CONSIDER

As the media overstimulate us with more provocative and shocking material, the ironic result is boredom. This creates the need to satisfy a lust for something even more sensational.

As each decency barrier is broken based on a desire for audience market share, our own sensibilities continue to be degraded in areas such as sex, violence, and exploitation.

The solution to avoiding this lurid sensationalism is a desire to be actively engaged in the wonder and joy God has placed in the world, to want to know and understand things that are true and beautiful.

GROUP STUDY

The Spiritual Dimension: As Christians, we do not live to satisfy our appetites but to love God with our entire being and to love our neighbors as ourselves. What appetites not yet under control inhibit our true purpose?

Group Approach: Where have we become jaded or bored with our Christian walk, perhaps because of overstimulation with worldly things? How can we help each other yield to God's control so that he will be back in first place?

Influencing Culture: Both the stick and carrot need to be employed, and if gentle persuasion doesn't work, we need to contact the purveyors of inappropriate material and boycott it if necessary. At the same time, turning off the TV may have an even greater shock value for some of our friends.

THE BRAWL AT THE PALACE

Sports and the Coarsening of the Culture

Note: This commentary was delivered by Prison Fellowship President Mark Earley.

By now, we have all seen footage from the near riot that broke out at an NBA game between the Detroit Pistons and the Indiana Pacers. There have been plenty of attempts to figure out what conclusions, if any, we should draw from what happened. Some sportswriters, such as Tony Kornheiser of the *Washington Post*, insist that it was an isolated incident. Others, such as Bryan Burwell of the *St. Louis Post-Dispatch*, see what happened as a consequence of cultural trends within the NBA, which include younger, less mature players and the NBA's uncritical embrace of hip-hop culture. While I tend to agree with Burwell, I think that there are other more widespread and troubling cultural trends that contributed to what happened in Detroit. In our ministry here at Prison Fellowship, we see the results every day in the constant filling up of our prisons.

One trend is the coarseness and incivility that has permeated American culture. Friends of mine tell me that they dread taking their kids to professional sporting events. The profanity, drunkenness, and boorish behavior of the fans make us all uncomfortable and set a bad example for any child. Ten years ago, unruly fans would have been asked to shut up or leave—now it's those who want to enjoy the game in peace who must make that choice.

The problem isn't limited to professional sports. A reporter for *USA Today* wrote about a fight that broke out at a coed slow-pitch softball game he attended. It's as if the entire country has, as we say in Virginia, forgotten its manners. This coarseness and incivility are fueled by a belief that self-expression is always good and inhibition is always bad. The past few decades have seen the triumph of what author Rochelle Gurstein calls "the party of exposure" that turned ideas such as manners, propriety, and decorum into synonyms for repression. It convinced our culture that, as Robert Bork ironically puts it, "Let all be told, let all be shown, and we will be a society of well-balanced individuals."

Of course, no such thing happened. A culture that has renounced inner restraints has only the cudgel of law to keep people from acting on their worst impulses. If shame isn't enough to keep you from making a drunken spectacle of yourself, then the sight of a rent-a-cop isn't going to stop you from throwing your beer on the court or charging into the stands to throw punches.

Athletes are, in many instances, the closest kids come to having heroes. The NBA and its advertisers have exploited this admiration to make our kids the biggest market for NBA-licensed apparel, expensive shoes, and soft drinks. Whether they want to admit it or not, athletes are role models, and they failed miserably that night. While events such as the brawl at the Palace are thankfully the exception to the rule, the beliefs that helped make it possible are not. We see the results every day in prisons all across America. Expulsions, suspensions, and even criminal prosecutions may be needed, but these won't change what most needs changing—a culture that has forgotten its manners. Only a good dose of repentance before a holy God is effective medicine for this cultural sickness.

TRUTHS TO CONSIDER

Our consumer culture is now telling us how to act and speak. The focus is on autonomy, on being answerable to no one so that we can indulge our impulses in any way that we please.

Your own reactions and behavior will do more to instill balanced judgment and appropriate behavior in your children than anything you say.

Children need adult role models that they can admire and emulate. Parents need to help them identify men and women of character who courageously make positive contributions to the world.

GROUP STUDY

The Spiritual Dimension: Do you command respect from your children based on proper role models, training, and nurture that are outlined in Scripture? Do you follow through with correction when they need it?

Group Approach: Does your extended church family give your children the extra care they need in a culture that is hostile to Christian values? Does your group behavior during church activities strongly counteract the kinds of acting out you frequently see at public events?

Influencing Culture: How does the respect and courtesy you show to your family members speak to those around you? Do your friends and neighbors see genuine love and harmony without the suppression of individual differences? How you treat others speaks volumes about the benefits of your Christian values.

INSTANT NEWS, BUT IS IT TRUE?

Why the News Makes Us Dumb

In 1730, a London wag began publishing something called the *Grub Street Journal.* Its purpose was to expose the unreliability of newspapers by showing how rival editors printed conflicting reports of the same events. The *Journal* became extremely popular, but ironically, people kept right on reading the discredited newspapers.

As C. John Sommerville writes in his book *How the News Makes Us Dumb,* "Even when we catch the papers in distortion . . . we still come back to them for more. We know it is insubstantial fare, like enchanted food, but we still need that daily fix."

How right he is! Sommerville played the Grub Street game in his own book—just listen to what he found. The *Wall Street Journal* announced one day, "Scores on College Entrance Tests Fall." On the same day, *USA Today* reported, "SAT Scores . . . Up."

On the same day that the *Washington Post* said, "Iran Offers to Accept Iraqi Kurds," the *New York Times* said, "Iran Is Said to Close Its Border to Iraqi Kurds." If I were a Kurd, I'd be a little nervous about that.

Bad as these headlines are, "the news" is inaccurate in a much deeper way. News people claim to give us "all the news, all the time," as CNN puts it. But this is absurd. By definition, "the news" is limited to whatever some editor decides to include in today's broadcast or newspaper.

But what about the thousands of other events that take place on a particular day that are not included? Many of those events may ultimately be judged far more important than the ones that have grabbed the day's headlines.

As Sommerville says, "Historians may eventually tell us that the world turned a corner at just that time. Maybe in some embassy or boardroom or laboratory or monk's cell, some lever was pulled that set history on a new course."

But these historic moments will never be "news" because they went unnoticed when they actually occurred.

In his book *Surprised by Joy*, C. S. Lewis urges against making young people read newspapers because "nearly all that a boy reads . . . will be known before he is twenty to have been false in emphasis and interpretation, if not in fact." Moreover, Lewis adds, "Most of it will have lost all importance."

"Most of what he remembers he will therefore have to unlearn; and he will probably have acquired an incurable taste for vulgarity and sensationalism."

Well, Lewis and Sommerville have a point—and I say that as one who is a news junkie. But if we really want to understand what's going on in the world, we should discipline ourselves not to get hooked on so-called "instant analysis."

The next time you're tempted to catch your third or fourth "news update" of the day, admit it: You're addicted. Now I don't say to stop reading newspapers or watching TV, but to balance it out by reading a good book—maybe a history book or one that discusses the great thoughts that, in fact, have moved history. It will help you to keep perspective and balance.

You may not learn the details of the latest scandal—but you *will* be acquiring what the Bible calls "better than jewels," and that is wisdom.

TRUTHS TO CONSIDER

We can be addicted to news even when it is known to be as unreliable as the latest rumor mill.

News coverage is always based on the personal choices of the news media and will never be completely objective or represent what is truly important in any given day.

As Christians, we need perspective, balance, and wisdom, not instant analysis, as we interpret the news, especially because an alternate worldview is often represented.

GROUP STUDY

The Spiritual Dimension: When do you become addicted or obsessed by things that either attract or worry you so that you don't live within the care and peace of God, focusing on his Kingdom and the things that really matter?

Group Approach: News bias is sometimes very subtle and needs to be probed for ideologies and hidden agendas. Share with others some examples of news from various media and identify their worldview and their agenda. How can you better detect and respond to media that distort events or present ideas counter to a Christian worldview?

Influencing Culture: Sometimes a slant consistent with a Christian worldview goes unheard in the media. Share your "unique" views so that others can apprehend a clear alternative to what they usually hear, read, and see in popular culture's media outlets.

SPIRITUALITY IN CULTURE

LIE 7

God accepts us as we are, and there are many ways to him.

Underlying Worldview: God is an impersonal evolving force, and we become emanations of that God as we fulfill our own self-appointed destinies, somehow harmonizing with the destinies of others through a subjective love that contains no ultimate judgment.

The New Age concept of God is certainly not one of absolutes. God can be perceived as being at the root or destination of our desires for such intangible objectives as universal freedom, economic and intellectual advancement, or a vague harmony with the universe and one another. Thus, we partake of God and become God. Though there are many varieties of New Age beliefs and practices, they tend to share an inclusive approach that features many roads as leading to the same God—a God who is not historical or personal, absolute or discriminating.

One critic calls this popular view of God and spirituality "Oprahfication." Talk-show host Oprah Winfrey's view begins with the assumption that truth is rooted in human experience and feeling, rather than the claims of Christian doctrine or faith in a transcendent, personal God.

Through our own efforts and techniques, we gradually grow in spiritual power, overcoming ignorance rather than sin and defeating any forces, including conventional morality, that would suppress our "true spiritual potential."

Secular psychotherapy, for example, uses techniques that replace religion by helping us to discover our true selves and reach our potential. In the film *Analyze This*, a mobster played by Robert De Niro seeks help from a psychotherapist played by Billy Crystal. In this comedy, Crystal shows De Niro the way to self-esteem and inner peace without having to change his behavior.

In substitution for a vanishing spirituality, we have rabid consumerism. Jack Welch, former CEO of General Electric, vowed after a heart attack to pursue the "good life" even more avidly, rather than make peace with God in the short time he had left. As most nonreligious people do today, Welch would probably protest that he has his own spirituality. The term *spiritual* has become ambiguous—in the pop culture, it can even refer to the lyrics of a rock band.

"Unity" is a mushy civil religious ecumenism that minimizes distinctive truths, even between such distinct religious orientations as Muslim and Christian, under the umbrella of tolerance. Postmodern values have also challenged the church with its emphasis on image over substance, with truth tailored to fit the preferences of the recipient. The culture has accepted the financial success of evangelical Christianity, saying that it's okay to be a Christian as long as you see it as a consumer choice—one option among many on the menu. Image over substance can also be seen in the postmodern church, where marketing and cultural accommodation override doctrinal content. In a TV commercial, Andre Agassi says that image is everything. The postmodern church relies on image for church growth, and some evangelical churches do so as well.

We have reached the state of early Christian days, when there was great ignorance of the Christian faith. The culture hasn't ceased believing in anything, but as G. K. Chesterton says, it believes in everything, including the latest fashionable superstition. *Time* magazine said that God was dead over forty years ago, but today we believe in gods and spiritualities of all kinds. For example, the Raelians are a UFO cult that want to clone a race of super humans and are suing the government. But they don't differ from many Americans who believe in necromancy, astrology, and other far-out superstitions.

In these times of great opportunity, this spiritual dimension allows us to make a stronger case for our faith. Let us speak and live persuasively in order to attract others to the wonderful news of liberation in Jesus Christ. We must let his light illumine and expose the darkness all around us.

"OPRAHFICATION" AND ITS DISCONTENTS

Our Mile-Wide, Inch-Deep Religious Culture

The weeks following the terrorist attacks on New York and Washington saw a noticeable increase in church attendance. Americans who hadn't been in a church for years suddenly felt the need to go to church. Millions of Americans watched televised memorial services from the National Cathedral in Washington and St. Patrick's in New York.

This turn to religious faith caught the notice of many cultural commentators. Columnist Peggy Noonan spoke for many people when she wrote that "God is back." A new survey, however, paints a somewhat different picture.

Poll results recently released by the Pew Forum on Religion and Public Life suggest that the post–September 11 spike in religious influence has flattened out. According to the poll, the percentage of Americans who believe that religion's influence on American life is on the increase has dropped to pre–September 11 levels.

Yet while religion as a whole may have seen its perceived influence wane since September 11, one religion, Islam, still seems to be benefiting from the post–September 11 surge. Fifty-four percent of Americans hold a favorable impression of Islam, which is significantly higher than at this time a year ago.

What's even more noteworthy is what Americans believe about the relationship between religion, morality, and truth. Sixty percent of Americans believe that growing up in a religious home makes it more likely that a child will be a moral adult. Yet less than half say that a belief in God is necessary to being a moral person.

Similarly, more than three-quarters of all Americans agree with the statement "Many religions can lead to eternal life." What's even more distressing, according to Pew, is that nearly half of the "highly committed" evangelicals polled agreed with that statement. Incredible!

The inevitable conclusion from these polling results is that religion in America has succumbed to what has been dubbed as "Oprahfication," which takes its name from the talk-show host Oprah Winfrey.

Columnist Terry Mattingly defines "Oprahfication" as the assumption that "all truth is based on human experiences, feelings, and emotions . . . as opposed to the claims of religious doctrine, transcendent faith, or cultural traditions."

Thus, the important thing about a religion is how it makes us feel, not whether it's true. In fact, questions about truth claims are considered impolite, uncivil, and even intolerant. If a particular belief makes a person happy, who are we to judge?

As Mattingly has written, this is the direction that American religion, including evangelicalism, is headed, and the numbers bear him out. This worldview causes people to see all religions, even those with diametrically opposed doctrines, as equally valid. And it may account for why regard for Islam rose after September 11.

Christians need to help people understand that religion is not a matter of sentiment but a matter of truth. Insisting that the truth claims of Christianity, and of other faiths, be taken seriously isn't "intolerant." On the contrary, it accords them the respect they deserve—something our "Oprahfied" religious culture can't and won't do.

TRUTHS TO CONSIDER

Truth is not just based on human experience but on the objective eternal truth revealed in the Bible.

Only one religion, Christianity, can lead to eternal life, and its truth claims contradict the truth claims of other religions. This makes those teachings from other religions false, and in the name of truth, this needs to be exposed.

We will go far beyond mere happiness in our Christian life, but our true purpose on this earth is obedience and sanctification, not personal gratification.

GROUP STUDY

The Spiritual Dimension: When have you focused on your own personal happiness rather than on the joy God promises, based on the redemptive work of his Son? Set your sights again on him.

Group Approach: Have you separated morality from a belief in God? If so, emphasize the link between the two to yourself and to others, anticipating growth in your own holiness as a result.

Influencing Culture: Show those who think that all religions lead to the same end that it's not intolerant but liberating to appropriate the exclusive truth of salvation in their own lives.

TRANSFORMATION WITHOUT REPENTANCE

Psychoanalysis and Evil in Analyze This

A murderous Mafia don is having an unexpected emotional crisis. He finds himself crying for no reason. Things he once did without thinking, such as pulling the trigger on an enemy, have become nearly impossible. What's a confused mobster to do?

In the film comedy *Analyze This*, the troubled mobster doesn't talk to a priest but goes to a psychoanalyst. It's another example of how psychotherapy has replaced biblical faith as the religion of choice in American culture.

Analyze This—a top box-office hit—stars Robert De Niro as a mobster named Paul Vitti and Billy Crystal as the psychoanalyst whose help Vitti enlists. The movie is undeniably entertaining as it takes hilarious jabs at the world of organized crime. But one thing it takes very seriously is psychoanalysis. In fact, it takes it so seriously that by the end of the movie, the murderous Vitti actually experiences a dramatic psychoanalytic breakthrough.

Vitti realizes that all his life, he's been saddled with feelings of guilt because at age twelve, when he saw his father gunned down in a restaurant, he did nothing to help. By understanding this and forgiving himself, Vitti has a cathartic breakthrough. After a good cry and a few words of apology to his dead father, Vitti is a new man. Suddenly the murderous anger isn't there anymore, thanks to psychoanalysis.

Of course, this would never happen in real life. Much of psychoanalytic theory has been totally discredited. As the *Los Angeles Times* put it, "Psychoanalysis' moment of triumph appears to have turned to ashes."

But you would never know this by going to the movies. In addition to *Analyze This*, the Academy Award–winning film *Good Will Hunting* also has as its lead character someone who successfully put his hopes in the hands of an analyst.

Why does Hollywood insist on putting faith in a discredited theory? In his book, *The Triumph of the Therapeutic*, sociologist Philip Rieff writes that psychotherapy has become the modern world's new sacrament. We once viewed life through a lens shaped by biblical religion, Rieff writes. But now the lens reflects the values of psychotherapy, such as the importance of self-esteem and inner peace.

This new religion has no place for sin. Its worldview teaches that people are not responsible for their actions. The evil they commit, whether it's lying to their spouse or killing a rival, is the result of unresolved inner conflicts, usually brought on by some childhood trauma.

That's why the emphasis in psychoanalysis is on insight, not repentance. But of course, if nothing is our fault, then we have nothing to repent of.

This is nonsense, as even secular critics of therapy acknowledge. And more than twenty years of working in prisons has taught me that only an encounter with Christ—one that leads to repentance—can turn a predator's life around.

If your unbelieving friends watch this new film, as they probably will, invite them to come up with even one instance in which psychoanalysis has turned a murderer into a nice guy. And then tell them about the one thing that can transform the worst among us: the glorious gospel of Jesus Christ.

TRUTHS TO CONSIDER

Contemporary films portray sinful behavior as a problem for the psychoanalyst. Everything can be resolved by understanding past hurts.

Psychoanalysis does not include a concept of sin and teaches that we are not responsible for our actions. The Bible makes it clear that we will be judged according to our deeds.

True peace and self-esteem come through repentance, which in turn gives us the power to turn our lives around.

GROUP STUDY

The Spiritual Dimension: In what areas do we find excuses for sinful behavior, blaming others and circumstances rather than seeking God's mercy through repentance?

Group Approach: How can we support the efforts of Christian counselors? Use this resource to help someone in your church who is hurting and needs direction and healing.

Influencing Culture: Solid biblical counseling is the Christian answer to psychoanalysis. How can you lead a needy unbeliever in that direction as a means of introducing him or her to the Lord?

A LIFE WELL LIVED
Spending His Way to Happiness

Twenty-three hundred years ago, Greek philosophers known as Epicureans believed that chance governed the universe. Since individuals had no influence over their circumstances, the most they could hope for was that their experiences would be pleasant.

This belief was somewhat inaccurately summed up in the phrase "Eat, drink, and be merry, for tomorrow we die."

While this epigram doesn't do justice to the Epicureans, it perfectly sums up the worldview of one of America's corporate giants, Jack Welch, former CEO of General Electric. Recent news reports about his most recent divorce have shed light on Welch's lifestyle.

Even after Welch retired, General Electric provided him with a luxury apartment on Central Park West, free travel on company jets, and good things of life such as flowers, furniture, opera tickets, and even stamps.

These disclosures about sticking GE with the tab for his lifestyle embarrassed Welch, who agreed to reimburse the company. But there's no evidence that Welch is rethinking his idea of the good life.

Quite to the contrary, during an appearance at a public forum, Welch was asked what he had learned from a brush with death seven years earlier. Had he had an epiphany during his heart surgery? His answer was, "I learned I didn't spend enough money." When pressed—they thought he was joking—he added that, after his bypass surgery, he vowed never again to drink wine that cost less than one hundred dollars a bottle—and he was completely serious.

What a sad answer! What's even sadder is that Welch is hardly unique in this regard. The past decade has been characterized by frenzied consumerism in which one's choice of olive oil, kitchen gadgets, underclothes, and cars have become a "spiritual" matter.

Spirituality as consumption, like Epicureanism, is the product of a purely materialistic understanding of the universe. After a century and a half of Darwinism, materialistic worldviews have deprived people of any sense of purpose in life. For many Westerners, chance does govern the universe. We are simply products of forces that did not have us in mind.

If that's the case, it makes sense to do all you can to maximize your material enjoyment. Whether it's drinking the best wine, eating the best food, or flying in a private jet, it makes no sense not to spend more money if this life is all there is.

But what a bankrupt and hopeless way to live! Christians know that chance doesn't govern the universe and that there's much more to our existence than this transitory life. Because of this, we never lack purpose. I get up every day excited that I've got something I can do to serve God, to help make a difference in the lives of others.

Every Christian ought to feel this way, and those who understand the gospel do. I remember Myrtie Howell, about whom I wrote in the book *Loving God*. Despite being in her nineties and in ill health, Myrtie was writing to dozens of inmates every week, leading many to Christ. I visited her in the nursing home, and she was full of joy and excitement.

This contrast between Myrtie Howell and an American business icon reminds us of why a biblical worldview is so important. Knowing where we've come from—and that we're created in the image of God—helps us to understand how we should live. It's what keeps us from confusing the "good life" with a life well lived.

TRUTHS TO CONSIDER

Those who believe that the universe is directed by chance have no sense of control or ultimate purpose, so they get as much pleasure out of life as possible because they think that is all there is.

People like Jack Welch, whose bank accounts are full and who hope the next material thing will satisfy them, are actually bankrupt, hopeless, and never really at peace. They waste resources that could be put to better use.

Let's not confuse the "good life" with a life well lived. As we serve others in the name of Christ, we have the best of everything to hope for—for all eternity.

GROUP STUDY

The Spiritual Dimension: Is your life oriented toward your next purchase, the next toy you can buy? Jesus said that a person's life does not consist of possessions but of the abundant life from above that he came to give.

Group Approach: Jesus says to give and it will be given back to you many times over. How can you as a church be set free from materialism by giving more away to those in need within your church, community, or parachurch ministry?

Influencing Culture: Many conspicuous consumers are really empty inside and looking for the real thing. Reach out to those caught up in rampant materialism. Love them for who they are, and try to reach some deeper needs that money can't satisfy.

VERY SUPERSTITIOUS

Belief in Contemporary America

The Raelians, a cult that worships UFOs, threatened to sue the federal government for interfering with their plans to clone a human being. The FDA insists that experiments such as the Raelians' must meet with its approval, which it won't give.

For their part, the Raelians claim that the FDA's refusal violates their beliefs, which teach them that human beings are the product of genetic experiments performed by extraterrestrials millions of years ago. They believe that cloning people is the key to eternal life.

While this is more than a little ridiculous, what's even more ridiculous is that the Raelians' beliefs aren't as far from the American mainstream as you might think.

In the 1960s, *Time* magazine asked on its cover, "Is God Dead?" The answer seemed to be that even if he wasn't, belief in the supernatural was on the way out.

What a difference three decades make! Americans have now embraced "belief" in a big way, so much so, in fact, that social critics and historians are referring to our times as another "great awakening." But wait a minute. Belief is surging, but what are people believing in?

Between 1976 and 1997, the number of Americans who believed in astrology grew from 17 percent to 37 percent. During the same period, the percentage of Americans who professed belief in reincarnation nearly tripled—from 9 percent to 25 percent. And without a doubt, crystal-ball makers are glad to hear that those who put stock in fortune-telling have nearly quadrupled—from 4 to 14 percent.

In addition, up to half of all Americans believe in necromancy (that is, conjuring up the dead), and millions of Americans believe in lucky numbers, alien visitations, and alien abductions. And this is only a sample of America's new credulity.

Clearly, this kind of spiritual awakening stands in marked contrast to the great awakenings of the eighteenth and nineteenth centuries. Those spiritual movements were grounded in historic Christianity. When men and women sought "spiritual growth," they turned to the God of the Bible.

But today, it's as simple as ABC, Anything But Christianity. In their attempt to find spiritual fulfillment without Christianity, Americans have become undiscerning as to what they believe. If it enables a person to feel "spiritual" without having to bother about being religious, no belief is too off-the-wall for some people.

This is to be expected. As G. K. Chesterton noted, when people cease believing in the biblical God, the problem isn't that they believe in nothing, it's that they believe in everything. Irrationality and superstition become the order of the day.

This situation leaves the church with both an opportunity and a challenge. All of this misplaced belief is, in fact, a tacit acknowledgment of the "God-shaped vacuum" within each human heart. Our challenge is to help our neighbors understand that this vacuum cannot be filled with superstition. It can only be filled by a relationship with the God of history—the one who created the vacuum within us.

TRUTHS TO CONSIDER

It's a lot easier to feel "spiritual" without conforming to rules and standards of a religion that involves sacrifice and commitment.

When people stop believing in the solid content of Christianity, they don't stop believing altogether; they become superstitious and believe in bits and pieces of many things.

This "spiritual awakening" is an awakening to deception that gives the church an opportunity to reach those who are seeking to fill a spiritual vacuum.

GROUP STUDY

The Spiritual Dimension: Have you at times fallen prey to some of the more subtle beliefs of the culture, such as the prosperity gospel or the god of technology? Replace this with the beliefs and values of your true faith in Christ.

Group Approach: More subtle forms of superstition can result from fear or anxiety rather than from a belief that God is totally involved in our lives and working for our good. Find someone in bondage and help to set him or her free from fear of circumstances or trust in other forces.

Influencing Culture: Seek to understand the spiritual hunger behind the vacuum left by the fading of the Judeo-Christian influence. Approach others from a position of satisfying the true needs behind these other spiritual movements.

MUSHY ECUMENISM
Incoherent Civil Religion

During a service at a large evangelical church, a Muslim leader—who had been invited to give the message—stood at the pulpit and declared, "All of us believe in Jesus. I believe in Muhammad and all the prophets. So our mission here is to introduce people to God." And then he added, "We believe in Jesus more than you do, in fact."

What a thing to hear in a Bible-believing church!

After 9/11, we saw all kinds of ecumenical services—from the huge one at Yankee Stadium, to the prayer service at the National Cathedral, to the celebration of Ramadan in the White House, to small celebrations all over America. And, yes, it's right to reach out to our Muslim neighbors—to offer love and support at a time when they may be feeling vulnerable. President Bush is absolutely right to reach out in friendship to Muslims—to lead the way in discouraging outbreaks of religious bigotry. But Christians must be careful not to allow support and acceptance of our Muslim neighbors to sink into a kind of mushy civil religion that obscures the truth about both Christianity and Islam. As I have been documenting, the two are not the same.

One dramatic difference is between Christianity's and Islam's understanding of Jesus. Christianity teaches that Jesus is part of the Trinity. He is God the Son who was offered as an atoning sacrifice on the cross to save his people from their sins. By contrast, the Koran denies that Jesus was crucified at all and claims that Jesus was no more than "a Messenger of Allah and His Word." Muslims reject the deity of Christ and his atoning sacrifice. That's a big difference. Contrary to what the Muslim leader said, Muslims do not believe in Jesus more than we do—this is pure nonsense.

To suggest that Christianity and Islam are basically the same is not only unfair to Christianity, it's equally unfair to Islam. It compromises both and thus creates massive worldview confusion. People need to know where the lines are drawn in order to think rationally about both Christianity and Islam.

Getting out the truth about how Christianity differs from Islam is more important now than ever. Just before the September 11 attacks, a Gallup survey showed that 45 percent of Americans had favorable views toward Muslim-Americans. Today, 59 percent do. Imagine it—Islamic extremists attack America, and we think more of Islam than before the attack!

This has happened because leaders on many fronts have cleaned up Islam. They've made a point of including Muslims in public religious events and of telling Americans that the terrorists hijacked a peace-loving religion. Those who dare to suggest otherwise, as some Christian leaders have done, are vilified.

While it's right to love our Muslim neighbors, we must redouble our efforts to make sure that our children and our neighbors know that all religions are not alike.

The same survey showing that more Americans view Muslims favorably also says that Americans—by a huge majority— believe that religion is gaining influence in American life. The critical question, of course, is what kind of religion is gaining influence. Is it the real thing or a mushy civil religious ecumenism? It's time for Christians—always lovingly—to make the truth known. All religious beliefs are tolerated—but not all are true.

TRUTHS TO CONSIDER

Muslims do not believe in Jesus more than Christians do; they do not believe that he is divine or even that he died on the cross.

Stating that Christianity and Islam are basically the same distorts both Christianity and Islam.

We can reach out to Muslims as Americans without sinking into a mushy civil religion that attempts to combine Islam with Christianity.

GROUP STUDY

The Spiritual Dimension: Some Muslims are very dedicated to their religion, even to the point of dying for their faith. Would you be willing to go to this extreme for the Christian faith? Why?

Group Approach: Attempt to befriend at least one Muslim. After a period of sacrificial love, reach out with the message of the gospel without criticizing Muslim faith. It's a step in the right direction.

Influencing Culture: Do your homework so that in discussing Islam and Christianity, you can make it clear that their practices are different and that the two religions have very different concepts of God.

AS LONG AS WE ALL GET ALONG

Selling Truth for Unity

Peter James Lee was one of the sixty Episcopal bishops who voted to approve the appointment of Gene Robinson, an openly gay man, as bishop of New Hampshire. Since the vote, Lee has faced stiff opposition from conservative evangelical churches in his diocese.

In his speech to the annual meeting of his diocese, Bishop Lee said, "If you must make a choice between heresy and schism, always choose heresy."

I can think of nothing more dangerous. What Lee is basically saying is that we can tolerate anything within the church just to keep the church together.

What would cause someone to think this way? Of course, there is much at stake economically in keeping things the way they are. Schism is considered the greater enemy because a pastor's retirement and church properties—not to mention a bishop's reputation—are threatened if a church breaks away from a denomination. But putting personal interest ahead of truth does not create real unity. Sacrificing truth on the altar of what we call unity is mere expediency.

The second reason for putting unity over truth is that American Christians of all stripes—evangelical and liberal—no longer take truth seriously. In a recent *New York Times* column, David Brooks said that Americans believe that "in the final days, the distinctions will fade away, and we will all be united in God's embrace. This happy assumption has meant that millions feel free to try on different denominations at different points in their lives, and many Americans have had trouble taking religious doctrines altogether seriously."

As a result, says Brooks, we tend to think that all people of good will are "basically on the same side." We practice religion that is easygoing and experiential, rather than rigorous and intellectual, and we "have trouble sustaining culture wars."

The result is that, like Bishop Lee, we've fallen into this mushy ecumenism, believing that doctrines and distinctions make little or no difference. But our forebears, particularly in the Reformation tradition, didn't shed their blood for retirement plans, buildings, or a cozy sense that everybody is okay. They shed their blood for truth.

Whether we're seeker-sensitive or liturgical, taking care of our retirement plans or building new additions, all other considerations are secondary to the preservation and defense of truth.

This applies to every church, not just the Episcopal Church. In my experience, other Bible-believing churches can sometimes be as unwilling to apply church discipline over matters of truth and morality as Bishop Lee was. One politician I know boasts about his faith while voting for gay rights and against the partial-birth abortion ban. He is not disciplined by his church in the name of truth, and he gets to speak in the pulpit time and again. Anything else, of course, might cause disunity.

As Pogo said, "We have just met the enemy, and he is us." It's all well and good for evangelicals to sit around and talk about "those crazy Episcopalians." But they're just reflecting what all of us do to a lesser degree. Lee's words ought to be a sobering wake-up call to all of us.

TRUTHS TO CONSIDER

"Unity" that is based upon opposing viewpoints where truth is at stake is not real unity at all.

Preserving church denominational unity is usually more a matter of selfish economic consideration and reputation than it is a principled stand for a united church.

Other Bible-believing Christians are also guilty to a lesser degree of preserving unity over truth by being lax in church discipline. They need to exercise this God-ordained mandate in a spirit of gentleness and wisdom.

GROUP STUDY

The Spiritual Dimension: At what times have you failed to confront a fellow believer about sin in order to get along or not rock the boat?

Group Approach: Without causing dissension or going on a witch hunt, examine with other members of your church the discipline process related to serious sin or heresy. Is there a need to take action in this area?

Influencing Culture: Demonstrate the inconsistencies of staying together for the sake of "unity" when individuals put forth views that are contrary to biblical truth. Show that it is the false belief that must be rejected, not the person.

IMAGE IS EVERYTHING

Postmodern Churches

A Baptist congregation was worried about declining membership and decided to do something about it. First, the pastor commissioned a market survey of the neighborhood. The survey found that people were put off by the word *Baptist*.

So the church changed its name.

Then the survey showed that people liked accessibility. So the congregation built a new building right by a freeway. They took down the crosses and other religious symbols and constructed a huge building with beamed ceilings and a stone fireplace.

It looked more like a dude ranch than a church.

Next the church threw out theological terminology. As the pastor explained, "If we use the words *redemption* or *conversion*, [people] think we are talking about bonds." So he banished all difficult or unpleasant terms such as *sin* and *guilt* from his sermons. The pastor even produced an abridged, easy-to-read version of the Bible.

In the end, the church became wildly successful. People loved it. It was McChurch for religious consumers.

I tell this story in my book *The Body* to illustrate the way that churches are capitulating to postmodernism. By that I mean a way of thinking that gets rid of objective teaching and panders to people's tastes—and thus turns religious belief into one more commodity on the market.

Postmodernists do not accept a religion because they think it's true but because they like it. Using the same reasoning, they might choose a particular soft drink.

Not long ago, I picked up a Christian book and was stunned to read the endorsements on the back cover. A Christian professor had written about the author, "I like the approach he takes to faith."

The professor did not say, "I think his approach is right," or "I think it's genuinely biblical." Instead, it was, "I like his approach to faith." But since when is faith a matter of liking? Since when did our likes or dislikes determine ultimate reality?

In postmodernism, even religion is reduced to a matter of personal taste. In postmodernism, we don't see ourselves as sinners who need to be justified but as buyers who deserve a break today. We don't ask, What is truth? Instead we ask, Will this make me happier or more fulfilled?

We come to church demanding consumer satisfaction.

Christians are called to stand against the spirit of the age—but first we need to identify it. Until recently, challenges to faith came from scientific rationalism. Christianity's teaching about miracles and the supernatural were denounced as irrational and unscientific.

Today, challenges to the faith come from a consumerist mentality. It's okay to be a Christian today—just so long as you treat it as a consumer choice, as one option among many.

In a TV commercial, tennis star Andre Agassi turns to the camera and says, "Image . . . is everything." That's postmodernism in a nutshell. Like the Baptist church with its market survey, postmodernist churches care more about image than about substance. They are ready to change their names, and even their teaching, to project an appealing image.

TRUTHS TO CONSIDER

In order to reach seekers, some churches are opting for the postmodern position that subordinates religious beliefs to the demands of the marketplace.

Instead of viewing ourselves as needing to change our behavior to conform to God's character, we pander to felt needs to achieve personal spiritual goals.

We need to focus on the substance of our faith rather than on its image in order to attract those who are hungry for the real thing and who will eventually see through superficiality.

GROUP STUDY

The Spiritual Dimension: We can get hung up on the image of our walk with God rather than on its substance. We have been given so much through our salvation in Christ and should celebrate these blessings. Do we get caught in the legalisms or appearances instead?

Group Approach: How can we as a church find a balance between speaking the language and understanding the needs and mindset of the culture and yet continue to uphold substance without compromising it?

Influencing Culture: People in the postmodernist culture applaud authenticity and resent manipulation. Can you communicate your willingness to understand their needs without twisting the message to lure them in?

UNDERGRADUATES WITHOUT CHESTS

Tending the Heart of Virtue

When Vigen Guroian began teaching a class on children's literature to his undergraduate students at Loyola College in Maryland, he invited his daughter's fourth-grade class in for some discussion. After talking about *Pinocchio*, the undergrads were shocked and embarrassed to find that the fourth graders had understood the book better than they had. Why was that?

The answer, Guroian says, is that we have neglected the development of the moral imagination. The college students literally were less capable of understanding the moral themes in the story of Pinocchio than the kids were.

As Guroian writes in his book *Tending the Heart of Virtue*, the undergrads noticed that the fourth graders were better at grasping "the nature and source of Pinocchio's temptations and backsliding, and they were less ready to excuse him for the behavior that got him into so much trouble and caused his father such grief."

His students even began to suspect that "maybe they had lost something in growing up—a sense of wonder that might have been better tended and retained" if they had been brought up reading books such as *Pinocchio*.

"Perhaps," Guroian concludes, "the fourth graders that they had met were actually nearer than they were to the wellsprings of human morality and were better served by reading *Pinocchio* than they had been by taking a required college course in ethics."

Guroian's book is subtitled *How Classic Stories Awaken a Child's Moral Imagination*, and in it he explains that children are born with a strong moral sense. They always want to know if a character in a story is good or bad. "This need to make moral distinctions," he says, "is a gift, a grace, that human beings are given at the start of their lives." But it is a gift that needs to be cultivated, or it will atrophy and disappear.

That's exactly what is happening, as Guroian's experience with college students has shown. "Our society," Guroian warns, "is embracing an anti-human trinity of pragmatism, subjectivism, and cultural relativism that denies the existence of a moral sense or a moral law." In this intellectual climate, the moral imagination is being starved.

One of the best remedies for this can be found in classic children's literature. Moral education is best accomplished through stories, through depictions of courage and the other virtues that show what they look like in action. A classic story such as *Pinocchio, Peter Pan* or *The Velveteen Rabbit* communicates vital truths about what it means to be human. It teaches us what bravery is, how to resist temptation, and how to practice love and self-sacrifice. A dry course on ethics simply cannot begin to bring these themes to life in the same way.

Why not pick up a copy of Guroian's *Tending the Heart of Virtue*. Reacquaint yourself with classic children's literature, and read it to your children or your grandchildren. Who knows? If you start early enough, by the time they're in college—even the most secular one imaginable—they just might graduate with as much moral discernment as they had when they were in the fourth grade.

TRUTHS TO CONSIDER

As a society, we have so given in to moral pragmatism and relativism that we have lost our moral imagination; we're unable to discern moral lessons in even the most basic art forms.

The educational system propagates an intellectual climate that stifles moral imagination while failing to promote the virtues that build our character.

By going back to the classics, such as classic children's literature, we can regain this moral imagination and pass it on to our children and others in creative ways.

GROUP STUDY

The Spiritual Dimension: Where do you find moral lessons and glimpses of God in literature? Find a novel or some other literary genre that has a Christian author who can inspire your moral imagination.

Group Approach: Set up a reading group that will take a major work of literature and mine its depths for spiritual truth. What can you gain here that you cannot learn from abstract doctrine or straight teaching?

Influencing Culture: Using great works of Christian literature, such as The Lord of the Rings, demonstrate that the great pleasure and the high artistry they offer are inextricably woven with the authenticity of the Christian message.

SOURCES

RIGHTS OF THE INDIVIDUAL, LIE #1

Checking Boxes: Transgender Chic

Fred A. Bernstein, "On Campus, Rethinking Biology 101," *New York Times*, 7 March 2004.

Lotem Almog, "ResCouncil Passes Co-ed Housing Resolution," *Brown Daily Herald*, 21 February 2003.

Jim Brown, "Another First for American Education: 'Gender-Blind' Dorms," *Catholic Exchange*, 16 June 2003.

Donald P. Myers, "A Changed Man," *Newsday* (biographical article about George Jorgensen).

BreakPoint commentary no. 040209, "Gender Blender: Adolescent Girls and 'Heteroflexibility.'"

BreakPoint commentary no. 030808, "Questionable Purposes: The Harvey Milk School."

BreakPoint commentary no. 010516, "Prom King Thinks He's a She."

BreakPoint commentary no. 961016, "Blurred Biology: How Many Sexes Are There?"

Phillip E. Johnson, *The Right Questions: Truth, Meaning, and Public Debate* (InterVarsity, 2002).

John Colapinto, *As Nature Made Him: The Boy Who Was Raised As a Girl* (HarperCollins, 2000).

Mike S. Adams, "A Queer Theory of Free Speech," *Townhall.com*, 15 January 2004.

For Whose Sake? Rosie and Gay Adoption

Glenn T. Stanton, "Examining the Research on Homosexual Parenting," *CitizenLink*.

Pete Winn, "Rosie's War," *CitizenLink*, 13 March 2002.

"Focus on the Family Gives the Facts on Gay Adoption," press release, 19 March 2002, http://www.family.org/welcome/press/a0020031.cfm.

BreakPoint commentary, "Outing the Truth: Do Gays Make Good Parents?" 30 March 1994.

Cal Thomas, "ABC's Rosie Scenario," TownHall.com, 19 March 2002.

"Rosie's Story," ABCNews.com, 14 March 2002.

Chuck Colson and Nancy Pearcey, *The Christian in Today's Culture* (Tyndale, 1999).

Glenn T. Stanton, "Why Children Need a Male and Female Parent," *CitizenLink*.

The Politics of Suffering: Stem Cell Research and Our Moral Ideals

Leon Kass, "Playing Politics with the Sick," *Washington Post*, 8 October 2004, A35.

Charles Krauthammer, "An Edwards Outrage," *Washington Post*, 15 October 2004, A23.

Jim Kelly, "The Wrong Path: Mourning Christopher Reeve," *National Review Online*, 21 October 2004.

Wesley J. Smith, "The 'Wrong' Cure: Adult Stem Cells Get the Shaft," *National Review Online*, 9 September 2004.

In an interview with *Reader's Digest*, Christopher Reeve admitted that embryonic stem cells "are not able to do much about chronic injuries."

Mark Zimmerman, "Why Can't This Nation Back Stem Cell Research?" *Baltimore Chronicle*, 4 October 2004.

Dr. Nigel Cameron, "Biotech Issues Increasingly Political," Council for Biotechnology Policy, October 2004.

Gareth Cook, "Harvard Teams Want OK to Clone," *Boston Globe*, 13 October 2004.

BreakPoint commentary no. 010813, "At the Edge of the Unknown: Assessing the Stem Cell Controversy."

BreakPoint commentary no. 020313, "Superman and Utilitarianism: Kindly Ignoring the Argument."

BreakPoint commentary no. 030225, "Cloning Superman: Are We Sweeping Away Human Dignity?"

BreakPoint commentary no. 030227, "'A Short, Philosophical Hop, Skip, and Jump': The Threat of Embryonic Research."

Dr. Nigel Cameron, "California's Bizarre Cloning Proposition," *BreakPoint Online*, 18 October 2004.

Dr. Nigel Cameron, "You Were a 'Dot' Once Too," *To the Source*, 19 October 2004.

Terence Jeffrey, "Cloning by Any Other Name Still Smells," *Townhall.com*, 11 August 2004.

Jane Burgermeister, "Stem Cell Patent Dispute," *Scientist*, 20 October 2004.

Charles Colson and Nigel Cameron, *Human Dignity in the Biotech Century* (InterVarsity, 2004).

UFOs, Little Green Men, and Cloned Babies: It's Time for a Ban

Take action: Call your congressman and senators. Urge them to pass a total ban on human cloning: Ban both reproductive and "therapeutic" cloning. The Capitol switchboard number is 202-224-3121. Or visit http://www.congress.org for mailing and e-mail addresses.

For further information:

Robin Toner, "Foes of Abortion Push for Major Bills in Congress," *New York Times*, 2 January 2003.

Denise Grady and Robert Pear, "Outrage over Cloning Claim," *New York Times*, 29 December 2002.

Stanley Kurtz, "Left Clones," *National Review Online*, 2 January 2003.

BreakPoint commentary no. 021217, "Opening Pandora's Box: Cloning at Stanford."

Daniel J. Bryant, Assistant Attorney General, Office of Legislative Affairs, U.S. Department of Justice, Testimony before House Government Reform Committee on Human Cloning, 15 May 2002.

Visit the Council for Biotechnology Policy and Americans to Ban Cloning Web sites for more information on bioethics and biotechnology.

"Debate of the Century." On June 7, 2002, Wilberforce Forum Dean Nigel Cameron debated Peter Singer of Princeton University on the topic "What Does It Mean to Be Human?" Dr. Cameron, deemed "the father of bioethics," argued the Christian worldview perspective: All human life is sacred, created in God's image. Dr. Singer, known for condoning infanticide, presented the extreme opposite view.

Blaise Pascal and Alban J. Krailsheimer (translator), *Pensees* (Penguin Books, 1995).

Darwin Made Me Do It: An Evolutionist Looks at Rape

Randy Thornhill and Craig T. Palmer, *A Natural History of Rape* (Cambridge, Mass.: MIT Press, 2000).

Born or Made?: The Gay Debate

Philip L. Bereano, "The Irrelevance of the 'Gay' Gene," spring 1996 issue of the *Professional Ethics Report*. Scroll down to the "Ethics, Law, & Public Policy Column" section.

Letter from John Paulk, Focus on the Family, July 2000. http://www.family.org/docstudy/newsletters/a0012066.html.

BreakPoint commentary, "Genetic Justification: The Search for the Gay Gene," 24 February 1997.

Thomas Schmidt, *Straight and Narrow: Compassion and Clarity in the Homosexuality Debate* (InterVarsity Press, 1995).

Support groups:

Exodus International http://www.exodusnorthamerica.org.

Regeneration http://exodusnorthamerica.org/resources.

National Association of Research and Therapy for Homosexuality http://www.narth.com.

Parents and Friends of Ex-Gays http://www.pfox.org.

New Direction for Life http://www.freetobeme.com.

Courage http://www.couragerc.net.

Kerusso Ministries http://www.kerusso.org.

Science without Limits: Reinventing Parenthood

Rick Weiss, "In Laboratory, Ordinary Cells Are Turned into Eggs," *Washington Post*, 2 May 2003, A01.

Mark Henderson, "New Artificial Egg Technique Eases Fears on Cloning," *The Times* (London), 2 May 2003.

Bill McKibben, *Enough: Staying Human in an Engineered Age* (Times Books, 2003).

BreakPoint commentary no. 030103, "Creating and Killing: Bioethics and the Future of Human Dignity."

BreakPoint commentary no. 021230, "So Close . . . So Far: *The Blank Slate* and Human Nature."

For more information on biotechnology and bioethics, visit the Council for Biotechnology Policy.

"A Call to Protect Human Dignity." At the Wilberforce Forum Dinner on February 6, 2003, Joni Eareckson Tada encouraged Christians to take a stand for the dignity and sanctity of all human life. She shared her personal testimony, her work with Joni and Friends, a ministry for the disabled, and her advocacy in Washington DC. Her remarks provide ample reason for Christians to speak up in the culture and in the public square.

C. S. Lewis, *The Abolition of Man* (1943).

Consenting Adults: Responding to a Cannibal

Theodore Dalrymple, "The Case for Cannibalism," *City Journal*, 5 January 2004.

John O'Sullivan, "Blind Alley of Nihilism," *National Review Online*, 6 February 2004.

Clare Murphy, "Cannibalism: A Modern Taboo," BBC News, 2 December 2003.

Roger Kimball, "Cannibalism: Why Not?" Armavirumque (weblog of the New Criterion), 7 January 2004.

Wesley J. Smith, "The Wrong Idea about Animal Rights," *Rocky Mountain News*, 3 January 2004. (Smith discusses PETA's take on cannibalism, which equates it with eating a steak.)

Austin Bramwell, "Mutilated Debate," *National Review Online*, 4 March 2004. (Bramwell uses another example of self-destructive behavior to show the danger of treating all desires as equal.)

Charles Colson and Nancy Pearcey, *The Problem of Evil* (Tyndale, 1999).

Arthur J. Dyck, *Life's Worth: The Case against Assisted Suicide* (Eerdmans, 2002).

Bearing Witness: The Martyrs of Uganda

"Memorial of St. Charles Lwanga and Companions, Martyrs," *Catholic Culture*, 3 June 2004.

Mike Crawley, " African Anglicans Shun US Money over Gay Policies," *Christian Science Monitor*, 19 April 2004.

Star Parker, "Black Pastors Join Gay-Marriage Debate," Townhall.com, 6 July 2004.

Jennifer Roback Morse, *The Marriage Revolution: Why We Need One and How You Can Help* (Spence, spring 2005). Visit Dr. Morse's marriage Web site.

Alan Cooperman, "Church 'Protect Marriage Day' Is Urged," *Washington Post*, 26 June 2004, A24.

Emotional Responses: Moral Sentiment Is Not Enough

James Davison Hunter, *Before the Shooting Begins: Searching for Democracy in America's Culture War* (Maxwell Macmillan, 1994).

What's Really "Harmful to Minors": Sex and Worldview

Frank York and Jan LaRue, *Protecting Your Child in an X-Rated World* (Tyndale, 2002).

Charles Colson and Nancy Pearcey, *The Christian in Today's Culture* (Tyndale, 1999).

David Crary, "U Press Book on Kids' Sexuality Called 'Evil,'" *Pioneer Press*, 3 April 2002.

Apples, Teachers, and Serpents: Academia's Assault on Our Children

Michael and Diane Medved, *Saving Childhood: Protecting Our Children from the National Assault on Innocence* (HarperCollins, 1999).

BreakPoint commentary no. 020429, "Sex and Worldview: What's Really 'Harmful to Minors.'"

Lynn Franey, "Many Criticize Professor's Writings on Pedophilia," *Kansas City Star*, 1 April 2002.

Jason Pierce, "Missouri House Votes to Eliminate Controversial Professor's Salary," CNSNews.com, 8 April 2002.

Jodi Wilgoren, "Scholar's Pedophilia Essay Stirs Outrage and Revenge," *New York Times*, 30 April 2002.

Edward M. Eveld, "Behind the Uproar: UMKC Professor's Experiences in Peace Corps and Beyond Led to Controversial Writings," *Kansas City Star*, 23 June 2002.

Stephanie Simon, "Some Claim Culture Plays It Too Safe with Sex," *Chicago Tribune*, 14 July 2002.

Robert Stacy McCain, "Porn Lawyer Charged in Brazil Girls Case," *Washington Times*, 24 July 2004.

"Generation Pro-Choice": The Battle for Their Hearts and Minds

Rock for Life is committed to offering the truth about abortion, infanticide, and euthanasia to America's youth through music and ministry: http://www.rockforlife.org.

Stand to Reason has great resources on pro-life issues, including the booklet "A Right to Know." See also STR President Greg Koukl's commentaries on abortion: http://str.org.

Lynn Vincent, "Growing Their Own," *WORLD*, 17 January 2004.

Visit NARAL's "Generation Pro-Choice" Web site at http:prochoiceamerica.org/generation/index.cfm. Similar sites include Planned Parenthood's "Teenwire," http://www.teenwire.com; Coalition for Positive Sexuality, http://www.positive.org; and Advocates for Youth, http://www.advocatesforyouth.org.

Visit the White House Web site, http://www.whitehouse.gov, to read President Bush's statement to attendees of the March for Life. Also read his remarks from last year's March for Life, http://www.whitehouse.gov/news/releases/2003/0½0030122-3.html.

Todd Billiot, "Students to Attend Pro-Life March," *The Advertiser* (Lafayette, La.), 19 January 2004.

See *BreakPoint Online's* "Worldview for Parents" page for ideas on how to talk with kids about issues like abortion.

T. Suzanne Eller, *Real Teens, Real Stories, Real Life* (River Oak Publishing, 2002). Also see Eller's new book, *Real Issues, Real Teens* (Life Journey, July 2004).

Colleen Johncox, "Defending the Helpless," *i.e.*, January 2001.

Michael J. New, Ph.D., "Analyzing the Effects of State Legislation on the Incidence of Abortion during the 1990s," Center for Data Analysis Report #04-01, Heritage Foundation, 21 January 2004.

Operation Outcry seeks to overturn the U.S. Supreme Court ruling in *Roe v. Wade* by mobilizing those who have been silent about the harmful effects of abortion.

Robert Hart, "Her Mother's Glory," *Touchstone*, January/February 2004.

BreakPoint commentary no. 030408, "A New Generation Gap: Abortion and Our Children."

BreakPoint commentary no. 030822, "The New Counterculture: Younger Evangelicals and the Search for Purpose."

Peter Kreeft, *Three Approaches to Abortion* (Ignatius, 2002).

Obvious but False: Common Views of Love and Courtship

J. Budziszewski, *How to Stay Christian in College* (Th1nk Books, 2004).

"College Life Today," a BreakPoint interview with Dr. J. Budziszewski.

J. Budziszewski, "'Little Platoons': God's Design for Our Relationships," *BreakPoint WorldView*, March 2003.

Read Dr. Budziszewski's "Office Hours" and "Ask Theophilus" columns at Boundless.

Kelly Monroe, *Finding God at Harvard* (Zondervan, 1997).

MARRIAGE AND THE FAMILY, LIE #2

"The Problem": The New Female Phenomenon

Betty Friedan, *The Feminine Mystique* (Norton, 1963).

Danielle Crittenden, *What Our Mothers Didn't Tell Us: Why Happiness Eludes the Modern Woman* (Simon & Schuster, 1999).

Ward and Ward Cleaver: The New Stay-at-Home Parent

Ginia Bellafante, "Two Fathers, with One Happy to Stay at Home," *New York Times*, 12 January 2004. (Reprinted by Council for Contemporary Families.)

Michael Foust, "Same-Sex Parenting: Does a Mom and Dad Make a Difference?" *BP News*, 16 January 2004.

David Usborne, "Children of the Revolution," *The Scotsman*, 17 January 2004.

Mike Allen and Alan Cooperman, "Bush Plans to Back Marriage Amendment," *Washington Post*, 11 February 2004, A01.

Pam Belluck, "Massachusetts Weighs a Deal on Marriages between Gays," *New York Times*, 11 February 2004.

Pam Belluck, "Unusual Sparring between Court Majority and Dissenters," *New York Times*, 6 February 2004.

Cathy Lynn Grossman, "Gay 'Civil Union' Not As Divisive As 'Marriage,'" *USA Today*, 13 January 2004.

Stanley Kurtz, "The 'Gay' Election," *National Review Online*, 10 February 2004.

Joseph Landau, "Misjudged: What Lawrence Hasn't Wrought," *New Republic*, 9 February 2004.

Maggie Gallagher and Linda Waite, *The Case for Marriage* (Doubleday, 2000).

Visit MarriageDebate.com.

Call 1-877-322-5527 to request the free BreakPointMarriage Amendment information packet, filled with helpful materials on the issue of same-sex "marriage," including the language of the Federal Marriage Amendment (also known as the Musgrave Amendment) and a chart showing its legal impact.

Sign BreakPoint's online petition in support of the Federal Marriage Amendment.

Family Values on HBO? Truth from Unexpected Sources

Mary Kenny, "Sex and the City Means Family Values," *The Spectator* (London), 16 August 2003.

Gina Dalfonzo, "Complicating the Issue," *BreakPoint Online*, 30 June 2003. (Also see "The Ick Factor.")

Marcia Segelstein, "Unforbidden Fruit," *BreakPoint Online*, 10 June 2003.

Rabbi Schmuley Boteach, "The Summer of Gay Love 2003," *Beliefnet*, 21 August 2003.

Lee Siegel, "Relationshipism," *The New Republic*, 11 November 2002.

J. Budziszewski, *What We Can't Not Know* (Spence, 2003).

Thomas Hibbs, *Shows about Nothing* (Spence, 1999).

Deceptive Rhetoric: Marriage and the Language of the Market

BreakPoint commentary no. 030122, "Roe: Thirty Years Later."

Barbara Dafoe Whitehead and David Popenoe, "Marriage and Children: Coming Together Again?" *The State of Our Unions 2003*, June 2003.

John Witte Jr., "The Meanings of Marriage," *First Things* 126 (October 2002): 30–41.

Danielle Crittenden, "The Cost of Delaying Marriage," *Boundless*, 1 February 2001.

Michael J. McManus, "Myths and True Meaning of Married Love," *Ethics & Religion*, 15 February 2003.

Visit Marriage Savers for more resources on marriage-building. http://www.marriagesavers.org.

"Why the Laissez-Faire Family Doesn't Work." At the April 4-6, 2003, BreakPoint conference, "Christians in the Marketplace," held in Colorado Springs, Jennifer Roback Morse spoke about the "laissez-faire family" and the new definition of freedom: "To be free is to be unencumbered by human relationships." The July/August issue of *BreakPoint WorldView* magazine includes an article adapted from her speech.

Jennifer Roback Morse, *Love and Economics: Why the Laissez-Faire Family Doesn't Work* (Spence, 2001).

Seven Brides for Two Brothers: Marriage and Foolish Consistency

Jonathan Turley, "Polygamy Laws Expose Our Own Hypocrisy," *USA Today*, 4 October 2004, 13A.

Travis Reed, "High Court Rejects Appeal by Tom Green," *Daily Herald*, 4 September 2004.

M. D. Harmon, "Does a Moral Slippery Slope Really Exist? Judge for Yourself," *Portland Press Herald*, 11 October 2004.

Christopher Cox, "The Marriage Amendment Is a Terrible Idea," *Wall Street Journal*, 28 September 2004, A22.

Carolyn Lochhead, "Gay Republican Castigates Party over Marriage Vote," *San Francisco Chronicle*, 1 October 2004.

What might happen in America? "Italian Denied EU Post after Gay Remark," Associated Press, 12 October 2004.

"Chuck Colson's Response to the Texas Sodomy Law Decision," Wilberforce Forum, 26 June 2003.

Charles Colson with Anne Morse, "Sowing Confusion," *Christianity Today*, October 2003.

BreakPoint commentary no. 030502, "Tolerance Run Amok: Gunning for Santorum."

BreakPoint commentary no. 030616, "Power Plays: Santorum and the Sex Lobby."

Charles Colson, "Feelings, Nothing More Than Feelings," Wilberforce Forum.

The Two-Income Trap: Mortgaging the Future for the Kids

Elizabeth Warren and Amelia Warren Tyagi, *The Two-Income Trap: Why Middle-Class Mothers and Fathers Are Going Broke* (Basic Books, 2003).

Visit No Excuses, http://www.noexcuses.org for more information on educational choice in low-income communities.

Maryanne Mary Buechner, "Parent Trap," *Time*, 15 September 2003.

Marilyn Gardner, "Two Incomes, More Debt?" *Christian Science Monitor*, 17 September 2003.

James Surowiecki, "Leave No Parent Behind," *New Yorker*, 11 August 2003, http://www.npr.org/features/feature.php?wfld=1423789.

Michael Lind, "Are We Still a Middle-Class Nation?" *Atlantic Monthly*, January/February 2004.

BreakPoint commentary no. 040102, "Life beyond the Cubicle: Where Do Our Priorities Lie?"

Brian Robertson, *There's No Place Like Work: How Business, Government, and Our Obsession with Work Have Driven Parents from Home* (Spence, 2000).

It Doesn't Add Up: When Two plus One Equals Too Many

Stanley Kurtz, "Heather Has 3 Parents," *National Review Online*, 12 March 2003.

Jennifer O'Brien, "Give Boy Three Parents, Court Asked," *London Free Press*, 7 February 2003.

Kelley O. Beaucar, "Homosexual Parenting Studies Are Flawed, Report Says," Fox News, 18 July 2001.

BreakPoint commentary no. 020404, "Born or Made? The Gay Debate."

Also see the October 22, 2002, "Worldview for Parents" page, "The Way God Made Them?"

"Legacy of Divorce," *Online News Hour* interview with Judith Wallerstein, author of *The Unexpected Legacy of Divorce* (Hyperion, 2000), January 2001.

Michael McManus, *Marriage Savers* (Word Publishing, 1995).

New Paltz Follies: Lawlessness and Democracy

"Bloomberg, New Paltz Mayor March in Gay-Inclusive Parade," NBC, 8 March 2004, http://www.nbc10.com/2903679/detail.html.

Jesse J. Smith, "More Gays Wed in New Paltz, But Without Embattled Mayor," *Daily Freeman*, 7 March 2004.

Matthew Cox, "New Paltz, N.Y. Mayor Says He Plans More Gay Weddings," *Bloomberg*, 3 March 2004, http://quote.bloomberg.com/apps/news?pid=10000103&sid=ayp3ok2mWoHg&refer=us.

Lea Brilmayer, "Full Faith and Credit," *Wall Street Journal*, 9 March 2004.

Thomas Sowell, "Gay Marriage Confusions," Townhall.com, 9 March 2004.

Lisa Schiffren, "How the Judges Forced the President's Hand," *New York Times*, 29 February 2004.

Stanley Kurtz, "Courts vs. the People," *National Review Online*, 4 March 2004.

Fred Bayles, "1913 Law Could Foil Plans for Gay Marriages in Mass.," *USA Today*, 9 March 2004.

BreakPoint commentary no. 040217, "Bucking the Trend: Courts Resist Lawrence."

BreakPoint commentary no. 040226, "An Epidemic of Lawbreaking: San Francisco's Gay 'Marriages.'"

SOCIETY AND TOLERATION, LIE #3

Regaining "Hard-Nosed Teachings": The Doctrine of Human Sin

Joseph Loconte, *The End of Illusions: Religious Leaders Confront Hitler's Gathering Storm* (Rowman & Littlefield, 2004).

Charles Colson and Nancy Pearcey, *The Problem of Evil* (Tyndale, 1999).

Read more about *Kristallnacht* ("Night of Broken Glass").

BreakPoint commentary no. 000614, "Dietrich Bonhoeffer: Agent of Grace."

Absolutes without Absolutism: True Truth

Art Lindsley, *True Truth: Defending Absolute Truth in a Relativistic World* (InterVarsity Press, 2004). To order, call 1-877-322-5527.

C. S. Lewis, *Surprised by Joy: The Shape of My Early Life* (Harcourt Brace, 1975 edition).

T. M. Moore, "Confronting Unbelief," *BreakPoint Online*, 1 June 2004.

Greg Koukl, "The Myth of Tolerance," *BreakPoint WorldView*, December 2003.

Visit Stand to Reason's Web site for more information on defending truth.

BreakPoint commentary no. 031223, "Meeting the Need for Truth: Reaching Out to Teens."

Hot Dog City: What's Wrong with Junk Culture?

Ken Myers, *All God's Children and Blue Suede Shoes: Christians & Popular Culture* (Crossway, 1989).

Image Is Everything: Losing Our Identity at the Shopping Mall

Alissa Quart, *Branded: The Buying and Selling of Teenagers* (Perseus, 2003).

The "Marketing and Consumerism" page of the Media Awareness Network includes links to resources for parents to teach children and teens about marketing and advertising, http://www.media-awareness.ca/english/parents/marketing/index.cfm.

The May/June 2003 *Mars Hill Audio Journal* includes an interview with Alissa Quart, http://www.marshillaudio.org/resources/segment_detail.asp?ID=453054396.

Call 1-877-3-CALLBP to receive the fact sheet "How to Keep Your Kids Unbranded," which includes facts and tips to help your kids become market savvy.

Sally Beatty, "Too Cool for School," *Wall Street Journal*, 15 August 2003.

"Sexist '60s Symbol Hot with Teen Girls," Netscape Network, http://channels.netscape.com/ns/atplay/package.jsp?name=fte/playboybunnylogo/playboybunnylogo&floc=wn-nn.

Laura Sessions Stepp, "Playboy's Bunny Hops into Teens' Closets," *Washington Post*, 17 June 2003, C01.

Deborah Roffman, "Way Too Much Fantasy with That Dream House," *Washington Post*, 22 December 2002, B01.

Bethany Patchin, "The Eye of the Beholder," *Boundless*, 2 August 2000.

BreakPoint commentary no. 020916, 16 September 2002, "Multiplying like Rabbits: Fashion's Assault on Our Children."

BreakPoint commentary no. 020617, "From Diapers to Thongs: Abercrombie and 'Outrageous Times.'"

BreakPoint commentary no.010315, "Mooks and Midriffs: Bypassing Parental Authority."

Michael and Diane Medved, *Saving Childhood: Protecting Our Children from the National Assault on Innocence* (HarperCollins, 1999).

Wendy Shalit, *A Return to Modesty* (Scribner, 2000).

Never Too Young: Teaching Your Kids about Civic Duty

Project Vote Smart provides a wealth of information on candidates, issues, and much more. Just plug in your zip code or a candidate's last name, and you'll find just what you need, http://www.vote-smart.org.

The mission of the Center for Civic Education is to promote an enlightened and responsible citizenry committed to democratic principles and actively engaged in the practice of democracy in the United States and other countries, http://www.civiced.org/index.php.

"Civic Education Increases Young People's Interest in American Government, New Study Shows," National Conference of State Legislatures press release, 22 September 2003, http://www.ncsl.org/programs/press/2003/pr030917.htm.

Karl T. Kurtz, Alan Rosenthal, and Cliff Zukin, "Citizenship: A Challenge for All Generations," National Conference of State Legislatures, September 2003, http://www.ncsl.org/public/trust/citizenship.pdf.

Brendan Miniter, "Why Doesn't Johnny Vote?" *Wall Street Journal*, 29 September 2003.

James Lemming, Lucien Ellington, and Kathleen Porter, "Where Did Social Studies Go Wrong?" Thomas B. Fordham Foundation, 1 August 2003, http://www.edexcellence.net/foundation/publication.cfm?id=317.

Seth Stern, "How to Get Gen Y to Carry ACLU Cards," *Christian Science Monitor*, 14 October 2003.

"Short Term Impacts, Long Term Opportunities," Lake Snell Perry & Associates and the Tarrance Group, Inc., March 2002, http://www.youngcitizensurvey.org/execsum-F.3011.pdf.

"Civics Lessons beyond the Classroom," NPR, 7 January 2003.

Catherina Hurlburt, "Fighting Apathy," *BreakPoint WorldView*, November 2002.

BreakPoint commentary no. 031022, "Doing Our Homework."

Call 1-877-3-CALLBP for a copy of "God and Caesar: The Logic of Christian Political Responsibility." This booklet ($5) addresses the issues of Christian engagement in the political process and the Christian stake in issues of public policy.

Multiplying like Rabbits: Fashion's Assault on our Children

Michael and Diane Medved, *Saving Childhood: Protecting Our Children from the National Assault on Innocence* (HarperCollins, 1999).

BreakPoint commentary no. 020617, "From Diapers to Thongs: Abercrombie and 'Outrageous Times.'"

BreakPoint commentary no. 010315, "Mooks and Midriffs: Bypassing Parental Authority."

"The Merchants of Cool: A Report on the Creators and Marketers of Popular Culture for Teenagers," *Frontline*, PBS, 2001, http:www.pbs.org/wgbh/pages/frontline/shows/cool.

Laura Sessions Stepp, "Nothing to Wear—From the Classroom to the Mall, Girl's Fashions are Long on Skin, Short on Modesty," *Washington Post*, 3 June 2002, C1.

Patti Edgar, "Zellers Pulls Shirts Linked to Porn Site," *Ottawa Citizen*, 26 June 2002 (archived article).

Mark Stewart, "Exposed: Sex Sells and Many Wonder If the Media Saturation Is Warping the Minds of Teens," *Washington Times*, 11 April 2000.

Alison A. Nieder, "Promoting Playboy: Los Angeles Manufacturer Wants to Cash In on Magazine's Cache," Apparelnews.net, 18 June 1999.

Wendy Bounds, "Can Aging Playboy Bunny Lure Women?" *Wall Street Journal*, 10 November 1998.

Bankrupt at Age Twenty-Five: Marketing to Teens, Tweens, and Kids

Alissa Quart, *Branded: The Buying and Selling of Teenagers* (Perseus, 2003).

BreakPoint commentary no. 031128, "Image Is Everything: Losing Identity at the Shopping Mall."

BreakPoint commentary no. 040810, "Beyond the Music (Video): MTV's Cultural Impact."

"Branded for Life: Catching 'em Young," *The Star* (Africa), 13 November 2003.

Jessica Johnson, "The Nerds Are All Right," *Globe and Mail* (Toronto), 3 May 2003.

G. Beato, "Sold Out," *Washington Post*, 26 January 2003, BW04.

Judith Martin, "The Battle of All Mothers," *Washington Post*, 11 May 2003, D02.

Caroline E. Mayer, "A Growing Marketing Strategy: Get 'em While They're Young," *Washington Post*, 3 June 2003, A01.

The "Marketing and Consumerism" page of the Media Awareness Network includes links to resources for parents to teach children and teens about marketing and advertising.

The May/June 2003 *Mars Hill Audio Journal* includes an interview with Alissa Quart.

Call 1-877-3-CALLBP to receive the fact sheet "How to Keep Your Kids Unbranded," which includes facts and tips to help your kids become market savvy.

Kay S. Hymowitz, "Tweens: Ten Going on Sixteen," *City Journal*, autumn 1998.

Sarah E. Hinlicky, "Me and My Mammon," *Boundless*, 1 February 2001.

Aceh and the Abyss: The Fog of Despair

Partial list of organizations ministering to tsunami victims: World Relief; World Vision; Youth for Christ Asia/ Pacific; Compassion International; Salvation Army; Catholic Relief Services; Samaritan's Purse; International Aid; Habitat for Humanity in India; National Christian Evangelical Alliance of Sri Lanka Also see list of groups provided by the State Department and the one provided by *Mission Network News* for other organizations helping tsunami victims.

Learn more about U.S. support for earthquake and tsunami victims at the White House Web site.

"Child Sponsors Needed for Tsunami Hit Areas," *Mission Network News*.

David Brooks, "A Time to Mourn," *New York Times*, 1 January 2005.

David B. Hart, "Tremors of Doubt," *Wall Street Journal*, 31 December 2004.

Mark Steyn, "On Tsunami's Shore," *Washington Times*, 4 January 2005.

Daniel Henninger, "Why We Need Politics: The Tsunami's Sorrows Will Need More Than Pity," *Wall Street Journal*, 31 December 2004.

Cal Thomas, "God and Suffering," *Townhall.com*, 4 January 2005.

Michael Novak, "Blaming God First," *National Review Online*, 5 January 2005.

Rob Moll and Ted Olsen, "Tsunami Weblog: The World Seeks Meaning," *Christianity Today*, 5 January 2005.

Dean Yates and Tomi Soetjipto, "Rescue Choppers Cheered in Aceh, Children Suffer," Reuters, 3 January 2005.

Patrick Lannin and Stephen Brown, "Tsunami Victims Prey to Crime from Asia to Europe," Reuters, 3 January 2005.

"Traffickers Threaten Aceh Orphans," CNN, 5 January 2005.

"Christians Ready to Reach Closed Muslim Countries with Christ's Love," *Mission Network News*.

See the "Worldview for Parents" page "Where Did Evil Come From?"

Daniel Sarewitz and Roger A. Pielke Jr., "Rising Tide: The Tsunami's Real Cause," *New Republic*, 6 January 2005.

Allen Hertzke, *Freeing God's Children* (Rowman & Littlefield, 2004).

Charles Colson and Nancy Pearcey, *The Problem of Evil* (Tyndale, 1999).

No Conservatives Need Sign Up: Postmodernism and Academic Freedom

"University Statement Regarding Scheduled Fall 2002 Class Titled 'The Politics and Poetics of Palestine Resistance,'" University of California-Berkeley press release, 10 May 2002.

Ellen Sorokin, "Women's Studies Mandates Seen As Threats to Free Speech," *The Washington Times*, 16 May 2002.

Gene Edward Veith, "God and the Academy," *World*, 7 October 2000.

Gene Edward Veith, "Can We Recapture the Ivory Tower?" *World*, 9 October 1999.

Armand M. Nicholi Jr., *The Question of God: C. S. Lewis and Sigmund Freud Debate God, Love, Sex, and the Meaning of Life* (Free Press, 2002).

Kelly Monroe, *Finding God at Harvard* (Zondervan, 1997).

Sarah Trafford, "True Confessions of a Women's Studies Spy," *C & F Report*, 31 July 2002.

An Inert Gray Blur: Depressed in the Midst of Plenty

Gregg Easterbrook, *The Progress Paradox: How Life Gets Better While People Feel Worse* (Random House, 2003).

Steven Martinovich, "A Problem with Prosperity?" *Enter Stage Right*, 12 January 2004.

BreakPoint commentary no. 040302, "Miserable in the Midst of Plenty: The Progress Paradox."

BreakPoint commentary no. 040303, "Scaring Witless: How the Media Distorts Reality."

J. A. Hanson, "The Cult That Unites Us," *BreakPointOnline*, 2001.

BreakPoint commentary no. 020821, "Secular Shortfalls: Faith and Suffering."

Ken Myers, "Worshipping Ourselves: Self-Obsession and the Denial of God," *BreakPoint WorldView*, December 2002.

Paul C. Vitz, *Psychology as Religion* (Eerdmans, 1994).

"You Can't Hug a Computer": The Problem with "Virtual Parenting"

Jim Buie, "Visitation Rights Are Becoming High-Tech," *Washington Post*, 15 June 2004.

Pamela Ferdinand, "'Virtual' Visits May Be Custody Solution," *Washington Post*, 13 July 2002.

Jim Buie, "A Virtual Dad's Journal," VirtualFamiliesandFriends.com.

Glenn Sacks and Dianna Thompson, "No Virtue in Virtual Visitation," *Boston Globe*, 12 July 2002.

Maryland's People's Law Library lists some more cases where the availability of virtual visitation helped persuade judges to let one parent move out of state, or even out of the country. (The site takes a pro-virtual visitation stance.)

Leslie Eaton, "Families Evolve, But Custody Wars Are Ugly as Ever," *New York Times*, 12 June 2004.

Joanna Grossman, "The Virtues of Virtual Parenting: Can the Internet Replace Visitation When a Custodial Parent Relocates?" *FindLaw*, 28 December 2001.

Leslie Carbone, "The Divorce Caste," *BreakPoint Online*, 27 September 2002.

Marcia Segelstein, "Intentional Marriage," *BreakPoint Online*, 16 June 2003.

Linda Waite et al., Does Divorce Make People Happy? Institute for American Values, 2002.

Quentin Schultze, *Habits of the High-Tech Heart* (Baker Book House, 2002).

BreakPoint commentary no. 030304, "More Than Duct Tape: Cyberculture's Values."

BreakPoint commentary no. 030305, "A Better Kind of Space: Real Community and Virtue."

See BreakPoint's sanctity of marriage resource page.

Call 1-877-322-5527 to request the free BreakPoint marriage amendment information packet and the free "Talking Points on Marriage and Same-Sex Unions." Also available is the Speak the Truth in Love kit (suggested donation: $25).

An Unstable Balance: Wanting It Both Ways

Read the spring 2003 issue of "InSight," the newsletter of the Institute for Advanced Studies in Culture that includes findings from the study mentioned in this *BreakPoint* commentary. Learn more about the Institute for Advanced Studies in Culture and its "Survey of American Political Culture."

"The Laissez-Faire Family." At the April 4–6, 2003, BreakPoint conference, "Christians in the Marketplace," held in Colorado Springs, Colorado, Jennifer Roback Morse spoke about the "laissez-faire family"—the government's approach to this foundation of society.

J. Budziszewski, "'Little Platoons': God's Design for Our Relationships," *BreakPoint WorldView*, March 2003.

James Davison Hunter, *The Death of Character: On the Moral Education of America's Children* (Basic Books, 2001).

Robert George, *The Clash of Orthodoxies: Law, Religion, and Morality in Crisis* (ISI Books, 2001).

Rules for a Reason: The World Rethinks Dating

Elizabeth Austin, "In Contempt of Courtship," *Washington Monthly*, June 2003.

BreakPoint commentary, 26 August 2003, "Family Values on HBO?"

Barbara Dafoe Whitehead and David Popenoe, "Why Men Won't Commit: Exploring Young Men's Attitudes about Sex, Dating, and Marriage," The State of Our Unions: The Social Health of Marriage in America, The National Marriage Project, 2002, http://marriage.rutgers.edu/Publications/SOOU/TEXTSOOU2002.htm.

Jennifer Roback Morse, "Why Not Take Her for a Test Drive?" *Boundless*, October 11, 2001, http://www.boundless.org/2001/departments/beyond_buddies/a0000498.html.

Candace Watters, "Finding a Husband," *Boundless*, 11 September 2003, http://www.boundless.org/2002_2003/departments/beyond_buddies/a0000796.html.

THE ARTS, LIE #4

Myth Meets Real Life: The Lord of the Rings and the Present Crisis

Charles Colson, "Finishing the Job," *BreakPoint WorldView*, November 2003.

BreakPoint commentary no. 030911, "Terrorism, War, and Evil."

Jeffrey Overstreet, "A Talk with the Stars of The Lord of the Rings: *The Return of the King:* John Rhys-Davies," *Looking Closer*, 5 December 2003.

Steve Beard, "Tolkien & Civilization," *National Review Online*, 17 December 2003.

BreakPoint commentary, 15 December 2003, "A Triumphant Return." See also the *BreakPoint* commentaries: "Preparatio Evangelica," "Now at a Theater Near You," and "Defrocking Frodo and the Death of the Imagination." Visit the Web site for *The Return of the King*.

Frank Rich, "The Mirrors of American Unease," *International Herald Tribune*, 12 December 2003.

Andy Seiler, "'Rings' Comes Full Circle," *USA Today*, 11 December 2003.

Andrew Coffin, "'Baptized imagination,'" *World*, 20 December 2003.

Michael H. Kleinschrodt, "Tolkien's Unlikely Heroes," *The Times-Picayune* (New Orleans), 12 December 2003.

J. R. R. Tolkien, *Lord of the Rings* (Houghton Mifflin, 1974).

See the BreakPoint with Chuck Colson Recommended Films List, http://www.pfm.org/BPtemplate.cfm ?Section=BreakPoint_Home&template=/ContentManagement/ContentDisplay.cfm&ContentID=11152.

A Passion for Getting It Right: The Power of the Image

Mark Gauvreau Judge, "Christ in Majesty," *BreakPoint Online*, 6 June 2003.

"Faith Guided Mel Gibson through 'Passion,'" *Miami Herald*, 29 June 2003.

Jane Lampman, "Capturing the Passion," *Christian Science Monitor*, 10 July 2003.

Raymond Arroyo, "The Greatest Story, Newly Told," *Wall Street Journal*, 7 March 2003.

David Limbaugh, "Mel Gibson's Passion for 'The Passion,'" Townhall.com, 9 July 2003.

Richard Corliss and Jeff Israely, "The Passion of Mel Gibson," *Time*, 27 January 2003.

Holly McClure, "A Very Violent 'Passion,'" *New York Daily News*, 26 January 2003.

Archbishop Charles Chaput, "Mel Gibson, 'The Passion,' and Critics Who Can't Wait," *Denver Catholic Register*, 28 May 2003.

"With a Brave Heart and Pure Soul," *Sydney Morning Herald*, 15 March 2003.

Julia Duin, "Mel Gibson Looks Right for Movie on Jesus," *Washington Times*, 7 July 2003.

Kamon Simpson, "Mel Gibson Brings Movie to City's Church Leaders," *The Gazette* (Colorado Springs), http://www.gazette.com/popupNews.php?id=408774.

Holly McClure, "Mel Gibson's Passion," Crosswalk.com, http://www.crosswalk.com/fun/movies/1195712.html.

Read an interview with Mel Gibson on *The Passion of the Christ* here, http://www.hollywoodjesus.com/passion.htm.

BreakPoint commentary no. 030611, "'The Last Acceptable Prejudice': Princeton's Double Standard."

Anne Morse, "Art Attack," *Boundless*, 10 July 2003.

Gary North, "Finding Nemo and My Moment of Truth," LewRockwell.com, 9 July 2003.

See the Wilberforce Forum's Recommended Films List, http://www.pfm.org/BPtemplate.cfm?Section=BreakPoint_Home&template=/ContentManagement/ContentDisplay.cfm&ContentID=11152.

A Religion for Heroes: Gods and Generals

Bill Kauffman, "The Civil War Returns," *American Enterprise*, March 2003.

"TAE Chats with Robert Duvall," *American Enterprise*, March 2003.

Learn more about the film *Gods and Generals* based on the book by Jeff P. Shaara, http://www.ronmaxwell.com/ggenerals.html.

Learn more about the film *Gettysburg* based on the book titled *The Killer Angels* by Michael Shaara (Ballantine), http://www.ronmaxwell.com/gettysburg.html.

Rod Dreher, "God Bless Ted Turner," *National Review Online*, 11 February 2003, http://www.nationalreview.com/dreher/dreher021103.asp.

Robert Koehler, "War Is Hell in Ponderous 'Gods and Generals,'" Reuters, 19 February 2003, http://reuters.com/newsArticle.jhtml?type=reviewsNews&storyID=2251533.

Robert K. Johnston, *Reel Spirituality: Theology and Film in Dialogue* (Baker Book House, 2000).

An Everlasting Playground: Understanding the Nature of Heaven

David Brooks, "Hooked on Heaven Lite," *New York Times*, 9 March 2004. (Archived article; costs $2.95 to retrieve. Or call 1-877-322-5527 for a copy.)

Adam Kirsch, "Paradise Lite," *Slate.com*, 5 February 2004.

David Kuo, "Gimme That New-Time Religion—a Play-Doh Jesus," *Los Angeles Times*, 8 March 2004.

C. S. Lewis, *The Great Divorce* (HarperSanFrancisco, 2001 edition).

BreakPoint commentary no. 020731, "As I Lay Dying: Worldview and Life's End."

BreakPoint commentary no. 040116, "Say It Ain't So, Dave: Evangelicals and the Cultural Mainstream."

Richard John Neuhaus, *As I Lay Dying: Meditations upon Returning* (Basic Books, 2002).

Mark Gauvreau Judge, "There and Back Again," *BreakPoint Online*, 11 June 2002.

T. M. Moore, "Knowing Scripture and the Power of God," *BreakPoint Online*, 2 March 2004.

Paul C. Vitz, *Psychology As Religion: The Cult of Self-Worship* (Eerdmans, 1994).

Cathleen Falsani, "The Next Great Awakening?" *Chicago Sun-Times*, 18 March 2004.

The Da Vinci Conspiracy: Distinguishing Fact from Fiction

Darrell Bock, "The Good News of Da Vinci," *Christianity Today*, February 2004.

Byron Barlowe, "*The Da Vinci Code*: Of Magdalene, Gnosticism, the Goddess and the Grail," *Leadership*, 7 January 2004.

Collin Hansen, "Breaking the Da Vinci Code," *Christian History*, 7 November 2003.

"Jesus, Mary and Da Vinci: Exploring Controversial Theories about Religious Figures and the Holy Grail," ABCNews.com, 3 November 2003.

See also Darrell Bock, "Was Jesus Married to Mary Magdalene?" ABCNews.com, 12 November 2003.

Sandra Miesel, "Dismantling the Da Vinci Code," *Crisis*, 1 September 2003.

Dr. James Hitchcock, "*The Da Vinci Code*'s Shaky Foundation: Gnostic Texts," *Beliefnet.com* [reprinted from the *Arlington* (Va.) *Catholic Herald*], 2003.

Cynthia Grenier, "Novel Gods," *Weekly Standard*, 13 September 2003.

G. K. Chesterton, *Orthodoxy: The Romance of Faith* (1908).

Jeffery Sheler, *Is the Bible True?* (HarperCollins, 1999).

Real Art: The Hope beyond Ground Zero

To learn more about this fascinating contemporary artist, visit Makoto Fujimura's Web site. Read his interview with James Romaine.

Learn more about the National Council on the Arts.

Both of these books from Square Halo include interviews with various artists, including Fujimura: Ned Bustard, ed., *It Was Good: Making Art to the Glory of God* (2000), and James Romaine, *Objects of Grace* (2002).

Kim I. Robbins, "Renaissance Man: Dan Gioia and the NEA," *BreakPoint Online*, 14 February 2003.

Also visit BreakPoint's Christians in the Arts page and the Wilberforce Forum's resource page on the arts.

Classically Sexy: Baring It All for Art?

Patrick Kavanaugh, "Keep Your Shirt On, Ms. Concertmaster," *National Review Online*, 28 February 2003.

Robert Taylor, "Hey, Babe, Nice Vibrato," *Contra Costa Times*, 9 March 2003.

BreakPoint commentary no. 020927, "Excellence on Display: MasterWorks Music Festival."

C. S. Lewis, *Surprised by Joy* (Harvest Books, 1975).

Steve Turner, *Imagine: A Vision for Christians in the Arts* (InterVarsity, 2001).

"Exit Jesus": God in the Public Square

Allie Martin, "U.S. Lawmakers Look into Religious Hostility Reports," *Agape Press*, 28 October 2004.

Liberty Legal Institute's paper, "Examples of Hostility to Religious Expression in the Public Square." (Free Adobe Acrobat Reader required.)

Nathan Burchfiel, "Conservative, Liberal Lawyers Resume Christmas Clashes," Crosswalk.com.

Cliff Kincaid, "Outlawing Thanksgiving Here and Abroad," *Accuracy in Media*, 22 November 2004.

"Bashing the Boy Scouts: One group Whose First Amendment Rights the ACLU Opposes," *Wall Street Journal*, 26 November 2004.

Susan Jones, "Congress Tries to Save Mt. Soledad Cross," Crosswalk.com.

Dennis Prager, "A Jew Defends the Cross," *Townhall.com*, 16 November 2004.

The Dangers of Reading: Dickens and the Social Order

Myron Magnet, *Dickens and the Social Order* (ISI Books, 2004 edition).

Charles Dickens, "The Noble Savage," *ClassicAuthors.net*. Originally printed in *Household Words*, 1853.

Stefan Kanfer, "And on the Right, Charles Dickens!" *City Journal*, winter 1999.

Myron Magnet, "What Use Is Literature?" *City Journal*, 1 July 2003.

G. K. Chesterton, *Chesterton on Dickens* (Ignatius, 1989 edition).

C. S. Lewis, *An Experiment in Criticism* (Cambridge University Press, 1992 edition).

Os Guinness and Louise Cowan, *Invitation to the Classics* (Baker, 1998).

Vigen Guroian, *Tending the Heart of Virtue* (Oxford University Press, 1998).

A Triumphant Return: The Return of the King

Visit the Web site for *The Return of the King.*

Steve Beard, "The Return of the King," Thunderstruck.org.

Jeffrey Overstreet, "Film Forum: Christian Critics Hail Third Rings, Harass Last Samurai," *Christianity Today,* 11 December 2003.

Monique Devereux, "The Return of the King—the International Verdict," *New Zealand Herald,* 9 December 2003.

Read more about *The Return of the King* at HollywoodJesus.com.

J. R. R. Tolkien, *Lord of the Rings* (Houghton Mifflin, 1974).

Kurt D. Bruner, *Finding God in the Lord of the Rings* (Tyndale, 2001).

See the BreakPoint Commentaries: "Preparatio Evangelica," "Now at a Theater Near You," and "Defrocking Frodo and the Death of the Imagination."

Roberto Rivera, "The Lord of the Rings," *Boundless,* 20 December 2001.

Gina Dalfonzo, "The Myth That Really Happened," *BreakPoint Online,* 23 December 2002.

Kelley Reep, "Between Two Masters," *BreakPoint Online,* 24 January 2003.

Colleen Carroll, "Tolkien, Transformer of Culture," *BreakPoint Online,* 19 April 2002.

Steven Garber, "Good Books, Bad Books," *BreakPoint WorldView,* January/February 2003.

See the *BreakPoint* with Chuck Colson Movie Recommendations, http://www.pfm.org/BPtemplate.cfm ?Section=BreakPoint_Home&template=/ContentManagement/ContentDisplay.cfm&ContentID=11152.

CHRISTIANS IN CULTURE, LIE #5

Abercrombie & Flinch: A Boycott That Worked

Learn more about the boycott against Abercrombie & Fitch, http://www.americandecency.org/abercrombie.htm.

Call 1-877-322-5527 to request the fact sheet "How to Keep Your Kids 'Unbranded,'" which includes facts and tips to help parents teach teens to understand how advertising and marketing works.

Read Joe Gibbs's letter to Michael Jeffries, president of Abercrombie & Fitch, http://www.americandecency. org/gibbs.htm.

Anne Morse, "'Field Guide' Bye-Bye," *National Review Online,* 1 December 2003.

Parija Bhatnagar, "Stripping Abercrombie," CNN, 4 December 2003.

Parija Bhatnagar, "Abercrombie: What's the Naked Truth?" CNN, 2 December 2003.

D. Parvaz, "Nudity, Sex Articles in Abercrombie & Fitch 'Magalog' Draw Fire," *Seattle Post-Intelligencer,* 3 December 2003.

"Abercrombie Ex-Bosses: Pretty Workers Favored," *Chicago Sun-Times,* 7 December 2003.

Joseph Sabia, "Abercrombie & Filth," *Cornell Review,* Freshman Issue 2001, 31 August 2001.

Karla Dial, "Megan vs. A&F," *Boundless,* 6 February 2003.

Roberto Rivera, "More Than Just Pants," *Boundless,* 10 June 1999.

William F. Buckley Jr., "Show Your ID before Reading," Townhall.com, 20 June 2001.

Martha Kleder, "Abercrombie & Fitch Sells More Sex Than Clothes," *Family Voice,* September/October 2001.

See the *BreakPoint* commentaries: "From Diapers to Thongs," "Not Your Father's Tweeds," "Bankrupt at Age Twenty-Five," and "Image Is Everything."

Gina Dalfonzo, "What Aren't You Kids Doing!?" *BreakPoint Online,* 4 June 2002.

SUV Spirituality: Jesus behind the Wheel?

George Will, "What Would Jesus Drive?" *Washington Post,* 28 November 2002, A47.

Michelle Cottle, "Jesus Drove a Civic," *New Republic,* 13 November 2002.

"Christian Concerts Spark Controversy for Chevy," *Detroit Free Press,* 23 October 2002.

Stuart Elliott, "Questions about G. M. Sponsorship," *New York Times*, 24 October 2002.

"Evangelical Leaders Join Criticism of Chevrolet-Sponsored Christian Music Tour," EEN press release, 6 November 2002. http://www.religionnews.com/press02/PR110702.html.

Stephen Bates, "The Jesus Market," *Weekly Standard*, 16 December 2002.

"What Is Hip?" *Christianity Today* editorial, 5 December 2002.

Frank Burch Brown, *Good Taste, Bad Taste, and Christian Taste: Aesthetics in Religious Life* (Oxford University Press, 2003).

Slothfully Tacky: The Scandal of Christian Merchandise

Stephen Bates, "The Jesus Market," *Weekly Standard*, 16 December 2002.

Jeremy Lott, "Jesus Sells: What the Christian Culture Industry Tells Us about Secular Society," *Reason*, February 2003.

BreakPoint commentary no. 030207, "Art as Torture: Rejecting Christian Ideas of Beauty."

C. S. Lewis, *Surprised by Joy: The Shape of My Early Life* (Harvest Books, 1975).

St. Augustine, *The Confessions of Saint Augustine* (Doubleday, 1988).

Frank Burch Brown, *Good Taste, Bad Taste, and Christian Taste: Aesthetics and Religious Life* (Oxford University, 2003).

Hit and Miss: Miss America Follies

George Archibald, "Miss America Told to Zip It on Chastity Talk," *Washington Times*, 9 October 2002.

George Archibald, "Pageant Permits Promotion of Chastity," *Washington Times*, 10 October 2002.

"Judges Sold on Miss America Pageant," letter-to-the-editor, *Chicago Sun-Times*, 1 October 2002.

Robert H. Knight, "Muzzling Miss America: Abstain from Discussing Abstinence, She's Warned," *Culture and Family Institute*, 9 October 2002.

Joel Mowbray, "The 'Right' Miss America," *National Review Online*, 23 September 2002.

Learn more about Project Reality. http://www.projectreality.org.

Peter Kreeft, *How to Win the Culture War* (InterVarsity Press, 2002).

Expelling the Founders: God and History in California

Read the Declaration of Independence.

Dan Whitcomb, "Declaration of Independence Banned at Bay-Area School," *San Diego Union-Tribune*, 24 November 2004.

"School Bars Declaration of Independence," *Smoking Gun*, 24 November 2004.

Dean E. Murphy, "God, American History, and a Fifth-Grade Class," *New York Times*, 4 December 2004.

Dr. Daniel L. Dreisbach, "A Godless Constitution?" *BreakPoint Online*, April 2000.

BreakPoint commentary no. 030710, "Wall of Separation: Text and Context."

See the "Worldview for Parents" page "America's Religious Roots."

For college students: Call 1-877-322-5527 for FIRE's Guide to Religious Liberty on Campus. This thorough guide explains how the legal and moral arguments for religious liberty apply differentially on public and private campuses. For other guides by FIRE, visit their Web site.

The Church's Great Challenge: Christians in the Marketplace

"Ethics, Enron, and American Higher Education: An NAS/Zogby Poll of College Seniors," *National Association of Scholars*, July 2002.

Dan Seligman, "Oxymoron 101," *Forbes*, 28 October 2002.

"Americans Are Most Likely to Base Truth on Feelings," Barna Research Online, 12 February 2002.

BreakPoint commentary no. 030717, "Taking Care of Business: Virtue in the Boardroom."

"Christians in the Marketplace," a Christian Mind in the New Millennium III conference, took place April 4–6, 2003, at the Cheyenne Mountain Resort and Conference Center in Colorado Springs. At this *BreakPoint* worldview conference, speakers—including Charles Colson, Mark Earley, Michael Novak, and others—discussed the role of Christian worldview in today's business sector and marketplace, how businesses should apply ethical standards to their practices, and how our work should be viewed as a calling, an opportunity to serve God in our businesses (audiocassette and CD sets are available at https://www.pfmonline.net/str_donation.taf?Site=BP_Item&Item_code =CSW03).

"A Time to Learn about Ethics. " Chuck Colson addresses Harvard Business School on developing a personal code of ethics (CD at https://www.pfmonline.net/str_donation.taf?Site=BP_Item&Item_code=CSW02017). The speech is also available in brochure form. https://www.pfmonline.net/str_donation.taf?Site=BP_Item&Item_code=BDBF1.

"How Now Shall We Work?" Charles Colson delivered a speech, "How Now Shall We Work?" to more than 600 workers in October 2001. He asked and answered five provocative questions, including, "Can we work well without God?" directing them to an audience of those in the marketplace. Colson's words provide Christians with practical tips on applying their faith at work (audiocassette at https://www.pfmonline.net/str_donation.taf?Site=BP_Item&Item_code=CSHSW).

"Truth in the Public Square." In June 2003, Charles Colson spoke to congressional members and their staff about the need to uphold truth in the public square, advocating moral truth as the basis of legislation and the need to make reasoned arguments based on natural law principles in order to make a significant influence in politics and public policy (CD at https://www.pfmonline.net/str_donation.taf?Site=BP_Item&Item_code=CDTPS).

J. Budziszewski, *What We Can't Not Know* (Spence, 2003).

Gina Dalfonzo, "Cheating Themselves," *Boundless*, 16 January 2003.

The BreakPoint Worldview Survival Kit for Students includes valuable books and resources, in a useful canvas satchel with a water bottle, to help your high school or college student develop a Christian worldview, https://www.pfmonline.net/str_donation.taf?Site=BP_Item&Item_code=UNKIT

Rebels for Life: The New Sexual Revolution

Colleen Carroll, *The New Faithful: Why Young Adults Are Embracing Christian Orthodoxy* (Loyola Press, 2002).

Agnieszka Tennant, "The Good News about Generations X & Y," *Christianity Today*, 5 August 2002.

Matt Kaufman, "A Shift Toward the Traditional," *Boundless*, 25 March 1999.

Learn more about World Youth Day. http://www.wyd2002.org/index.php

Rock for Life is committed to offering the truth about abortion, infanticide, and euthanasia to America's youth through music and ministry, http://www.rockforlife.org.

Find more international, national, and local pro-life youth organizations, http://www.prolifeinfo.org/4.

The World Youth Alliance promotes "the dignity of the person at the international level, encouraging solidarity between the developed and developing worlds, building a culture of life," http://www.worldyouthalliance.org.

See the findings from UCLA's Higher Education Research Institute's "American Freshman 1998" survey (statistics about opinions on abortion are at the end of the press release), http://www.gseis.ucla.edu/heri/press98.html.

Janet Gilmore, "Youths more conservative than their elders on issues involving religion and abortion, new UC Berkeley survey reveals," University of California-Berkeley press release, 24 September 2002, http://www.berkeley.edu/news/media/releases/2002/09/24_youth.html.

Lydia Saad, "Public Opinion about Abortion—an In-Depth Review" (see section on "Gender, Religion, and

Other Group Attitudes Toward Abortion"), The Gallup Organization, 2001, http://www.gallup.com/poll/specialReports/pollSummaries/sr020122viii.asp.

Frederica Mathewes-Green, "The Oneida Experiment: What We Have Discovered about Not-So-Free Love," *Touchstone*, November 2002.

Peter Nixon, "Abortion and the Law," *Sursum Corda*, 11 November 2002.

The New Counterculture: Younger Evangelicals and the Search for Purpose

BreakPoint commentary no. 030821, "The Third Millennium Church."

BreakPoint commentary no. 030408, "A New Generation Gap."

Robert E. Webber, *The Younger Evangelicals: Facing the Challenges of the New World* (Baker, 2002).

"Gen Y Goes to War," *Wall Street Journal*, 28 March 2003.

Daniel Henninger, "The Anti-Woodstock," *Wall Street Journal*, 4 April 2003.

John Leland, "A Movement, Yes, but No Counterculture," *New York Times*, 23 March 2003.

Peter Perl, "Crash Course," *Washington Post Magazine*, 22 June 2003, W10.

Nathan Finn, "The Protest Culture," *Boundless*, 3 April 2003.

Cathy Young, "Turnabout in Campus Radicalism," *Boston Globe*, 14 April 2003 (reprinted on FreeRepublic.com).

Vicki Haddock, "The Young Back the War," *San Francisco Chronicle*, 23 March 2003.

Mark Gauvreau Judge, "The Resenters," *BreakPoint Online*, 21 February 2003.

Stuart Buck, "The End of Religion?" *BreakPoint Online*, 2 July 2003.

Johannes L. Jacobse, "The New Faithful: A New Great Awakening?" *BreakPoint Online*, 6 March 2003.

As students you know prepare to enter college, consider sending them the BreakPoint Worldview Survival Kit for Students (also a great gift for high school students), packed with books and resources critical to helping them grapple with the conflicting worldviews they'll encounter. It now includes a CD of a speech Charles Colson delivered at Brown University, "Can the Ivy League Teach Ethics?" in which he called for teaching absolute truth in higher education, https://www.pfmonline.net/str_donation.taf?Site=BP_Item&Item_code=UNKIT.

Hugh Hewitt, *In, but Not Of* (Thomas Nelson, 2003).

Prisoners' Kids and the State of the Union: A Faith-Based Solution

Joseph Loconte, *God, Government and the Good Samaritan: The Promise and Peril of the President's Faith-Based Agenda* (Washington, D.C.: The Heritage Foundation, October 2001).

"President Names New Faith-Based & Community Initiatives Director," White House Office of the Press Secretary, 1 February 2002.

Faithful unto Death: The Plight of Burmese Christians

Benedict Rogers, "Faith Unbroken: Persecuting Christians in Burma," *Crisis*, June 2004.

Learn more about the crisis in Burma, and what you can do, from Christian Solidarity Worldwide.

Learn more about the Free Burma Rangers.

Visit the Free Burma Coalition Web site.

Benedict Rogers, *A Land without Evil: Stopping the Genocide of Burma's Karen People* (Monarch Books, 2004).

BreakPoint commentary no. 040503, "Touching the Untouchable: India Targets Christian Converts."

"Paramilitary Hindu Group to Restrict Christian Conversions," *AsiaNews*, 26 May 2004.

Learn more about helping the persecuted Church at Stand Today's Web site.

Kristin Wright, "Standing with the Persecuted Church," *BreakPoint Online*, 6 November 2003.

Nina Shea, *In the Lion's Den* (Broadman and Holman, 1997).

Loving Mondays: Business as a Calling

John D. Beckett, *Loving Monday: Succeeding in Business without Selling Your Soul* (InterVarsity Press, 2001).

Michael Novak, *Business as a Calling* (Free Press, 1996).

A Compassionate Law: Signing the Sudan Peace Act

Learn more about the Sudan Peace Act on BreakPoint's Sudan links and action page, http://www.breakpoint .org/Breakpoint/ChannelRoot/TopicsGroup/PoliticsAndPublicAffairs/Sudan+Links+and+Action.htm.

BreakPoint commentary no. 020918, "Standing Firm: Fighting Unspeakable Evil."

BreakPoint commentary no. 020605, "An Envoy Reports and a Letter Is Sent: Signs of Hope for Sudan."

Paul Marshall and Lela Gilbert, *Their Blood Cries Out* (Word, 1997).

THE MEDIA, LIE #6

TV Unplugged: Solving the Entertainment Dilemma

Dan Ackman, "The FCC Is Not Amused," *Forbes*, 4 February 2004.

Nekesa Mumbi Moody, "Jackson, Timberlake Apologize for Flash," Associated Press, 3 February 2004.

Leonard Pitts Jr., "What Was Really Exposed on National Television," *Seattle Times*, 8 February 2004.

Katy Kelly, Kim Clark, and Linda Kulman, "Trash TV," *U.S. News and World Report*, 16 February 2004.

BreakPoint commentary no. 040203, "Only a Matter of Time: Why the Super Bowl Incident Isn't Surprising."

Ken Myers, *All God's Children and Blue Suede Shoes: Christians & Popular Culture* (Crossway, 1989).

Chris Jones, "When Is Bad Publicity a Bad Career Move?" *Chicago Tribune*, 8 February 2004.

BreakPoint commentary no. 020208, "Must-Close-Your-Eyes-TV."

Neil Postman, *Amusing Ourselves to Death* (Viking, 1986).

Thomas Hibbs, *Shows about Nothing* (Spence, 1999).

Peter Kreeft, *How to Win the Culture War* (InterVarsity, 2002).

Marketing Deviant Lifestyles: Social Messages for Sale?

Harvey Gallagher Cox, *The Secular City: Secularization and Urbanization in Theological Perspective* (Macmillan, 1966).

Fidelity and the Creative Class: An Impossible Goal

Roberto Rivera, "Lives of Optional Desperation," *BreakPoint Online*, 11 November 2004.

Roberto Rivera y Carlo, "Destructive Myths: Love Onscreen," *Boundless*, 11 November 2004. (See also "Pursuing Happiness.")

Lee Siegel, "Relationshipism," *New Republic*, 11 November 2002. Note: some profanity.

Caryn James, "Partners Who Cheat but Tell the Truth," *New York Times*, 8 December 2004.

BreakPoint commentary no. 030826, "Family Values on HBO? Truth from Unexpected Sources."

BreakPoint commentary no. 041130, "Taking Sides: Kinsey."

Mark Gauvreau Judge, "Kinsey on Film," *BreakPoint Online*, 12 November 2004.

BreakPoint commentary no. 040728, "De-Lovely Couples: Mocking Marriage."

BreakPoint commentary no. 040218, "Ward and Ward Cleaver: The New Stay-at-Home Parent."

Jeffrey Overstreet, "Review of Closer," *Christianity Today*, 3 December 2004.

Jonathan V. Last, "Live. Young. Girls." *Weekly Standard*, 3 December 2004.

Frederica Mathewes-Green, "Not Even Close," *National Review Online*, 3 December 2004.

Richard Florida, *The Rise of the Creative Class* (Basic Books, 2004).

Mike McManus, *Marriage Savers* (Word, 1995).

Our Shrinking Culture: Movies and Cultural Literacy

Roger Ebert's review of *The League of Extraordinary Gentlemen* in the *Chicago Sun-Times*.

Jeffrey Overstreet, "Film Forum: The League of Flat and Uninspired Gentlemen," *Christianity Today*, 17 July 2003.

Joe Baltake, "Extra-Odd 'Gentlemen,'" *Sacramento Bee*, 11 July 2003.

Louise Cowan and Os Guinness, eds., *Invitation to the Classics* (Baker, 1998).

E. D. Hirsch, *Cultural Literacy: What Every American Needs to Know* (Vintage, 1988).

Thomas Hibbs, *Shows about Nothing* (Spence, 1999).

T. M. Moore, "Culture, Cultures, and Pop Culture," *Findings* (spring 2003).

T. M. Moore, "Nurturing the Soul," *BreakPoint Online*, 29 April 2003.

Darren Hughes, "Seeking 'Holy Moments' at the Movies," *Findings* (spring 2003).

Vigen Guroian, "On Fairy Tales and Moral Imagination," *BreakPoint Online*.

Gene Edward Veith Jr., *Reading between the Lines* (Crossway, 1990).

David Lyle Jeffrey, *People of the Book: Christian Identity and Literary Culture* (Ferdmans, 1996).

Alan Jacobs, *A Visit to Vanity Fair* (Brazos, 2001).

Vigen Guroian, *Tending the Heart of Virtue* (Oxford University Press, 1998).

William J. Bennett, *The Book of Virtues* (Simon & Schuster, 1993).

Star Power and Suffering Children: Exploiting Celebrity

Adam Cohen, "When Not Knowing a Celebrity Could Prove Fatal," *New York Times*, 29 December 2002.

To learn more about spinal muscular atrophy and what you can do to help, visit the Families of Spinal Muscular Atrophy Web site. http://www.fsma.org.

Bob Dart, "I'm No Expert, but I Play One on TV: Congress's Love Affair with Celebrities," *Austin American-Statesman*, 10 June 2002.

"More and More Celebrities Using Fame to Back Causes," *Dallas Morning News*, 26 December 2002.

Darrell M. West and John M. Orman, *Celebrity Politics* (Prentice Hall, 2002).

Ken Myers, "Celebrity, Hedonomics, and Popular Culture," an address to Congress members and staff, *BreakPoint Online*.

Learn how you can make a difference in the culture with the BreakPoint Culture of Life Packet. It includes the booklet *Building a Culture of Life: A Call to Respect Human Dignity in American Life* and a *BreakPoint This Week* special broadcast CD that includes an interview with Wilberforce Forum Fellow William Saunders, Human Rights Counsel and Senior Fellow in Human Life Studies for Family Research Council, along with a speech, "Bioethics and the Clash of Orthodoxies," by Dr. Robert George, http://www.pfmonline.net/products.taf?_function=d&IC=COLPT.

It's All about Profit: Exploiting Kids for Cash

Craig F. Garfield, M.D. et al., "Alcohol Advertising in Magazines and Adolescent Readership," *Journal of the American Medical Association* 289, no. 18 (14 May 2003): 2325.

Adam Marcus, "Magazines Shower Teens with Alcohol Ads," ABC News, 14 May 2003.

Steve Jordahl, "Teen Mags Targeted with Booze Ads," *Family News in Focus*, 16 May 2003.

Visit the Web site for the Center on Alcohol Marketing and Youth (CAMY) for more information on this topic. http://camy.org.

"Summary: Youth Exposure to Alcohol Advertising," CAMY.

"Radio Daze: Alcohol Ads Tune in Underage Youth," CAMY, April 2003.

"The Merchants of Cool," *Frontline*, PBS, 2001.

Kimberly Erickson, "Youth Facts: Alcohol and Youth," Institute for Youth Development, 1 October 1998.

Charles Colson, *Answers to Your Kids' Questions* (Tyndale, 2000).

Benjamin Wiker, *Moral Darwinism: How We Became Hedonists* (InterVarsity, 2002).

Reality or Something Like It: Reality TV and Boredom

Richard Winter, *Still Bored in a Culture of Entertainment: Rediscovering Passion and Wonder* (InterVarsity, 2002).

Bill Carter, "Reality TV Alters the Way TV Does Business," *New York Times*, 25 January 2003.

J. Budziszewski, "The Vixenette," *Boundless*, 23 January 2003.

Gloria Goodale, "Even Reality TV Producers Turn Some Ideas Down," *Christian Science Monitor*, 28 January 2003.

Gloria Goodale, "Changing Channels," *Christian Science Monitor*, 7 February 2003.

Gina Dalfonzo, "Not Dead Yet: Shame Exists—for Now," *BreakPoint Online*, 2 May 2002.

Roberto Rivera, "Survivor Ex Nihilo: Creativity in the New Wasteland," *BreakPoint Online*, 1 August 2000.

BreakPoint commentary no. 030314, "Torture TV: Creating a 'Lust for Cruelty.'"

The Brawl at the Palace: Sports and the Coarsening of the Culture

Tony Kornheiser, "A Stern Test for the NBA," *WashingtonPost*, 23 November 2004, D01.

Bryan Burwell, "The NBA Is Hip-Hopping Its Way Out of the Mainstream," *St. Louis Post-Dispatch*, 22 November 2004.

Jeff Zillgitt, "Fans Make the World Go 'Round and Other Brawl Theories," *USA Today*, 29 November 2004.

"Sell Sport, Not Thuggery," *Palm Beach Post*, 24 November 2004.

Bill Simmons, "Tale of the Tape," ESPN, 22 November 2004.

George Neumayr, "Rap Sheets," *American Spectator*, 23 November 2004.

Shawn Macomber, "Sporting Chance," *American Spectator*, 29 November 2004.

Ben Mathis-Lilley, "Fight! Fight! Fight!" *Slate*, 23 November 2004.

Sally Jenkins, "With Artest, a Human Quality," *Washington Post*, 26 November 2004, D01.

Mike Wise and Sally Jenkins, "An Enigma in the Hall of Infamy," *Washington Post*, 28 November 2004, A01.

Bill Littlefield, "Full Court Mess," *Washington Post*, 28 November 2004, B01.

Daniel Henninger, "From McLuhan to Artest," *Wall Street Journal*, 3 December 2004.

Todd Boyd, "Beyond Black and White," *Charlotte Observer*, 1 December 2004.

Alan Drooz, "Playing the Blame Game: Maybe We Need to Blame the Game," *San Diego Union-Tribune*, 29 November 2004.

Rochelle Gurstein, *The Repeal of Reticence* (Hill & Wang, 1996).

Karen Santorum, *Everyday Graces: A Child's Book of Good Manners* (ISI Books, 2003). Bono of U2 refers to this book as "also a book of manners for rock stars." We might add it's useful for college and professional athletes as well.

Hugh Hewitt, *In but Not Of: A Guide to Christian Ambition* (Nelson, 2003). This book provides readers with valuable insights, wisdom, personal experiences, and advice on how to rise in the world and achieve the kind of radical success that honors God.

Instant News, but Is It True? Why the News Makes Us Dumb

C. John Sommerville, *How the News Makes Us Dumb* (InterVarsity, 1999).

BreakPoint commentary no. 030827, "The British Are Not Coming—Film at Eleven."

Mark Gauvreau Judge, "Journalism 101," *BreakPoint Online*, 15 January 2003.

BreakPoint commentary no. 030520, "Trouble for the Gray Lady: Truth or Consequences at the *New York Times*."

The Worldview Resource Directory and *Worldview for Teens: A Resource Guide* contain information on valuable resources that will help you strengthen your biblical worldview.

See the list of Chuck Colson's favorite books at BreakPoint.org.

Scott Larsen, ed., *Indelible Ink: 22 Prominent Christian Leaders Discuss the Books That Shape Their Faith* (Waterbrook, 2003).

C. S. Lewis, *Surprised by Joy* (Harvest Books, 1975).

SPIRITUALITY IN CULTURE, LIE #7

"Oprahfication" and Its Discontents: Our Mile-Wide, Inch-Deep Religious Culture

Peggy Noonan, "God Is Back," *Wall Street Journal*, 28 September 2001.

Rod Dreher, "More Oprah," *National Review Online*, "The Corner," 20 March 2002.

"Americans Struggle with Religion's Role at Home and Abroad," *The Pew Forum on Religion & Public Life*, 20 March 2002.

LaTonya Taylor, "The Church of O," *Christianity Today*, 1 April 2002.

Charles Colson and Nancy Pearcey, *The Christian in Today's Culture* (Tyndale, 1999).

Transformation without Repentance: Psychoanalysis and Evil in Analyze This

Philip Rieff, *The Triumph of the Therapeutic: Uses of Faith after Freud* (Harper & Row, 1966).

A Life Well-Lived: Spending His Way to Happiness

Philip Kennicott, "Rich with Irony," *Washington Post*, 14 October 2002, C1.

"Divorce Duel Reveals Welch's Perks," CNN, 6 September 2002.

Robert Trigaux, "Welch Divorce Will Deflate Superhero Myth," *St. Petersburg Times*, 24 March 2002.

Michael Novak, *Business as a Calling: Work and the Examined Life* (Free Press, 1996).

Charles Colson, *Loving God* (Zondervan, 1996).

Richard John Neuhaus, *As I Lay Dying: Meditations upon Returning* (Basic Books, 2002).

The Epicurus and Epicurean Philosophy Web site offers more information on the history of this school of thought.

Very Superstitious: Belief in Contemporary America

"The New Superstition in the Midst of a Knowledge Explosion; Americans Embrace Irrational Fears." *Boston Globe*, 2 January 2001, E1.

"Sold on Spirituality." *Boston Globe Magazine*. 3 December 2000, 19.

Gabler, Neal. "Culture Wars; A Victim of the Third Great Awakening," *Los Angeles Times*, 14 January 2001, M1.

Mushy Ecumenism: Incoherent Civil Religion

Read Willow Creek Community Church's Statement regarding Muslim Visit to Willow Creek, http://www.pfonline.net/features.taf?ID141.

For more on understanding Islam, read Chuck Colson's "When Night Fell on a Different World: How Now Shall We Live?" http://www.pfonline.net/features.taf?_function=detail&Site=BPT&Item_Code=BCWNF.

As Long As We All Get Along: Selling Truth for Unity

Faith McDonnell, "Primate of Sudan Expresses Grief over Situation in the Anglican Communion," Institute on Religion and Democracy, 2 February 2004.

Caryle Murphy, "Virginia Episcopalians Avert Split over Gay Bishop," *Washington Post*, 1 February 2004, C07.

"Diocese Says Gay Bishop Should Not Be Cause of Split," *New York Times*, 2 February 2004.

Julia Duin, "Heresy Better Idea Than Schism?" *Washington Times*, 31 January 2004.

Ross Mackenzie, "Reason vs. Openness and the Impending Episcopal Schism," Townhall.com, 23 October 2003.

BreakPoint commentary no. 040116, "Say It Ain't So, Dave: Evangelicals and the Cultural Mainstream."

BreakPoint commentary no. 011218, "Mushy Ecumenism: Incoherent Civil Religion."

Matthew Spalding and Joe Loconte, "In Defense of Marriage," Heritage Foundation, 19 November 2003.

"Trouble in the Church." In this interview with BreakPoint managing editor Jim Tonkowich, Dr. John Yates II, senior minister of the Falls Church in Falls Church, Virginia, discusses the current crisis in the Episcopal Church: the election of Gene Robinson, a practicing homosexual, to be bishop of New Hampshire. They discuss how the Church should approach the issue of homosexuality. This CD also includes a lecture by Dr. J. Budziszewski in which he discusses homosexuality and same-sex "marriage" from a Christian perspective.

"Mass. Court: Gay Civil Unions Not Enough," Fox News, 4 February 2004.

Rev. John C. Rankin, "A Conversation with Homosexual Advocates," *BreakPoint Online*, 27 October 2003.

Call 1-877-3-CALLBP to request the complimentary Marriage Amendment information packet, which includes articles on marriage and family by William Bennett and Stanley Kurtz, the Evangelicals and Catholics Together statement on marriage, the text of the Federal Marriage Amendment, and a chart from the Alliance for Marriage outlining the legal impact of the amendment. Also available is the BreakPoint Speak the Truth in Love resource kit ($25), which includes CDs, booklets, articles, and more to help you speak effectively and compassionately on the issue of homosexuality and marriage.

Image Is Everything: Postmodern Churches

Charles Colson with Ellen Santilli Vaughn, *The Body: Being Light in Darkness* (W, 1996).

Undergraduates without Chests: Tending the Heart of Virtue

Vigen Guroian, *Tending the Heart of Virtue: How Classic Stories Awaken a Child's Moral Imagination* (Oxford University Press, 1998).

ABOUT THE AUTHOR

CHARLES COLSON is a popular author, speaker, and radio commentator. A former presidential aide to Richard Nixon and founder of the international ministry Prison Fellowship, he has written several books that have shaped Christian worldview thinking, including *How Now Shall We Live?* In 1993 he was awarded the prestigious Templeton Prize for Progress in Religion.

Resources That Support
The *How Now Shall We Live?*
Worldview Message

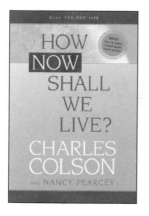

How Now Shall We Live?

Gives Christians the understanding and tools to confront bankrupt worldviews and to redeem every aspect of culture. *Hardcover ISBN 0-8423-1808-9; softcover ISBN 0-8423-5588-X*

How Now Shall We Live?
Devotional 365 meditations on how to be a countercultural Christian. *ISBN 0-8423-5409-3*

Answers to Your Kids' Questions
A guide to help parents know how to talk to their kids about the worldview issues they face every day. *ISBN 0-8423-1817-8*

Developing a Christian Worldview series, *How Now Shall We Live?* worldview issues in a format for individual and group study:

Science and Evolution *ISBN 0-8423-5583-9*

The Problem of Evil *ISBN 0-8423-5584-7*

The Christian in Today's Culture *ISBN 0-8423-5587-1*

COMING SOON:

How Now in Real Life series:

How Now Shall We Live as Parents? ISBN 1-4143-0164-2

How Now Shall We Live in the Workplace? ISBN 1-4143-0165-0

Lies That Go Unchallenged series:

Lies That Go Unchallenged in the Media and Government ISBN 1-4143-0167-7

Complete How Now Shall We Live? adult and youth video curriculum
Available from LifeWay Church Resources:

LifeWay Church Resources
Customer Services, MSN 113
One LifeWay Plaza
Nashville, TN 37234-0113

Fax (615) 251-5933
Catalog orders (800) 458-2772
Order from online catalog at www.lifeway.com/shopping

OTHER TYNDALE BOOKS BY CHARLES COLSON

Burden of Truth — Practical help for handling difficult issues
that collide with culture. ISBN 0-8423-0190-9

Justice That Restores — Charles Colson's legacy statement
about criminal justice. ISBN 0-8423-5245-7